P9-CCY-857

*To Ellen, Nick and Mike for
their support and understanding.*

*To my parents, Ralph and Barbara,
for their guidance and encouragement.*

Contents

Preface *ix*

Chapter 1

Crisis management and *The Crisis Counselor* **1**

Quick evaluation:
How does crisis management apply to your business? 1
How do you define a business crisis? 3
What are some examples of crises that could strike any business? 3
What is the likely impact of a crisis? 10
What is crisis management? 15
What is "The Crisis Counselor mindset"? 16
How can a business thrive from a crisis? 24
What are the most important aspects of crisis management? 29
How do I determine whether my company is vulnerable to a crisis? 38
Tips to consider 39

Chapter 2

Where could your business get tripped up? **41**

Quick evaluation:
How vulnerable is your business to a crisis? 41
How do crises typically occur? 43
Is it possible to recognize warning signs in advance? 47
What are the best ways to determine vulnerabilities in my business? 53
How would we conduct a vulnerabilities analysis in my organization? 55
What do we do with our list of vulnerabilities? 65
How often should we conduct a vulnerabilities analysis? 77
Tips to consider 78

THE CRISIS COUNSELOR

The executive's guide to avoiding, managing and thriving on crises that occur in all businesses

Jeffrey R. Caponigro

Copyright © 1998 by Jeffrey R. Caponigro

All rights reserved. No part of this book may be reproduced or transmitted in any form or by any means, electronic or mechanical, including photocopying, recording or by an information storage and retrieval system, without permission in writing from the publisher.

Published by

Barker Business Books Inc.

4000 Town Center, Southfield, Michigan 48075

Publisher's Cataloging-in-Publication Data
Caponigro, Jeffrey R.
The crisis counselor : the executive's guide to avoiding, managing and thriving on crises that occur in all businesses / Jeffrey R. Caponigro. – Southfield, Mich. : Barker Business Books, 1998
p. cm.
Includes index.
ISBN 0-9659606-0-9
1. Strategic planning. 2. Crisis management. I. Title.
HD30.28 .C37 1998 97-77202
658.4' 056 dc21 CIP

01 00 99 ꙍ 5 4 3 2 1

Printed in the United States of America

Chapter 3

Preventing crises in your business **81**

Quick evaluation:
Will a preventive approach work at my business? 81

How can businesses prevent crises from occurring? 83

How do warning signs turn into crises? 89

What can be done to prevent *potential* crises from becoming *real* ones? 94

Tips to consider 97

Chapter 4

How to plan for a crisis **99**

Quick evaluation:
Has my business planned sufficiently for a crisis? 99

What is meant by planning for a crisis? 101

What is the best way to plan for a crisis? 107

What is a crisis management team? 109

What is a crisis-management plan? 114

What is crisis-simulation training? 120

What is media training? 125

What written materials can be developed in advance of a crisis? 130

What is the best way to get others to buy into the idea of crisis planning? 132

Tips to consider 133

Chapter 5

The crisis itself **135**

Quick evaluation:
What is there to know about a crisis? 135

How will our business know when a crisis has occurred? 137

Are some crises more difficult to manage than others? 142

What stages typically occur over the life of a crisis? 142

What is typically the objective of managing a crisis? 146

What should be our strategy in a crisis? 146

Tips to consider 149

Chapter 6

What should we say and do? **151**

Quick evaluation:
How do you know what to say and do during a crisis? 151

How communicative should we be during a crisis? 154
What are some general tips for communicating during a crisis? 157
What do we do if we get contradictory advice? 163
Communicating with your employees 165
Communicating with your customers 181
Communicating with the news media 191
Who should be our company spokesperson in a crisis? 203
What sort of training should we consider for our spokespersons? 208
What are some techniques reporters may use to trick someone? 210
How do we know if we are successful in our communications with the media? 214
How do we increase the opportunity to receive fair treatment by the media? 216
Communicating with other publics 220
Tips to consider 226

Chapter 7

Monitoring, evaluating and making adjustments **229**

Quick evaluation:
How will we know whether or not we are successfully managing our crisis? 229

How will we know when our problem should still be considered a crisis? 231
What do you mean by monitoring and evaluating a crisis? 232
What reports can we generate to senior management regarding the process? 238
In what ways might we consider adjusting our management of the crisis? 241
When is it okay to stop monitoring and evaluating the crisis? 245
How do you know when the crisis has ended? 246
Tips to consider 248

Chapter 8

Insulating your business **251**

Quick evaluation:
Are there other steps companies can take to prepare themselves for a future crisis? 251

What type of insulation does a business need? 253
What are the best ways to help insulate a business? 255
What are some ways to establish and maintain a crisis-management culture? 255
How can a business establish and maintain high levels of goodwill? 256
How can conducting an ongoing PR program help insulate a business? 260
What are public relations objectives? 264
What is meant by strategy for targeting specific publics? 265
What are some examples of public relations tactics? 266
What else can help insulate our company from the damaging effects of a crisis? 268
Tips to consider 270

Chapter 9

Putting it all together **273**

What are the most important points covered in *The Crisis Counselor*? 273
How can I get others to appreciate the importance of crisis management? 275

Glossary 277

Index 280

Preface

A fruit market. A *Fortune 500* company. A law firm. A computer-services business. A hospital. A dry cleaners. A school district. A university. An automotive supplier. An accounting firm. A bank.

All of these businesses have one thing in common – they face problems every day. Many are managed quickly and dissolve. Others fizzle out on their own. And, many others erupt into crisis situations that needlessly damage corporate reputations and executives' careers.

These crises aren't necessarily the high-profile, sensational ones covered on the front pages of newspapers or the covers of business magazines. They're not necessarily the ones that are easy to brush off as the type that "will never happen to *our* business."

All businesses face more common crises that, in their own ways, can be as scary and potentially damaging for their individual organizations as the Bhopal disaster was to Union Carbide, the Valdez oil spill was to Exxon, and the breast implants' crisis was to Dow Corning.

These "common" crises include employee downsizings, negative media coverage, corporate lawsuits, government probes, damaging quality problems, product recalls, boycotts and strikes, an unexpected death of a senior executive, and many others.

Businesses of all types – from the smallest, entrepreneurial startup to the largest, most powerful corporation – need to be aware of ways to prevent crises from occurring and how to manage them before they ignite into potentially debilitating and crippling events.

The Crisis Counselor is a practical reference guide for any aspiring executive, CEO, business owner, franchisee, attorney, accountant, marketing professional or anyone else who wants to broaden his/her perspectives about managing a business in the most effective and enlightened way.

This book was written recognizing that *most* businesses operate without sufficient concern about managing the most fragile of assets – their reputations.

Many continue to feel the management concept of planning for a crisis makes a lot of sense. However, most just don't do it. The reasons for putting off are many, and you can almost hear the mantra of those saying, "We have a well-managed company, and a major crisis will never occur in our business."

The problem actually begins when they think of *crises* only as the high-profile, spectacular ones causing catastrophic results, and they forget about the ones that – like termites –weaken and gnaw away at the foundation that led to the company's success. When the damage is finally identified and confirmed as something to be taken seriously, it's often much too late to fix the problem without lengthy, costly repairs to the heart of the foundation – its credibility, reputation, loyalty and trust.

Even if you agree a crisis *could* occur in your business, it is too easy to set aside *crisis planning* in favor of keeping up with the day-to-day pressures of running the business.

Executives talk about "disaster control" or – what you may have heard called – "crisis communications." A primary premise of *The Crisis Counselor* is that this is only a small part of the crisis-management process. You will learn how many crises can be prevented and managed effectively by focusing on the larger crisis-management continuum. This includes identifying vulnerabilities in an organization; preventing crises from occurring; planning for crises; recognizing when a crisis ignites; communicating during a crisis with your employees, customers, news media and other important publics; evaluating your crisis work and making adjustments along the way; insulating your business to protect it from a future crisis; and, beginning the process again with identifying any new vulnerabilities.

This is a new way of thinking in business, and the most effective business executives and owners have *The Crisis Counselor* mindset.

I hope you like the unusual format of this book. It is intended to be a quick, easy-to-read book that offers specific tips and techniques you can immediately implement in your business or department. Most of the book is written in Q&A format to make it possible to digest in small, bite-sized portions. It describes *The Crisis Counselor* perspective in preventing and managing crises and, through specific tips and anecdotes, provides practical and easy ways for you to incorporate them at your work.

Every chapter – except for this Preface and Chapter 9, the conclusion – includes a quick test you can take to assess your level of crisis preparation. And, each of those chapters features a bulleted list of tips to consider for immediate application in your business or department.

To get you into the swing of things, here are some answers to a few questions you might have on your mind:

How can *The Crisis Counselor* help me?

If you run a business, manage a department or are trying to work your way up the corporate ladder, learning and adapting *The Crisis Counselor* principles will help broaden your perspectives and make you more effective. It will provide a strong foundation of knowledge that will help *structure* your way of problem solving and managing your planning, communications and reputation.

Why is *The Crisis Counselor* different than others on crisis management?

Nearly every book written on the subject has focused on critiquing high-profile crises you've seen reported by the news media. Plane crashes. Product tamperings. Oil spills. Plant explosions. Product recalls. They provide insight into the crises and offer professional criticism on ways the situations could have been better managed. Others on the subject offer extremely academic, theoretical solutions to planning for and managing crises. Both types of books are interesting reading. However, I've always felt they didn't help the real business executive, who would have to translate those thoughts into practical steps that can be taken in an individual business.

This book is very different. It is a practical guide that makes it easy for the reader to apply the information to his/her own company or department. It is much easier to read and absorb than any previous crisis-management book. It features crises that could likely affect *any* type of business, at *any* time, and includes examples to which every executive can relate and integrate in their businesses.

What should I expect in *The Crisis Counselor*?

As you progress through the chapters, you'll begin to see the ways each part of *The Crisis Counselor*'s crisis-management process works together with the other. The bulleted tips at the end of each chapter will provide the cement you'll need to build a strong and effective foundation for your company or department.

You should expect to become increasingly enthusiastic as you string together the concepts and determine the most effective ways to apply them. I hope you enjoy the journey.

CHAPTER 1

Crisis management and *The Crisis Counselor*

How does crisis management apply to your business?

Take a few minutes to ask yourself the following questions:

1) Has your company or department ever experienced a crisis situation?

2) Do you think it might someday experience a crisis?

3) Have you ever played a part in managing a crisis?

4) Have you participated in managing a crisis that you thought could have been handled more effectively with greater preparation?

5) Do you wonder why some crises seem to come and go, while others appear to linger and take on a life of their own?

6) Are you concerned your company or department is vulnerable to a crisis?

7) Would you feel more comfortable if you were more knowledgeable in this area?

8) Do your instincts tell you that something should be done now to help prevent a crisis in your company or department from occurring or escalating in severity?

9) Are you sometimes confused by the advice you read or are given on this subject?

10) If you agree with the advice offered in this book, are you prepared to put it to immediate use within your company or department?

Evaluation:

0 - 3 "yes" answers	Your business is more fortunate than most or you might be underestimating the potential for a crisis in your business.
4 - 6 "yes" answers	Your business is vulnerable to a crisis. If it hasn't occurred already, you're quite fortunate. This chapter will help provide a basic overview on crisis management.
7 - 10 "yes" answers	You've lived through one or more crises, or will experience one soon. You are likely in a business that is extremely vulnerable to crises. This chapter and the remainder of *The Crisis Counselor* should be extremely helpful to you.

Managing serious problems in a business is not an art or a science. It's actually more like learning to play golf. You can learn to play golf by reading books and having someone explain how to do it, but nothing can replace getting on the course or the driving range and actually swinging the golf club. You'll never be a good golfer without actually playing the game, but you can improve your progress by learning as much possible about it off the course.

The management of serious problems – and ensuring they don't erupt into events that cause irreparable damage to your business – is something that can be only slightly more difficult than playing golf on an ice pond. And, if unprepared and unsure, it is usually about as enjoyable as falling through the ice and holding on for your life.

The Crisis Counselor is intended to help improve your management instincts and judgment the next time you are faced with a business crisis. Several ways exist to increase your awareness of impending problems, to determine ways to prevent them, and to react effectively if a crisis occurs. There's only one problem. Developing a common, fail-safe solution for all business crises is like grouping fingerprints. It can't be done because every one is different.

What you *can* learn, however, is an effective thought process and management mindset for managing crises effectively with the minimum amount of disruption and negative impact to your business – and to your career.

Let's begin this journey by starting with the basics – the definition of a crisis and what can be done to swat it before it turns into a swarm of killer bees. We will get more specific in subsequent chapters as we follow the path toward crisis-management success: identifying vulnerabilities, preventing crises from occurring, planning for a crisis, communicating after the crisis occurs, evaluating and making adjustments and beginning the process over. Also, we will discuss later one of the most important concepts in the entire book: insulating the business to protect it from future crises.

How do *you* define a business crisis?

A crisis is any event or activity with the potential to negatively affect the reputation or credibility of a business. It is typically a situation that is – or soon could be – out of control.

What are some examples of crises that could strike any business?

- **Employee layoffs/ downsizings.** Nearly every layoff, restructuring and downsizing results in employee anxieties, loss of employee loyalty and uncertainty about the future.

- **Financial results below expectations.** Companies suffer crises when they fail to meet the financial expectations of their owners, shareholders, employees, market analysts or the media. If the company has surprised any of its publics, the business usually pays for the breech of trust. Credibility suffers, employee morale plummets and, in the case of a publicly held company, the stock price plunges. It turns into a crisis when mistrust escalates, the company's market value drops, management changes occur and the company struggles to gain back its previous form.

- **Poor employee morale.** This can bite every business. Poor morale can result when employees feel overworked or mistreated. Some or all employees may feel they should be better paid and appreciated. They may have a deep need for more regular and consistent communication. Although nearly every business faces this situation more frequently than it would like to admit, it can escalate to crisis proportions when it significantly affects productivity, profitability and perhaps even workplace safety.

- **Corporate lawsuits.** Every business is susceptible to a lawsuit. Take your pick. You can get sued by former employees, customers, investors, competitors, community residents and the list goes on. Lawsuits almost always are uncomfortable for a business and can put your company in a bad light.

- **Discrimination/ harassment claims.** Your business also can be struck by the ever-increasing list of ways people feel injustices and inequities exist against them. This includes discrimination against sex, race, age, appearance, religion, sexual preference and carriers of the virus causing AIDS. Harassment claims are similar in their sensitivity. Those include various forms of harassment which are most often either sexual or racial. Failure to manage or prevent these situations with the utmost compassion and aplomb can lead to a serious crisis from it which can take years to recover.

- **Negative media coverage.** A successful business is one that is in control. So, it's particularly frustrating to senior executives who find they can't control the news media – which can report on anything it wants at any time. A particularly negative story, or series of stories, in a daily newspaper or monthly magazine, or on a local television or radio station, can turn into an immediate crisis for a company. Possible negative media coverage of this type could be related to how the business treated one or more of its customers; accusations made by a disgruntled employee; information based on its finances; or damaging allegations about a senior executive.

- **Damaging rumors.** The promulgation of myths, misconceptions and rumors are another way a company can experience a major crisis. They could be related to the sale of the business, negative customer comments, speculation about a senior executive's behavior or fear about the reliability of a major product line. Some may simply be innocent questions not intended to harm the business, or some are questions maliciously raised by a former employee or major competitor to cause significant damage to the business.

- **Product defects or quality problems.** These could range from simple problems about your products or services that place your business in a negative light, yet ones which can be fixed or repaired. Or, they can be catastrophic problems that are more difficult to mend or justify. They might escalate to a product recall or make it necessary to kill a brand or product line altogether.

- **A mistake in technology.** Technology *can* cause crises in most businesses. Viruses and bugs can shut down or create havoc into the daily operations of your company's computer system. Incorrect data can be provided by a computer incorrectly programmed. Your online connections might fail, making it impossible to communicate with specific customers. Increased vulnerability for most businesses exist as technology expands and organizations of all sizes take advantage of and rely on it.

- **Violent threats or actions by a disgruntled current/former employee.** Poor employee morale, on an individual or company-wide basis, also can be a precursor to a more severe situation. One or more disgruntled employees can turn into angry employees, who can become – in rare occasions – *violent* employees. This is an excellent example of a warning sign that can go easily undetected and ignored. This type of crisis can cause long-lasting scars for a business and its employees, and can be one of the most difficult to manage and recover from.

- **On-the-job accidents.** These occur most frequently at manufacturing facilities and high-risk businesses. Most are ordinary accidents that cause little, long-term damage to an organization. They turn into crisis situations when an employee or customer is maimed or killed on the premises of the business, or harmed due to a mistake made by the company or a failure of its product. This is another way of eroding confidence, credibility and trust in a company. If mismanaged, the situation can escalate into one that affects a business for a long period of time.

- **The sudden death of a senior executive.** Every business has one or more senior executives who are extremely important to its current and future success. This is typically the Chief Executive Officer, but also could be the Chief Operating Officer, the Executive Vice President, a Vice President of a division or even one of the company's top sales performers. A crisis can exist when one or more of these key leaders dies suddenly – which most often happens from by car accidents, heart attacks and plane crashes. This is a situation that every business should consider to ensure it can react quickly and effectively to avoid a gap in leadership, company direction and stakeholder confidence.

- **Loss of a major customer account.** The loss of a major customer account, one that is a high percentage of your overall business, can immediately precipitate a crisis. The crisis can occur when employees, other customers, vendors, the news media and, perhaps, others begin to question the company's abilities and health. The company's credibility is weakened and its reputation is damaged. The manner in which this is managed dictates whether it becomes a non-issue that soon goes away, or becomes a prolonged crisis with debilitating effects for the business. This is at the essence of *The Crisis Counselor* and what you will learn in this book.

- **Government probes or fines.** A major crisis looms over a business when the state or federal government conducts an investigation into possible wrong-doings by the company. A preliminary examination can escalate into a comprehensive probe, which can lead to major penalties. This can emerge with the investigation by any regulatory body. If it is a sizable case with a big-time penalty, you can bet it will draw considerable, negative attention to your business.

- **Damage caused by an Act of God.** Your business could be greatly affected by a tornado, flood, hurricane or lightning strike. This can force your business to temporarily close its doors or cause a loss of productivity from which it can take months to recover. The ability to make fast adjustments and recover quickly is the difference between a manageable problem and a full-blown crisis.

- **Boycotts, strikes or pickets.** An organized boycott against your business can occur when a large number of people rally behind a common cause that involves your company or products. This often, but not always, arises from actions taken by one or more associations or unions. For instance, the National Association of Retired Persons may persuade its membership and other senior citizens not to shop at your retail chain as a way to pressure you into hiring more older employees. The United Automobile Workers of America may encourage members of all unions not to buy a specific muffler if the manufacturer recently tried to bust the unions representing its employees. Strikes and pickets can occur in front of businesses by disgruntled union members and upset customers and community leaders, if they feel the company will not listen to them through more conventional means. A crisis occurs when these situations are mismanaged, and lead to reduced business, productivity and morale.

- **The corporation as a takeover target.** A publicly held company can be a target for an unwanted acquisition that can escalate into a public campaign to persuade board directors and shareholders to vote against the company and for the courting party. These challenges can get particularly uncomfortable for a company since the takeover attempt questions the organization's existing management and lays doubt on the future of the business. Employees, customers and others are usually uncertain of whom they should support and confused about the situation. Failure to effectively manage a situation of this type, almost always leads to a full-blown crisis and – on most occasions – new ownership.

Example: A crisis strikes a local bank

A regional bank has the largest number of branches in the state. Many of its branches are old and will soon be refurbished to be more customer-friendly for their growing number of customers.

Its busiest branch is in an older part of town and includes a high percentage of older customers. On a particularly busy afternoon, one of the octogenarian customers was waiting in the teller line, which had grown to about 15-people deep, and began raising his voice about the slowness of the line.

"What do we need to do to move this line along? Doesn't anyone know what they're doing around here?" the man complained loudly.

His remark drew quite the attention. The Manager looked at him from his desk and then went back to work.

"I hate this place," the man screamed. "This is the slowest bank I've ever been in. You're a bunch of incompetent fools."

The Manager walked over and politely asked the man to leave the premises. The man refused and the Manager asked the security guard to escort him from the bank.

"What's the matter, you don't like to serve old people?" the man said loudly as he limped from an old war injury out the front door. "What do you have against old folks like me?"

Two months later, the Manager received a call from the bank's Legal Counsel to inform him that the bank was being sued by the "old man who caused the disturbance a few weeks ago."

The Legal Counsel said: "He's suing us for age discrimination. He said he has the backing of the state's leading senior-citizens association. His attorney told me we clearly discriminate against senior citizens in a number of ways including our lack of rampways and sidewalks, the small type we use on our brochures and bank forms, and the rock-and-roll music we play in the branch. He said they will implement a campaign to get all senior citizens to boycott the bank. We need to make sure this doesn't happen again. But first, we need to apply some disaster control to this situation. I just don't know what to do."

Three lessons to learn

The regional bank's experience reinforces several key points from which we can learn:

1) **Identify your company's vulnerabilities and do something about them.** The bank's vulnerabilities included its lack of rampways and sidewalks, the music it played in the bank branch, the small type in its brochures and bank forms and the long lines that frustrated some customers. These were warning signs that the bank failed to notice or do anything about.

2) **Consider ways to improve the bond with your customers.** Nothing is more important than treating customers with respect and dignity. The bank manager who ignored the man complaining and "went back to work" should have been reprimanded for his lack of customer empathy. If necessary, he should have been replaced.

   The bank is located in an older part of town, and has a high percentage of older customers. It should have sought ways to improve the relationship with this segment of its customer base. This could be done by conducting customer focus groups or establishing a community-customer advisory group that meets regularly at the bank to offer input and suggestions. The bank should build up its goodwill with its older customers by identifying appropriate community projects and activities throughout the year to show its support (i.e., sponsorships, employee participation, special senior-citizen services).

3) **Solve the problem before it turns into a larger one.** Upon notification by the man's attorney, the bank should work to immediately solve the problem. The bank would like to avoid expensive litigation, negative publicity, a possible boycott by senior citizens and a significant loss of business. If possible, the bank needs to solve the problem in its early stages by showing the man – in a compassionate and understanding way – that other ways exist to solve the problem without litigation. In an effort to do so, the bank

would offer to meet with the man, apologize for the situation and describe the changes the bank has made to ensure it won't occur again (i.e., sidewalks, rampways, new music in branch). The bank representative could describe the idea of a customer advisory panel and ask if the man would be willing to serve on it. The bank should allow the man to feel he has made his point and has helped to improve the bank where he thought of as an important customer. He might consider dropping the litigation and may eventually become the bank's most-loyal supporter.

◆

What is the likely impact of a crisis – particularly one that isn't managed effectively?

It usually includes one or more of the following:

- **A significantly damaged reputation.** This is usually damage to the reputations of both the company and the people who are deemed responsible for either causing the problem or for not making the correct decisions to fix it. Many businesses have been unable to recover from bungled crises. Plenty of high-level executives were forced to make unwanted career changes after being labeled as the one who "caused the crisis" or "couldn't manage the problem."

- **Damage to the credibility, trust and confidence in the business.** These all shape the *reputation* of a business. It takes a long time to prove to employees, customers, vendors, the media, regulators and others that you and your business are credible, trustworthy and dependable. Unfortunately, a poorly managed crisis can destroy these key attributes in only a matter of hours and days. And, once you have broken the trust, it can take years and sometimes even decades to repair the damage.

- **Loss of employee loyalty.** A mismanaged crisis is among the fastest ways to lose the loyalty and support of your employees. A crisis showcases a company's leadership and all visible actions by management are magnified and evaluated by employees. It is a great opportunity to reinforce to employees your leadership and effectiveness. A mismanaged crisis often means a tremendous loss of employee loyalty that is frequently unrecoverable for the leadership team and the business

- **Lower sales.** The fallout from a large-scale crisis and a damaged reputation is almost always a decrease in sales. Customers aren't as attracted to your products or services, and they can more easily justify going somewhere else to fulfill their needs. Even if they still prefer your products or services, they may feel the crisis has you preoccupied and unable to keep focused on their needs.

- **Reduced profits.** Profits drop at most businesses experiencing a crisis due to the deadly combination of lower revenue *and* higher costs. Increased expenses occur in a number of areas that wouldn't be needed if the crisis hadn't occurred.

- **Necessary costs to help minimize damage caused by the crisis.** These costs could include hiring a crisis-management or public relations firm, conducting a news conference, sending overnight-mail letters to customers, holding a video conference, making scores of long-distance phone calls, incurring inordinate facsimile and photocopier charges, traveling to special meetings of customers and suffering the effects of lower credit ratings.

- **A decreased level of employee productivity.** During and after a crisis in a business, employees are almost always less productive – unless you can use the crisis to galvanize employees to become better focused and motivated. Most of the time employees are preoccupied with the crisis. They have to vent and talk about it among their colleagues. They often gossip and spread rumors. They might also feel less inclined to invest a strong effort for a company that they may feel betrayed them in some way.

- **A preoccupation to solve the crisis that greatly reduces the time and budget available to spend on profit-enhancing activities.** Perhaps the greatest negative of a crisis is its ability to steal the focus away from a company. A successful business is strongly focused on what it takes to be successful. Usually this is a passion for exceeding the expectations of their customers and an outstanding plan and execution for making that happen. A crisis throws that empowering focus aside, often without a business realizing it, while the company is preoccupied with fixing the problem. How did the crisis happen? How can we ensure it won't happen again? What should we do now? What will our employees think? How can we ensure we don't lose business from this? What can we do to bounce back from the problem?

- **Senior-level personnel changes.** Often the senior-level carnage from a crisis is spectacular. Presidents and CEOs are asked to resign or are terminated by their boards of directors. Executive Vice Presidents, Senior Vice Presidents, Vice Presidents, Directors and Managers of departments all find themselves in a vulnerable position, and many are replaced. It's like the professional sports team with a losing record. Players are traded, coaches are fired and other changes are made. After all, someone needs to take the blame and if there can be a fall-guy (or gal) – who can be cut like a tumor from the organization – then usually this will be done. Learning crisis-management skills can greatly improve job security.

- **Major product/service enhancements.** A crisis can force some unwanted and costly changes in the products or services offered by a company. This can involve a complete shift in the marketing of your products/services or perhaps dictate more aggressive changes – including killing a brand or giving up on a market segment altogether.

- **Corporate name change.** A crisis can force an expensive name change if the damage to a company's reputation is so severe that it needs to build an entirely new identity. This has happened with companies such as International Harvester, which changed its name to Navistar to build a new identity after a major union problem. Building a new corporate identity can cost large companies millions of dollars and take several years to achieve market acceptance.

You mentioned "unexpected necessary costs to help minimize damage caused by the crisis." What costs would likely become necessary?

Costs could include one or more of the following:

- **Fines or penalties.** These can include fines or penalties for breaking laws or not meeting regulatory requirements related to the environment, product safety, workforce and labor, building standards, among other possibilities. Costs add up quickly here for attorneys, consultants, lobbyists, auditors, in addition to the fine or penalty itself.

- **Litigation.** This includes costs to fight litigation in the courts or settle it before it gets that far. Costs include court fees, the settlement amount, rising insurance premiums and the stream of attorneys sinking their teeth into the legal action.

- **Crisis-management/public relations consultants.** Many businesses don't have on-staff expertise in the areas of crisis management or even public relations in general. Retaining a consulting firm will be costly to help get the bone out of your company's throat and to work on ways to rebuild the goodwill that was depleted by the crisis. If you feel the business is vulnerable to a crisis, it's best to retain this type of expertise *before* the crisis occurs because a front-end investment might save considerable expenses when a crisis eventually erupts.

- **Media-information materials.** If a crisis occurs that draws the attention of the news media, you may need to develop and distribute information to help describe the crisis, your position related to the crisis, your company and products/services, and other items. This might be in the form of news releases, fact sheets, backgrounders, position statements, opinion-editorial articles, by-lined stories or video news releases. In addition to the time involved to develop the items, other costs could include fees to a public relations firm to help prepare and distribute the materials; printing and production costs; overnight-mail and postage rates; facsimile and photocopier charges; fees for transmitting information to the news media through PR Newswire, BusinessWire or another media-distribution service; satellite costs for transmitting video news releases or backgrounders to television stations.

- **Airfare and lodging.** The company's crisis may force you or some of your staff to schedule unexpected trips to meet with employees, customers, political leaders, regulators, community residents or news media. With the cost and hassles of airline travel and hotel visits today, and the lost time out of the office, this can have a large impact on business in a short period of time.

- **Information pamphlets.** A crisis often forces a business to increase its level of communication with employees, customers and other publics. This might include incurring costs to develop pamphlets in the form of "questions and answers" or "myths vs. facts" or a restatement of the organization's mission. The information could include background or rationale on the situation, and the adjustments being made to ensure a future problem doesn't occur. Based on the quantities needed, the costs to print and distribute the pamphlets could be several hundreds or thousands of dollars.

- **Direct-mail costs.** In some cases, it becomes necessary to mail large quantities of letters, flyers, pamphlets or brochures to communicate during and after a crisis. This expense includes costs for printing, labels, postage and envelopes.

- **Teleconferences or videoconferences.** A crisis may force a company to communicate quickly and simultaneously with large numbers of employees, distributors, customers, analysts or media in many different cities. This may be done through telephone conference calls or videoconferences. The rates for both can be costly, and the effort to coordinate such an undertaking is time intensive.

- **Targeted advertisements.** Paid advertisements are often used when a crisis occurs at a business and it finds its most important messages are not being communicated by the news media or making a sufficient impact with the company's key publics. These are typically advertisements published in newspapers or select trade publications. The costs involved include possible fees to an advertising or public relations firm, production costs, overnight/courier charges and the cost to actually purchase the advertising space.

- **Media monitoring costs.** You will want to track what the media are reporting about your company during and after a crisis occurs. It is important to monitor media reports to be aware of what your employees, customers, vendors and others are learning about your situation. Monitoring the media will also help keep you abreast of any errors made in news reports, and to help determine future strategies and tactics. Several media-monitoring services exist – such as Burrelle's, Luce, Bacon's and Video Monitoring Services. In addition, coverage can be monitored by research services such as MAID's Profound® service and Find/SVP. Internet monitoring services, such as Minnesota-based eWorks, Inc., exist to identify and track companies or issues being discussed in websites, newsgroups or cyberspace chat rooms.

- **Extraordinary on-line fees.** In an effort to communicate with others and to further monitor reports on your company, your business could incur significant costs involving on-line fees. This could include costs for electronic mail and bulletin boards – if you don't have a dedicated line for that purpose – and to monitor on-line services such as Lexis-Nexis, DataTimes, and others.

What is "crisis management"?

Crisis management is the function that works to minimize the potential damage of a crisis to a business, and helps gain control of the situation. Within the context discussed here, crisis management works to minimize the damage to a company's reputation and to take advantage of any benefits that can be obtained from a crisis.

Isn't "crisis management" just a different way of saying "disaster control" or "crisis communications"?

No. The most effective executive thinks of crisis management as a wide range of principles and activities. Disaster control or crisis communications is done after the crisis has already occurred. Crisis management is a series of specific activities that is best understood as part of a process, referred to by the author as "*The Crisis Counselor* mindset."

The Crisis Counselor mindset

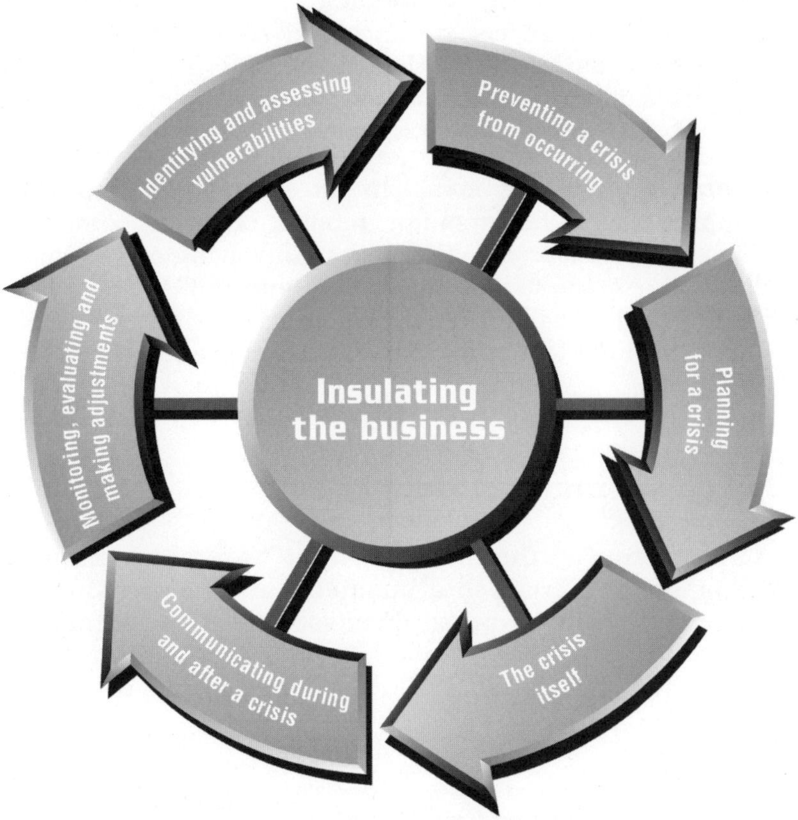

So, what is "*The Crisis Counselor* mindset"?

"*The Crisis Counselor* mindset" is putting the most effective crisis-management philosophy to best use in a business. It is a series of activities and management steps to help prevent, manage and thrive on business crises. After this chapter, the remainder of the book addresses each area with its own chapter. The mindset is as follows:

1) **Identify and assess vulnerabilities in an organization.** Almost all crises are preceded by some type of warning. The successful business spots early warning signs and makes necessary adjustments to ensure they don't turn into crises.

The first step in *The Crisis Counselor* mindset is to identify the vulnerabilities or weak spots in an organization and assess the potential damage that could be caused by each. (This is covered in Chapter 2.)

2) **Prevent the vulnerabilities from erupting into crises.** The successful business works to ensure the vulnerabilities don't negatively affect the company. Tough decisions are made decisively, and procrastination to address the organization's Achilles heels doesn't exist. (This is discussed in greater detail in Chapter 3.)

3) **Plan for a potential crisis.** The successful company believes every business will someday experience a crisis and recognizes its potential damaging effect. The investment of time and budget to plan well in advance for ways to effectively manage a crisis helps prevent the huge negative fallout from a poorly managed crisis. The most successful businesses consider potential worst-case scenarios, and conduct as much advance planning and preparation as possible. (Learn more about this in Chapter 4.)

4) **Identify when a crisis has occurred and determine actions to take.** The successful business recognizes a crisis when it has occurred and acknowledges the necessity for quick action. After all, a problem can't be fixed until the problem is recognized. A major key to effectively managing a crisis is taking fast, decisive action in an attempt to nip it while it's still at manageable proportions. The problem needs to be fixed first, and then the crisis needs to be managed through effective communications. (This is covered in Chapter 5.)

5) **Communicate most effectively during a crisis.** Once a business begins addressing the problem, the next step is to determine at what level the company should communicate with its employees, customers, regulators, shareholders, news media and other important publics. The communications need to be open, honest and credible. Failure to communicate to the extent expected and desired by the various publics almost always leads to serious, often long-term, problems for a business. (This is discussed in Chapter 6, including specific recommendations for communicating with employees, customers, news media and other important publics.)

6) **Monitor and evaluate the crisis and make adjustments along the way.** It can be difficult to know whether you are making the best decisions during and after a crisis. The successful business recognizes the importance of monitoring the opinions and behavior of the company's key publics during and after a crisis, and making necessary adjustments along the way. It may be necessary to adjust the messages being communicated, the publics being addressed and the manner in which you are communicating. (This is discussed in greater detail in Chapter 7.)

7) **Insulate your business through activities intended to enhance your organization's reputation and credibility.** One of the most important factors in how a business is affected by a crisis is its reputation going into the crisis. The successful business works hard throughout the year – not just in times of crisis – to earn the respect, confidence and trust of its key publics: employees, customers, vendors, regulators, politicians, community leaders, news media and others. The goodwill equity earned by the business helps insulate it from a crisis just like solid insulation helps keep a home comfortable during a bad winter. (This is covered in Chapter 8.)

So, who should be The Crisis Counselor in an organization?

The Crisis Counselor is any business owner, executive, franchisee, sales person, marketing or public relations professional, accountant, CEO, CFO or others who – through their crisis-management principles and actions – prevent and manage problems that arise in their everyday business lives. The Crisis Counselor would be the person or persons who take the lead to ensure the company's reputation is preserved and protected before, during and after a crisis. In a small flower shop it might be the franchisee or the day manager. In a law firm it would likely be the Managing Partner, unless its size enables it to have a senior public relations officer on staff. At a hospital, the most appropriate person would be the senior public relations officer or either the CEO or COO.

Should every business have someone who is responsible for being its primary Crisis Counselor?

Yes. Ideally, *everyone* in the organization should have *The Crisis Counselor* mindset and understand the ways to prevent and manage crises that could occur in the business. At the least, every business should have a Chief Crisis Officer (CCO), just as one has a Chief Executive Officer, Chief Operating Officer, Chief Financial Officer and Chief Information Officer. The CCO might likely be the most senior public relations officer already existing in the organization. If your business doesn't have an on-staff public relations officer, the responsibility could be given to the CEO or COO, or perhaps to a senior executive specializing in crisis management at a well-respected public relations firm.

What does someone with *The Crisis Counselor* mindset do within a business?

The Crisis Counselor – whether it be the business owner, CEO, a manager or a trained public relations executive – would likely conduct one or more of the following activities on an ongoing basis:

- **Provides input on a business strategy.** Someone with *The Crisis Counselor* mindset has a broad-minded, objective way of thinking that serves an organization well in the area of business strategy. Even if this person isn't the CEO or owner, he or she can provide helpful insights on strategies and tactics related to managing the company's reputation.

- **Establishes a crisis-management strategy.** The Crisis Counselor helps establish a crisis-management gameplan and culture in the business. She pushes the senior management toward being a crisis-ready organization, and ensures that many of the principles covered in this book are integrated in the business.

- **Identifies specific objectives that can be achieved.** The Crisis Counselor in an organization helps identify crisis-management objectives that can be met and works toward specific ways to meet them.

- **Identifies and assesses the vulnerabilities of a business or department.** The Crisis Counselor helps a business look at its blemishes and Achilles heels. The counselor may encourage the company to conduct a comprehensive vulnerabilities analysis (see Chapter 2), or ensure an internal review and discussion on the matter.

- **Recommends ways to prevent the most likely crises from occurring.** The Crisis Counselor in a business suggests ways to ensure the organization's vulnerabilities don't turn into crises. He recognizes that most crises are preceded by some type of warning and will work with others in the business to heed the warning signs.

- **Establishes a crisis-management team to help plan for a crisis.** The Crisis Counselor takes the initiative to establish a crisis-management team in the business well before a crisis occurs. The crisis team will help identify vulnerabilities, consider worst-case scenarios and plan for ways to ensure the crisis will be managed effectively when it occurs.

- **Develops information and materials.** The Crisis Counselor recognizes that development of information and materials in advance of a crisis will be one less necessary step when a crisis actually occurs. These might include a news release, media kit, pamphlets, customer letters, employee memoranda, fact sheets and backgrounders. Although initial "drafts" will need updating and revising – based on the actual crisis that has occurred – the initial drafts will save considerable time when a crisis erupts and evolves. The Crisis Counselor won't necessarily develop the materials himself, but he will ensure they are being done by someone.

- **Helps ensure communications activities before, during and after a crisis.** The Crisis Counselor recognizes that communication is often the most important variable in determining the effects of a crisis on a business. She helps ensure that someone in the business, or at a retained public relations firm, will properly plan and implement communications activities before, during and after a crisis.

- **Identifies and trains possible company spokespersons.** The Crisis Counselor may help identify those who will represent the business in media interviews, speaking appearances and employee meetings. He knows the importance of an effective, well-trained spokesperson, and helps ensure those who will fulfill that function in a crisis will be well prepared.

- **Ensures all the business' publics are communicated with in a priority manner and with the most appropriate spokesperson.** The Crisis Counselor in a company makes sure all of its publics are being addressed during and after a crisis. She also ensures a sufficient amount of goodwill exists with each of the organization's most-important publics to help insulate the company for the inevitable crisis that will occur in the future.

- **Continually evaluates strategies and tactics, and makes adjustments when necessary.** The Crisis Counselor keeps an ear on the organization's railroad tracks. He helps identify when strategies and tactics should be adjusted during and after a crisis, and when the business should stay on the track it is following.

Can this responsibility be shared?

Yes. In larger organizations it would likely be shared between a senior public relations officer and someone in senior management – perhaps the person who has the ultimate responsibility for the public relations function. In a smaller organization, it might be shared between the owner/franchisee/CEO and another senior-level executive. Or, in many cases, the responsibilities could be shared between a senior manager and a public relations firm. In some instances, it is the sole responsibility of the CEO/owner.

Example: The Chief Crisis Officer and the team

The university boasts the highest enrollment of students in the state. Despite the large student population, the school has had an outstanding record of on-campus safety and is considered among the most student-friendly universities in the nation.

Unfortunately, during this year's unusually hot summer, two students were victims of on-campus sexual assaults while walking home from night classes. It had been nearly 20 years since crimes of this magnitude occurred on campus, and the university's students, employees and faculty were both frightened and frustrated.

The university's administration had previously conducted some planning to prepare for such a crisis, but it hadn't realized the strangle-hold these incidents would have on the campus community.

The VP-University Relations was designated as the crisis leader – the Chief Crisis Officer – until further notice. Several university leaders stepped up to share the crisis-management responsibilities. The President and the VP-University Relations were designated as the only two spokespersons approved to publicly discuss the situation, but some confusion existed as to which person would be used for what purpose.

"When should I be the spokesperson and under what circumstances would you prefer to be?" the VP-University Relations asked of the President.

"Let's just play it by ear," replied the President. "Handle as much of it as you can, and I'll do the rest."

The VP-Public Relations worked to compile facts about the university, including its outstanding safety record, and worked to coordinate all media inquiries and requests. The Director of Security worked with the appropriate law-enforcement agencies to lead toward the arrest of the person or persons who assaulted the students, and to work on ways to improve security on campus.

A number of other university officials helped develop strategies and implement activities to ensure the school's primary publics felt everything possible was being done to achieve a safe and secure environment for students, employees and faculty. Everyone involved said they wished they had been better prepared to manage such a crisis.

Three lessons to learn

The university's crisis helps reinforce these important points:

1) **Clearly identify a Chief Crisis Officer.** The VP-University Relations was designated as the crisis leader. In this case, the university did this *after* the crisis. Ideally, it should have been done *before* the crisis, to further reduce the decisions necessary during the crisis.

2) **Limit the spokespersons and clearly identify their roles.** The university was smart to limit the number of people authorized to be official spokespersons. In many cases, a business is best served limiting the number of spokespersons to only one. This is done to limit the risk of communicating incorrect and inconsistent information. However, since little advance planning had been conducted, the VP-University Relations and the President were unsure and unclear about their roles as spokespersons. One way to have segmented the roles would be to have the VP-University Relations handle all routine requests for information and brief interviews (after first being screened by the VP-Public Relations). The President would be used for major interviews and personal appearances in front of student, faculty and community groups to show her concern and to explain changes to on-campus security policies and procedures.

3) **Consider worst-case scenarios and plan for them.** Although the university had an outstanding safety record, a process to consider possible worst-case scenarios would have revealed the possibility of such on-campus crime. The university could have considered what information or materials would be necessary if or when such crimes occurred. It would have found that information would need to be prepared on the university's safety record, security procedures, safety policies and enforcement records. In this situation, the university had to develop the information after the crisis had already occurred and when its people were already scrambling to fulfill other needs and requests. You would be surprised what can be done in advance of a crisis that will save considerable time and problems when one actually occurs.

◆

You mentioned a business can "thrive" from a crisis. How can that happen? Aren't all crises inherently bad?

Believe me, I'm not saying a business should want a crisis to occur. But, there are times when a crisis can be beneficial to a business. This indirect "benefit" has the potential of occurring only when a crisis is managed effectively.

Here are some possible *positive* benefits a business can experience during and after a crisis:

- **Increased visibility and name recognition.** If nothing else, a high-profile crisis provides substantial visibility for a business. In most cases, it is certainly visibility a company could do without. In rare occasions, when a crisis is managed skillfully, the *positives* gained by the situation can outweigh the negatives. This benefit is easier to obtain when the business is "victimized" by a crisis rather than the "culprit" *causing* the crisis. For instance, if your business is shut down because of a natural disaster – such as a hurricane – it is much easier to gain the support and understanding of your customers, vendors, employees and others. If your business is shut down because you underestimated the amount of parts needed to sustain production at its current level, you are much less likely to benefit from it. In any case, the problem needs to be solved quickly and effectively to have people saying, "Gee, that must be a great company to have managed that situation so successfully. We ought to look into them."

- **An opportunity to show competency/leadership.** Crises offer excellent opportunities to make or break a CEO or whoever is in charge of managing the problem. Many CEOs have become legendary figures based on how they took charge, showed strong leadership and helped solve serious problems. These include former Chrysler Chairman Lee Iaccoca (1979 government bailout and 1986 odometer situation), former Johnson & Johnson Chairman James E. Burke (1982 and 1986 Tylenol tamperings), and General Motors' former legal counsel and current Vice Chairman Harry Pearce (1994 GM truck side-impact allegations by NBC-TV). Leaders are transformed every day into superstars in all types of organizations by demonstrating their strong leadership in managing crises. In times of crises, some leaders not only emerge unscathed, but actually improve their reputations and careers. They usually achieve this by doing the following:

1) Moving on the problem quickly and showing strong commitment to solving it immediately.
2) Demonstrating unwavering confidence, but not arrogance, in following through with his/her gameplan.
3) Showing remorse and compassion to the people affected by the crisis. If the company made a mistake, the leader will apologize for it.
4) Immediately making changes in the organization to ensure the crisis won't occur again, and communicating this to the company's key publics.
5) Ensuring that his/her leadership is visible. This doesn't mean handling everything alone, but making sure the leadership is clearly visible as the problem is being managed.
6) Assuming the responsibility and ultimate blame, if necessary; but, sharing the credit and accolades if they come along the way as well.

- **Improved relationships.** Crisis situations don't always mean insurmountable problems and strained relationships between you and your key publics – such as your employees and customers. If a crisis is managed properly, it can provide great opportunities for stronger bonds and healthier, long-term relationships with those you count on for your organization's success. However, this can only happen if you have previously earned their goodwill and trust (see Chapter 8) and treat them in the following ways:

  1) Communicate with them about the situation, and describe specifically what you would like them to do and why it is necessary.
  2) Treat them as a respected team member. Persuade them to help in a sensitive and compassionate manner.
  3) Show your genuine appreciation for their help.

4) Keep them updated.

5) Continue treating them well long after the crisis over.

- **Necessary changes are made.** Some businesses sorely need to be fixed. Their leaders either don't recognize the problems exist or simply don't want to invest the time or energies to fix the situation. Many just hope the problem will go away by itself. This may involve restructuring the company – and terminating unproductive employees and destructive managers – or changing a product that no longer meets customer needs. A crisis can be the impetus to make the type of changes that should have been made anyhow. A crisis can provide the motivation and incentive to convince the leader to make the type of changes that will eventually strengthen the organization. It's too bad that some organizations need a crisis to push them toward improvement, but it occurs every day in business.

Why should I concern myself with crisis management, if I'm not a CEO or in public relations?

The Crisis Counselor philosophy is an essential part of effective leadership and management – the ability to plan for difficult times and work to ensure the negatives are minimized when they occur.

Everyone in an organization has a responsibility to their employer – regardless of their positions – to help ensure the company's sales, profits and reputation are enhanced by the contributions they make on a day-to-day basis. They need to help protect the company's most-valuable asset – its reputation – by ensuring they are prepared for the inevitable crisis situation and can react decisively and confidently to successfully minimize damage caused by it.

Everyone at all levels in business today is held more accountable than ever. Companies are making decisions every day on which people make the greatest contributions to the organization and which have the best perspectives on the business and its future challenges. Employees who understand and practice crisis management greatly improve their value and potential for career growth in their businesses.

What are some of the biggest *mistakes* companies make in managing crisis situations?

The most common mistakes are **failing to heed warning signals** and **not planning for a crisis in advance**. These are covered in later chapters. Other typical mistakes include the following:

- **Being too slow to make decisions.** When a crisis occurs in a business, it needs to be addressed quickly and with insight. Failure to do that within a reasonable period of time leads to frustrations, misinformation and lack of support. You can't be afraid to make decisions in a crisis.

- **Failing to communicate with *all* necessary publics.** A common mistake in a crisis is communicating only with a select group of publics when the situation dictates that others are affected as well. This occurs frequently when businesses notify customers about a situation, but fail to adequately inform their employees about it. Or, they notify customers and employees but those most affected – vendors, for instance – aren't notified until they've already heard about it third-hand from someone else. The act of communicating during a crisis needs to be done *comprehensively*. A good rule of thumb is to treat those various audiences they way *you* would want to be treated if you were one of them. If you think they should know about the situation, or would *like* to know about it, then communicate with them before it's too late. After all, *keeping* their support is much easier than trying to win it back once it's lost.

- **Not preparing information materials in advance.** It is surprising the level of planning that can be done in advance of a crisis (see Chapter 4). By considering possible worst-case scenarios, and what might be needed if a crisis were to occur, an organization can develop a number of items before the crisis erupts. These might include fact sheets describing the business and its history, products and services; biographies and photographs of your top people; and, video footage showing your operation in action.

- **Failing to return phone calls from the news media.** Many businesses make the mistake of gladly talking with a news reporter if a positive story is on the horizon, but refuse to cooperate when a problem occurs and the coverage could be negative. Failing to return phone calls and to treat reporters and editors with courtesy and decency are common mistakes that will only fan flames, making the problem worse. If the media feel you are running scared or trying to evade any blame or attention, they will likely come after you with long fangs and powerful jaw muscles.

- **Saying "no comment" to media questions.** Here's a common mistake that is akin to wearing an "I'm guilty" sign around your neck. So many ways exist to say nothing harmful to questions asked that you should never need to say "no comment" to a question you'd rather not answer. However, these responses need to be considered in advance and put in writing for future reference, if necessary. A major key to managing a crisis effectively is to avoid the impression you are being evasive, failing to recognize the problem or shirking responsibility. It doesn't mean you need to tell them everything you know. It means you step up and tell them what you can (or would like), and have a solid reason for why you need to stop there. Don't say "no comment." See Chapter 6 for more thoughts on the news media and for an example of a way to say "no comment" without using those words.

- **Not obtaining input, feedback and questions from publics.** A common mistake businesses make in managing a crisis is the failure to provide mechanisms to hear from their publics. This includes receiving their ideas, suggestions, input and criticism, and providing them opportunities to ask questions and receive timely answers. This is often accomplished in one-on-one meetings, group meetings, town-hall gatherings, toll-free phonelines, suggestion boxes, electronic mail and survey questionnaires. Failure to do so almost always leads to frustrations, rumors and perhaps even a larger crisis.

- **Being unwilling to make necessary adjustments.** Not all advance planning pans out the way it was first conceived. And, not all decisions work as well as desired. Adjustments are inevitable during the management of a crisis, and – based on information and input gathered – you need to maintain flexibility to make necessary adjustments along the way.

- **Listening to the wrong people.** When a crisis occurs, everyone has an opinion on how to solve it. Input and advice may be offered by your management team, employees, customers and the news media. Your spouse will have an opinion, so will your next-door neighbor and the person who cuts your hair. You may even have slightly conflicting opinions from those you expect to help set overall strategy. For instance, your organization's legal counsel might instruct you not to say anything to anyone – even if news media, community leaders or customers want information. Your public relations counsel might instruct you to be communicative by proactively informing your key publics about the situation. To whom should you listen? The decision is different for every situation and should be based on past experience, professional instincts and information gathered about the situation at hand.

- **Being misleading or dishonest.** Although it occurs less frequently, a serious mistake is made when a business is deliberately misleading or dishonest during a crisis. In either case, an organization's credibility and trustworthiness can be shattered in a matter of minutes. If one cardinal rule exists for managing a crisis, it is that you should never intentionally lie or mislead someone whose support is important to the success of your business. It isn't worth the possible side-effects that may take years to mend if you are caught.

What are the most important aspects of crisis management?

Each of the parts are important. Effective crisis management is a *process*, not an *event*. It is an ongoing, systematic and disciplined process that a business should follow to help identify vulnerabilities, prevent crises from occurring, plan for those most likely to occur, communicate effectively during and after a crisis, monitor and evaluate the situation, and make adjustments as necessary.

In most cases, a crisis is preceded by some type of warning sign that should be heeded. This will be discussed in a subsequent chapter. However, when a crisis is not preceded by a warning sign, it makes the preparation done to plan for a possible crisis absolutely essential.

How can you tell whether a crisis is managed well?

Unlike *mis*managed crises that often receive considerable negative media coverage or linger for several days, weeks or months, a *well*-managed crisis is often more difficult to detect. Here are a few ways to identify a crisis which is managed successfully:

- **The problem seems to go away after a few days.** The best sign of a well-managed crisis is that the situation becomes a forgotten after-thought in a relatively short period of time. This often occurs when the organization effectively manages the situation, takes the blame for the mistake and apologies (if appropriate), and gives the strong impression the problem has been rectified and that life goes on.

- **The crisis doesn't receive any further media coverage after the initial stories appear.** Often times a crisis will receive significant media coverage one day and, if managed effectively, may never be reported about again. This often happens when the company was accessible and open with the news media, and avoided any impression of being defensive and afraid of the situation. If the business makes the situation appear as if it is well under control, and does so in a confident manner, the news media may determine that the story is no longer newsworthy. The story dies a quick death and the problem is forgotten – due to the crisis-management techniques practiced by the company.

- **The organization's publics are supportive.** A sign of a well-managed crisis is the sustained support received by the organization's various publics (e.g., employees, customers, vendors, community leaders, regulators, analysts, investors, news media). If they are hanging in there with you during difficult times, it undoubtedly means three things:

    1) You had previously earned a fair amount of goodwill with each.

    2) You have communicated well with them during the crisis.

    3) The other aspects of the crisis have been managed well by you.

- **The company gives the strong impression the crisis is under control.** A business can actually convey a sense of leadership and management in a crisis. Do they appear to be running from the crisis, hoping it will just go away? Is anyone panicking? Does it appear they know what they're doing? Is the business controlling the crisis or has the crisis taken control of the company? Employees, customers, vendors and other key publics usually can tell whether a business is managing a crisis well, and the company itself can play a major part in sending a positive message. This is done by one or more of the following ways:

1) Be prepared in advance so you can move quickly and effectively during and after a crisis.

2) Communicate specific messages with each of your publics, and give them opportunities to offer feedback and ask questions.

3) Ensure your leadership and company spokespersons give the impression of control. They can't look like they're scared to death or are on the verge of a panic attack.

4) Respond in a timely way to inquiries about the crisis, so you don't give the impression of being evasive or uncooperative.

- **The spokesperson seems to be well prepared and competent.** When a crisis occurs that puts your business in the spotlight, you will need someone to represent your organization to answer questions from the media and others. Depending on the nature of the crisis, this could be one or more of the following: the company's owner, the Chief Executive Officer, a plant manager, a department director, a public relations representative, or someone else in a similar leadership position. Those representing your business in a crisis play a major role in the perception of whether or not your crisis is being well managed. They are most likely to give that impression if they are the following:

  1) Well prepared with specific core messages to communicate and reinforce, and answers to both routine and difficult questions that may arise.

  2) Articulate and well spoken.

  3) Compassionate and able to connect with people through proper eye contact, vocal tone and body language.

4) Not rattled easily – and can maintain their composure when the pressure tightens.

5) In a position of authority in the company.

- **Company sales, profits and productivity rebound quickly or aren't negatively impacted at all.** A business that manages its crisis well finds that sales, profits, productivity and stock price aren't negatively affected over a long period of time. Some don't suffer at all. The ability to bounce back after a crisis is directly related to the proficiency in managing the crisis. If the crisis has damaged your company's reputation and credibility, the consequences suffered will surely include a major impact on sales, profits and productivity. If they recover quickly, or aren't affected at all, you've probably done an excellent job of managing the crisis.

- **The company's reputation and credibility remain unscathed.** Reputation and credibility are difficult to measure, so how can you tell whether they have suffered damage in a crisis? Well, if you are looking at a business that just experienced a crisis, how do you feel about the company now? Has the crisis, and specifically the manner in which the business managed the crisis, affected your impression of the company? Do you still trust the company? If the crisis has occurred at *your* business, what feedback are you receiving that indicates how your reputation and credibility have been affected? The reputation and credibility of a business aren't negatively affected – over the long term – in a well-managed crisis. And, in some cases, they can actually be *improved* by a crisis managed extraordinarily well by a business.

You've mentioned "publics" several times. What do you mean by "publics" or "targeted publics"?

Publics are individuals or groups of people or organizations with similar characteristics that are important to the success of your business. "Targeted" publics are those that should be focused on and addressed in a priority manner. The following are publics for many organizations:

- Company employees
- Current customers

- Potential customers
- Directors of the company's board
- Investors
- Financial analysts
- Distributors/ franchisees
- Suppliers
- News media
- Community residents
- Government officials and politicians
- Regulators
- Labor officials

Publics need to be described as specifically as possible. For instance, employees in a bank can be grouped in at least four distinct categories: tellers and other branch employees, senior-level branch executives, senior-level executives at corporate headquarters and other employees at corporate headquarters. Each public might receive specific messages tailored exclusively for it. And, a different spokesperson might be considered for one or more of the publics.

In most cases, the effectiveness of the communications during a crisis is greatly enhanced by a more segmented and defined body of publics.

What are some ways publics can be *segmented* for more effective targeting and communication?

Take a fresh look at the publics affecting your business, and consider some of the different ways each can be segmented or separated. Here are a few ways each of the following publics can be segmented – you may think of others:

- **Company employees.** Hourly; salary; full-time; part-time; senior officers; managers; corporate headquarters staff; and those located at off-site plants, branches or offices.

- **Current customers.** Large, medium and small volume; local, regional, national and international; long term; project-only; potential for future cross-selling; fastest payers; and, slowest payers.
- **Potential customers.** Hottest; most-desirable; those currently talking with us; former customers with the potential to return; large, medium and small volume; local, regional, national and international; long term; and project-only.
- **Directors of the company's board.** Chairman; executive-committee members; internal management on the board; and, those from outside the company.
- **Investors.** Institutional; individual; company ownership; high, medium or small volume; local, national or international; buy-side; and, sell-side.
- **Financial analysts.** Industry; buy-side; sell-side; and, local, regional, national and international.
- **Distributors/ franchisees.** Highest volume; large-, small- or medium-sized markets; longest term; and, local, regional, national or international.
- **Suppliers.** Large, medium and small volume; local, regional, national and international; most-to-least important to the success of the business; and, those accepting the most flexible payable terms.
- **News media.** Local-community media; industry/trade media; newspapers; magazines, radio stations; broadcast television; cable television; and, reporters, editors, columnists, and producers.
- **Community residents.** Key opinion leaders; block-club directors; CEOs of major area businesses; gadflys; high-, medium- and low-income; and, those within a short distance from your business.
- **Government officials and politicians.** Local, national or international; political affiliation; legislators on committees related to your industry; legislative sponsors on bills related to your industry; and, governors, county executives, mayors, and council members in areas where operations exist.

- **Regulators.** Industry-specific; state; federal; primary staff contacts; directors; engineers; and, public affairs contacts.
- **Labor officials.** Industry-specific; union-specific; local stewards; national officials; and, contract negotiators.

How often are crises actually preceded by some sort of warning sign?

It all depends on the type of crisis it is. Most of the time, some sort of warning sign does precede a crisis. For instance, a problem with a violent, disgruntled employee is often preceded by several emotional confrontations or indirect threats made to other employees. If the problem isn't addressed in a direct and decisive manner, it can lead to a more serious outburst and full-blown violent crisis. Losing a major piece of business is often preceded by some previous problems with the customer.

Example: Making the wrong call

The corporate Internet provider specializes in secure websites and intranets for businesses in this suburban market. Its clients include some of the area's largest and most successful car dealerships, for which the company has developed individual intranets.

The dealerships' sales staffs use the intranets to communicate with their sales managers and determine the pricing on each of their new and used automobiles. The parts and services departments check inventories and pricing in their areas as well. The Internet provider maintains a firewall security system using encryption and passwords to ensure their websites can't be breached by hackers or the competition.

The Internet provider has found it difficult of late to find sufficient numbers of qualified and experienced employees. Client demands and growing new business have forced the company to ask under-trained workers to perform highly technical tasks for their top clients. This didn't prove to be a problem until the largest of the company's automobile dealerships said its intranet firewall had been penetrated.

"I've been told by two friends at our competitors that we are the laughing stock at their dealerships," said the car dealer, who called in panic one night around 7 p.m. He asked for his client contact who had just left the office for the evening. He spoke with one of the newer employees. "Someone penetrated our firewall, and our competitors now know all of our pricing on our automobiles, parts and repair and body-shop services. This will cost us thousands of dollars in lost profits. You better find out what the problem is and get it solved right away."

The junior employee said: "Sir, I rather doubt your site's firewall has been penetrated. It's highly unlikely that happened. I understand that's never happened with our clients, which is why I joined this company. You're probably overreacting. I'm sure they learned your information from some other source. Can you trust all your sales people? I'll have my boss call you tomorrow."

"Don't tell me I'm overreacting, young woman," said the car dealer. "Tell your boss he just lost a client. I want our site deactivated immediately. Do you hear me?"

When the Internet company's President learned of the situation the next day, she called to apologize to the client and worked to eventually win back the client. She felt obligated to give his dealership free Internet service for the remainder of the year, which cost the company thousands of dollars.

She later analyzed the situation with her management team and said, "We've learned several valuable lessons. First, we need to listen to the warning signs. We knew we had put under-trained employees in inappropriate positions. That firewall mistake would not have been made by a more experienced person. Second, we should always have a manager-level person working on site to manage customer calls at all times. And, third, we need to better train our employees to be more customer-oriented. Believe me, it will take a long time before we recover from this crisis."

Three lessons to learn

The Internet provider learned these three lessons from which all businesses can benefit:

1) **Ensure all employees in contact with customers are properly trained.** Most businesses train their employees, but few do it very well. The Internet provider had an inexperienced person who was under-trained and under-qualified to communicate with customers. Look at your own business. Do employees in contact with your customers really understand their needs and how they count on your company to help them? Do they have a solid understanding of *all* your publics and how they are important to your business? Do they know how to react appropriately to a disgruntled customer?

2) **Don't accept work unless your business can do it well.** The Internet provider recognized that growing client demands had forced it to place under-trained workers to perform highly technical jobs for their clients. Although turning down business is one of the least desirable options a business can consider, it is much better than accepting work that can't be done successfully. In this case, the Internet provider should have ensured that all of its programmers and technicians had the expertise to meet and exceed customers' needs. Failure to do so is no different than manufacturing alarm clocks that don't quite tell the right time, and hoping the customer won't notice. Of course, it is much better to fix the problem with the alarm clocks before manufacturing any additional ones. This sounds so obvious, and it often is in a *manufacturing* business. It is a more difficult call in a *service* organization.

3) **If your business makes a mistake, admit it and work fast to fix the problem.** The President of the Internet company was smart to personally call the customer, to apologize and to offer an incentive for the client to continue working with the company (and as a goodwill gesture for the mistake and the way it was handled). Remember this adage: "If your business messed up – fess up." When customers and others are irate, they want to get a strong sense that you see the problem, understand the seriousness of it and are sorry for the mistake. Failure to do so almost always leads to prolonged frustrations, strong disagreements and loss of trust between the two parties. In many cases, it leads to a lost customer, possible litigation and a seriously damaged reputation.

◆

What can I do to determine whether or not my company or department is vulnerable to a crisis?

The most effective way is to ask questions and be perceptive about any warning signs that should be addressed. A comprehensive way to do this is through a *vulnerabilities analysis,* which is discussed in the next chapter. However, take a few minutes now to sit back and consider any obvious areas of vulnerability that quickly come to mind about your business. Jot them down on a piece of paper and consider them as you read the next few chapters.

Closing thoughts

The Crisis Counselor mindset is a new way of thinking about your job and helping your business become as strong and crisis-ready as possible. It involves identifying vulnerabilities, preventing crises from occurring, planning for a possible crisis, communicating effectively during and after a crisis, making adjustments along the way and beginning the process over again. It includes "insulating" your business – on an ongoing basis throughout the year – by building up goodwill, credibility and trust with the organization's most important publics. You'll wish you had a thick padding of insulation when your business faces its next crisis.

These concepts are discussed in greater detail through the remainder of the book. You can prevent a lot of headaches and worrisome nights by having *The Crisis Counselor* mindset in looking at your business today and into the future. Your business and your career will be better for it.

Tips to consider

- **Learn to think like a Crisis Counselor in managing your business or department.**

- **Encourage everyone in your organization to manage with *The Crisis Counselor* mindset.**

- **Name someone in your organization as your Chief Crisis Officer.**

- **Determine the application of crisis-management principles for your business or department.**

- **Recognize that crisis management is more than simply after-the-fact "disaster control" – do as much advance planning as possible.**

- **Heed warning signs that a crisis might be right around the corner.**

- **Assess the vulnerabilities of your business or department and do something about them.**

- **Determine *your* role in the crisis-management process for your company.**

- **Develop a list of your company's most-important publics and list them in priority order.**

- **Don't consider your publics as a single, homogeneous group. Segment them as much as necessary by considering their similarities and differences. You'll be glad you did when it's time to determine how best to communicate with them.**

- **Consider ways to demonstrate to your key executives the importance of crisis management.**

CHAPTER 2

Where could your business get tripped up?

How vulnerable is your business to a crisis?

Take a few minutes to answer these questions:

1) Is your business relatively well known in its industry?

2) Is your business relatively well known in the community/city in which it operates?

3) Are the news, business or trade media interested in your company?

4) Is your business in a strictly regulated industry?

5) Has your organization received more than its share of lawsuits?

6) Are disgruntled current or former employees a problem at your business?

7) Is your business led by a high-profile person in the industry or community?

8) Is your business, its industry or the executives at your company considered controversial in any way?

9) Is your company's stock publicly traded?

10) Has your business experienced a crisis during the past five years?

Evaluation:

0 - 3 "yes" answers	Your business is significantly less vulnerable to a crisis. Will any of these things change during the next few years?
4 - 6 "yes" answers	Plenty of potential exists for a crisis. Begin to look at your business' warning signs in a different way. This chapter will help.
7 - 10 "yes" answers	Move quickly to establish priorities and plan ways to address your vulnerabilities *before* they turn into crisis situations.

A road in your community sorely needs work. Large potholes are two-feet deep. A soft shoulder needs to be rebuilt. The lines need to be restriped. The asphalt needs repaving.

You might intentionally avoid traveling on the road until it is fixed, as you consider the possible risk of using the road. You'd rather not take the chance the potholes might cause a flat tire, or the soft shoulder could force your car to slide into the roadside ditch. Or that the hard-to-see lines in the road might lead to a serious accident. It's not worth the risk. "I'll work around the road on my way home," you say.

On the other hand, you might not even think about the road's problems – even though you travel on the road everyday – until it's too late. You wish you would have thought about these warning signs and did something about them. Your car's front end is out of alignment and an expensive wheel cover fell off after kissing a most vicious pothole. You destroyed your best pair of shoes slopping through the ditch retrieving the wheel cover that couldn't be salvaged anyhow.

Sometimes warning signs are noticed and sometimes they are not. And sometimes they are ignored altogether. Have you ever driven around a "Road Closed" sign and driven down a street that clearly is under construction or dangerous in some way? You slither your way down the road and, on occasion, somehow avoid the trouble. This reinforces that it really wasn't such an insurmountable problem and strengthens your courage or ignorance for the next time.

Business is much the same way. Warning signs occur all the time. Manageable problems that exist today are tomorrow's crises if ignored or worked around. The successful executive is the one with *The Crisis Counselor* mindset – recognizing a company's vulnerabilities as warning signs that have the potential of growing into costly crises.

The key to a winning organization is identifying vulnerabilities and assessing whether they are small problems easily managed or potential combustibles ready to ignite at the smallest provocation. This chapter helps describe the warning flags that may be waving in your business. You'll learn how to identify and assess them so you can decide what – if any – action should be taken to ensure they don't further disrupt your business.

How do crises typically occur?

Crisis situations usually occur from the simple day-to-day work performed in a business. Sometimes they occur by management mistakes which build up through a long period of time, or by only one slip up that causes extreme damage to the organization.

Sometimes a company is *victimized* by a totally unexpected event. A fire, plant accident or the sudden death of a senior executive can occur with little or no warning. Or, other events can occur such as a tampered product, a damaging rumor spread by a competitor or a significant lawsuit against the company.

Crises have many faces. They occur at different times and in varying ways. They can come in as a small problem and, if mismanaged, can escalate into a serious company-threatening disaster. Some crises *begin* as explosive disasters that immediately debilitate a company, while others hang around like a bad virus and kill by a thousand tiny cuts.

Aren't crises *unpredictable* though?

Some crises *are* difficult to predict and foresee. However, *most* crises are preceded by an incident, a mistake or a tell-tale sign that can tip you off to a crisis before it occurs. The problem is we get too busy and preoccupied in the day-to-day management of our businesses to take the time to put out the brush fire before it erupts into an inferno. The warning sign either goes unnoticed or is ignored for something more pressing – perhaps in favor of the extra sale or something easier with which to deal.

What type of organizations are most vulnerable to a crisis?

All businesses eventually experience some form of crisis. Those which seem to be most vulnerable, however, include businesses with one or more of the following characteristics:

- **Businesses that have recently experienced a crisis.** Businesses should *learn* from crises. It would make sense that those which recently experienced a crisis should be the most prepared to avoid a future one. Lightning never strikes twice in the same place, right? Some feel, using that logic, the airline that just suffered a plane crash is the safest to fly. However, the odds are that – if your business has suffered a crisis recently – it is more likely than one that hasn't to suffer another one soon. Two reasons for this include: the previous crisis showed the company is vulnerable to a crisis; and, the business is often preoccupied fixing the previous crisis and may not notice the warning signs of another on its heels.

- **Those in highly regulated industries.** It makes sense that the more rules your business must follow, with serious consequences for violators, the more vulnerable you are to a crisis. The crisis could be in the form of a product recall, environmental fines, labor-related penalties, stressful government probes and other costly investigations. These can significantly damage the reputation of your business which, even beyond the cash outlay for fines and penalties, can take years and even decades to overcome.

- **Businesses with financial difficulties.** Your business is more likely to suffer a crisis when it is suffering financial troubles. When this occurs, a business is more likely to overlook a warning signal because it is preoccupied with other, more immediate matters. Financial troubles can also deplete the amount of goodwill earned by a business with some of its key publics. This occurs most frequently with suppliers who are not being paid on time, and, in some smaller companies, with employees who are faced with pay reductions or delays in cashing their checks. Without the strong support of your key publics, a business is significantly more likely to suffer a crisis.

- **High-profile companies with well-known CEOs.** Some businesses have owners or CEOs who are heralded as "superstars," "brilliant" and "geniuses." They have received substantial amounts of media coverage and have helped make their companies and themselves newsworthy through their success and leadership. The *positives* from this almost always outweigh any potential negatives. However, a negative by-product of the increased profile is that a crisis experienced by the company and CEO become more newsworthy.

- **Publicly held companies.** Businesses that are publicly owned are more vulnerable to crises for several reasons. They are highly regulated (i.e., Securities and Exchange Commission), have a greater number of publics to please (i.e., shareholders, investors, analysts), and are covered by media that focus primarily on publicly held businesses (e.g., *The Wall Street Journal, Investor's Business Daily, Forbes*). They need to disclose all "material" events occurring in the business and can't easily solve a problem over time with little fanfare, as can a privately held business.

- **Fast-growing companies.** Businesses experiencing rapid growth are vulnerable to crises because they have hired employees who may not be adequately trained or experienced. They may be entering previously uncharted markets by the company. And, keeping up with the day-to-day work has left the business with little time to consider its vulnerabilities, heed its warning signs and work to prevent crises from occurring.

- **Those with market share among the top three in their industries.** These companies are usually covered closely by industry analysts and trade media. Their actions and decisions are scrutinized and second-guessed. These businesses may feel others are waiting for any slip, flinch or mistake that can be sensationalized and used to damage the company. An otherwise manageable vulnerability in this company can easily be catapulted by competitors, analysts, media and others fanning the flames.

- **Start-up businesses.** New businesses face extreme challenges during their early months and years to avoid major crises that could negatively affect their financial positions, marketing potential and future health. They are most vulnerable to crises because they haven't yet established a broad base of goodwill and support among a broad range of publics (e.g., employees, customers, prospects, suppliers, news media). Start-up businesses often have few management staff and employees who can help prevent vulnerabilities from turning into crises. They also may not have the financial resources to purchase the equipment, technology and other systems that would help reduce their vulnerabilities.

- **Businesses with absentee ownership.** These include businesses whose owner, CEO or franchisee are not on site to personally experience the challenges of the crisis and to see they are managed swiftly and effectively. These can include multi-store franchise operations, where the franchisee is not on-site and rarely visits the outlet, or branches of retail stores, banks, fitness centers or wholesalers.

- **Businesses with high stress and unfavorable working conditions.** Every business nowadays has an abundance of stress as it is forced by competitive pressures and economics to achieve more results with less resources. However, some businesses are clouded by an inordinate amount of workplace stress. This often occurs through the combination of pressure to meet tight deadlines; extremely demanding management; workers/employees feeling underpaid and underappreciated; little sense of accomplishment due to the relentless workload level; and, a working environment that only adds to the stress levels. These pressures can result in disruptive and even violent behavior by disturbed employees, which has occurred at U.S. Postal Service outlets in Michigan and Texas.

Is it *really* possible to recognize warning signs in advance?

Warning signs are recognized through discipline and perspective. This is the essence of crisis management. It includes being aware of potential problems and vulnerabilities that creep into businesses and can erupt into crises.

Have you ever bought a new car then begin to notice how many of those models are out on the road? It may seem like there's one at every stoplight. They go unnoticed until you become interested in them. Then, you notice virtually every one that drives by.

Crisis warning signs are similar. Without *The Crisis Counselor* mindset, the warning signs will likely go unnoticed through the hecticness of pressing deadlines, increased demands and ringing telephones.

However, if something occurs in the business that just doesn't seem right, it allows an opportunity for someone to heed the warning and consider whether something should be done to help prevent combustion. The enlightened manager and leader recognizing vulnerabilities are like the old Fram oil filter advertising line: "You can pay me now, or pay me later." You can address the situation or problem, to possibly avoid a larger problem, or you can hope it goes away and potentially face more disastrous results in the future.

Certainly, not every vulnerability or warning sign becomes a crisis situation. But, an outstanding business includes managers and employees who believe the signs *can* become crises. The warning signs need to be taken seriously and provide an opportunity for someone to consider their possible short- and long-term effects.

Example: The association misses the clues

The association of architects was the nation's largest. Its membership totaled 75,000 professionals but a second association for architects was formed two years ago and had begun to slowly depress the numbers of those renewing their memberships in the older association.

The executive director of the association was growing increasingly unpopular within the organization as he didn't take kindly to criticism or new ideas, for that matter.

"I ought to know what our members want," said the executive director. "I've been the head of this group before most of our members graduated from elementary school. We've run a pretty darn successful association up to this point, and nothing's going to change that. Believe me, the new association is getting only those members who we didn't want anyhow. Most of them are losers, and we're glad to get rid of them."

The board of directors were occasionally uneasy about the tyrannical executive director, but no one wanted to address the problem.

"Oh, that's just him," said one board member. "He's been like that for years. He keeps everyone in their place, which most people need at one time or another."

The current volunteer chairman, serving a one-year term, said quietly to a fellow member of the board: "He probably needs to move on, but you can bet your house we're not going to tackle that during my chairmanship. I have enough problems back at my firm, I don't need this to make my life even more miserable."

The membership, however, began to get increasingly impatient with the direction of the association.

One member wrote in a letter to the board chairman, "The new association is kicking our behinds. We can't operate the same way we did 25 years ago. When was the last time we surveyed our membership to ask what type of programs they'd like to have? Do you even know what the satisfaction level is among the membership? Why do you think so many members are leaving the association? When was the last time the executive director actually listened to a suggestion and followed through with it?"

The board chairman read the letter, shook his head and asked his secretary to file it – along with other similar letters he had received lately on the same subject.

Six months later, the chairman received a letter from the same person. He said he wasn't satisfied the problems were being addressed, and he and the other 25 architects from his large firm were resigning from the association. He also said he would write a letter to the 1,350 members from his local chapter to encourage them to switch to the new association as well. The letter also said, "I understand the same thing is being considered by several other chapters across the country. It's too bad you didn't address the problem when you had the chance."

Three lessons to learn

The association example reinforces several key points:

1) **Warning signs precede most crises.** Here's an example where even the most hard-headed of us would have caught on to a possible crisis in the oven. These included: an out-of-touch executive director; the lack of a regular membership feedback vehicle (i.e., membership satisfaction survey); a decline in membership while the new association is growing swiftly; and ignoring letters from members. Plenty of opportunities existed to address the situation, fix the problem and evade the crisis.

2) **Problems rarely go away by themselves.** Human nature usually leads us down a slippery slope in the area of solving problems in business. It often is easier to ignore the problem than to address it. Procrastination creeps in and it is put off for another day. Or you convince yourself that it will resolve itself. The truth is, problems rarely resolve themselves. The association chairman was clearly hoping the problem would evaporate – or, at least, not interfere with his one-year term. The chairman should have realized that not only do problems rarely go away by themselves, but – more often than not – they worsen like an abscessed tooth that could have been fixed easily with a dentist visit when it first began hurting months earlier.

3) **Fix the problem and strive for some *positives*.** Don't delay addressing problems if warning flags are waving fiercely. The pain you will face today by fixing them will be far less than the consequences if you don't. Also, take the time to determine if there are ways to turn the potential problem – which you've now addressed – into a *positive* opportunity. The association could have sent a strong message to the membership by replacing the executive director, and communicating a 10-point plan for increasing member satisfaction through the end of the year. The plan could have included a comprehensive membership survey, a new member advisory panel, a new toll-free phone line to obtain member ideas and answer member questions, and a new bulletin sent via electronic mail to members every two weeks. Warning signs can help tip off potential crises and also act as catalysts for achieving strong positives. Solve the problem and then consider the steps necessary to take advantage of the *positive* opportunities.

◆

Couldn't a business be bogged down by a management team who worries about every little vulnerability that could potentially turn into a crisis – no matter how unlikely it may be that it will?

Absolutely. A business could become unnecessarily bureaucratic, indecisive and paranoid if it stopped to concern itself with every little organizational pimple. However, it is extremely unlikely any business would become preoccupied to the point of gridlock. Things move too quickly in business.

It is more likely that an organization – with *The Crisis Counselor* mindset – will recognize the larger, unsightly warts and make a quick decision on whether and what action should be taken to address them.

But, doesn't this suggest a more conservative, risk-averse management style that could cripple a business?

Not at all. This provides an environment for just the opposite. CEOs and managers can be wonderfully innovative and creative when they know warning signs will be noticed and handled effectively. Risks can be taken in an organization only if the culture includes the discipline and ability to recognize unusual events and address them immediately and competently.

CEOs or managers who *don't* take risks or fail the test of innovation are often those fearful that the most-obvious blemish will go undetected. The fear of a malignant tumor can be crippling to an organization. Today's risk takers are those who are confident that the crisis-management philosophy of identifying and managing vulnerabilities *exists* in their businesses.

What are some examples of warning signs that can lead to potential crises?

The following are some examples of warning signs and the potential crises that could occur if the situation evolves:

Warning signs	*Potential crisis*
Disgruntled employee(s)	➲ **Violence at the workplace**
Disappointing financial results	➲ **Negative media coverage** **Staff downsizings** **Morale problems**
Customer complaints	➲ **Product recalls** **Loss of business** **Product-liability lawsuits**

Warning signs	***Potential crisis***
Elderly CEO or senior executive	Sudden or serious injury
Ignored advice from attorneys, accountants or tax consultants	Fines or penalties Negative media coverage Loss of credibility/trust
Sloppy environmental procedures	Fines or penalties Expensive lawsuits Loss of credibility/trust
Cutbacks in research and investment	Loss of market share Poor financial performance Damaged reputation
Insufficient employee-orientation programs	Serious quality problems Accidents Loss of customer business
No succession plans	Poor performance while preoccupied with internal organization and responsibilities
No business plan	Poor performance due to lack of strategies/tactics and long-term plan
No crisis-management plan	Mismanaged crisis Negative media coverage Damaged reputation

The Crisis Counselor mindset

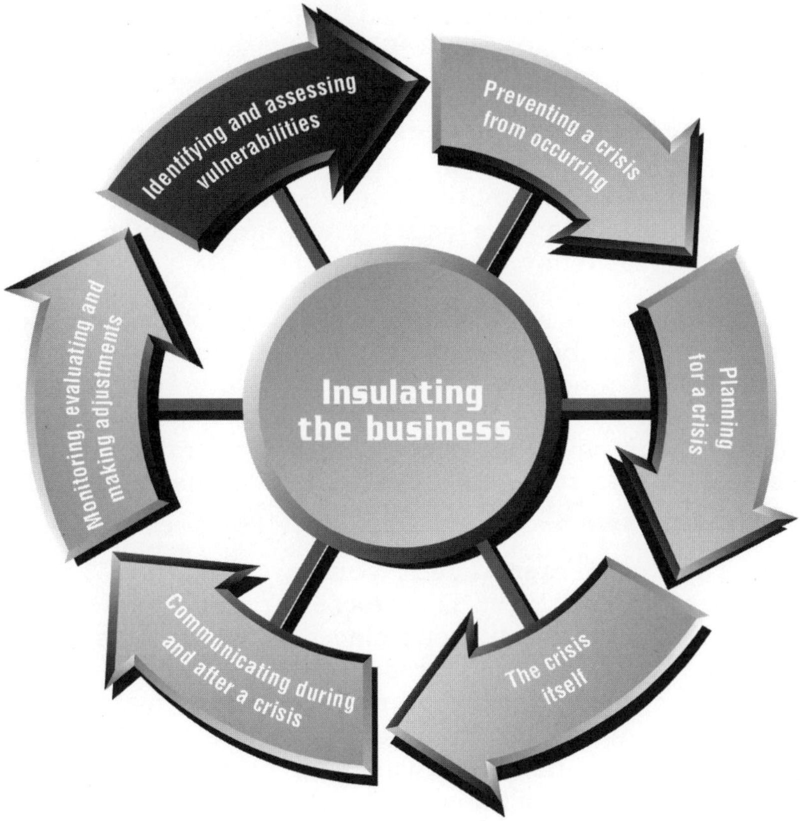

What are the best ways to determine the vulnerabilities in my business?

The best ways to determine the vulnerabilities include:

- **Recognize that addressing your vulnerabilities *now* will be less painful than facing the consequences later.** You first have to get yourself and your business strongly committed to identifying your vulnerabilities. The first step is to recognize *every* business has vulnerabilities that can turn into crises, if not properly managed, and *your* business is no different. Then, strongly commit to the notion that it will be far more painful to *delay* addressing your vulnerabilities than if you address them immediately.

- **Step away from the day-to-day business to honestly consider things that could be done better.** Where is the business most vulnerable to a major crisis? What small problems, if left unattended, could grow into crises for the business? What could be done differently in the business to help reduce the risk of a crisis? Answer these questions about your business today.

- **Consider the consequences of the weaknesses.** How painful will it be for the business – and you, personally – if you don't address the vulnerabilities immediately? What type of short- and long-term damage could you suffer? Make a list of the consequences today.

- **Seek input from your employees.** Work with your employees to obtain their thoughts about the vulnerabilities and ways they can be best managed. This will provide some ideas you may have not considered, and also obtain their support and buy-in to make the changes. Develop a list of employees you could meet with to discuss this, and schedule one or more meetings to do so.

- **Ask your customers about your organization, its products and people, and ideas they have for improvement.** Contact a select group of your customers to seek ideas on ways to improve your service, products and people. Unlike the employee group, you wouldn't necessarily mention that the focus is primarily on vulnerabilities – but, rather, on ways to improve their satisfaction with your company. This approach will still reveal specific vulnerabilities to be addressed without needlessly sharing all your blemishes with your customers. This is usually best accomplished in personal meetings with the customers, but can also be accomplished through telephone surveys, mailed questionnaires, focus group sessions and customer advisory panels. Decide which approach to take today.

- **Establish industry benchmarks to determine *best practices* and where your business falls short in each area.** Learn as much as possible about other businesses in your industry. Which businesses in your industry have the best reputations? What do they do particularly well? What can be learned from them? In what ways should we change to eliminate our vulnerabilities? Develop the list of businesses today, and determine a plan for obtaining information about them.

What is the most comprehensive way to determine our vulnerabilities?

The best and most thorough way is to conduct a comprehensive ***vulnerabilities analysis***. This involves breaking out your company's key publics to obtain their help in identifying vulnerable areas in the business, along with specific ways to reduce their potential damage or to eliminate them altogether. The publics you should consider include:

- Your senior management team
- Managers of key regions, divisions or departments
- Staff employees (including secretaries and clerks)
- Distributors or sales representatives
- Key customers
- Trade media or any other reporters who closely cover your company
- Select suppliers/vendors

How would we conduct a ***vulnerabilities analysis*** in my organization?

First, you should consider the following:

- **What type of information do we want to obtain from each of your publics?** Develop a list of the things you'd like to know and the people you feel should be contacted. The publics to consider could include your employees, customers, suppliers, financial or industry analysts, regulators, and select news reporters who cover your business and/or industry.

- **What would be the most cost-effective way to obtain the input from each of the publics?** Consider whether this should be done at a face-to-face meeting, through a telephone survey, a focus group session, an advisory group discussion or a mailed questionnaire. It may be more appropriate for you to meet personally with the CEO from one of your customer companies than to expect her to complete a written questionnaire or participate in a focus group meeting. A select group of other customers could be contacted through a telephone survey. Your employees could be asked to complete a written questionnaire. Determine the most appropriate way to contact your specific publics.

- **Who should obtain the information?** Determine who is the most appropriate person to contact each of the people to be interviewed. For example, the CEO of your customer company should be contacted by your CEO, if possible. Other customers could be contacted by a senior executive in your business, or by a research firm with the capability of conducting hundreds of interviews in a short period of time. Your employees, who could be asked to complete the written questionnaire, might receive a memo attached to the survey from your CEO or senior human resources officer. The cooperation and insight you receive will be directly related to whether the most appropriate person from your business is involved in asking the questions or endorsing the project.

- **How many people should we interview or obtain input from?** Once you determine what you'd like to learn, who you should contact and who should obtain the information, the next step is to determine the number of people necessary to interview. For instance, if your primary customer base consists of only six key people in the purchasing departments, then you might want to contact all six people. If the CEO and only one other person makes the buying decision to work with your business, then contacting both of them is important. But, let's say your business has 3,500 employees worldwide. How many of those are necessary to contact? It all depends on how those publics break out (i.e., hourly, salary, management, plant workers, union, non-union) and the reliability or confidence level that those contacted will accurately represent the opinions of the others not contacted. In most circumstances, for a group of 3,500, a reasonable sample to interview might be in the 150-400 range – again, depending on the nature of the publics and how you will use the information.

- **When do you want to complete the analysis?** The approaches necessary to conduct the analysis will be affected by when you want complete it. If you want it completed within a week, for instance, you will want the immediacy of contacting people through the telephone, electronic mail or a swiftly scheduled meeting. If you can wait a few weeks for the results, you might conduct a series of focus group meetings, a dozen or so personal meetings and a telephone survey of several hundred consumers.

- **How much budget can be earmarked for this?** If the answer is "zero," then you know you won't be conducting a telephone survey of "several hundred consumers." What budget can be committed to the vulnerabilities analysis to ensure it is done professionally and effectively? Will you hold focus group sessions? Will a mailed questionnaire be used? Should an outside public relations firm and/or a research agency be retained to help plan and implement the project? You can answer these questions by first determining the level of budget available. Or, determine the best way to complete the project, identify all possible costs and seek the appropriate approvals.

- **Who will spearhead the project and do the work?** Should you retain the services of a public relations firm to help you conduct the work, or handle it all with internal resources? The third-party perspectives of a respected outside firm can be extremely useful and may help enhance the credibility of the analysis. And, some of those interviewed may be more likely to open up and honestly comment on your business if asked by someone seen as an impartial outsider.

How long does it take to conduct a *vulnerabilities analysis*?

Again, it all depends. The varying factors include the *number* of interviews, the length of each interview, the methodology used to obtain the information, and the number of people used to conduct the interviews, tabulate, prioritize and analyze the results. It also depends on the size and complexity of your business. If you have only 10 employees and a dozen customers, it will take far less time than the company which has 10,000 employees, five divisions, 300 distributors and 30,000 customers. A comprehensive vulnerabilities analysis could take several days, a few weeks or four or five months.

What are some effective ways to obtain each public's input?

The following is a list of key publics and one way you might consider obtaining their input:

Public	***Methodology to consider***
☐ **Your senior-management team**	☑ **One-on-one, face-to-face interviews**
☐ **Managers of regions, divisions or departments**	☑ **One-on-one interviews, a telephone survey or focus sessions**
☐ **Staff employees**	☑ **A written questionnaire**
☐ **Distributors or sales representatives**	☑ **A telephone survey**
☐ **Key customers**	☑ **One-on-one, face-to-face interviews**
☐ **Trade media or reporters from other media who closely cover your business**	☑ **A telephone survey**
☐ **Select suppliers/vendors**	☑ **Telephone survey or mail-back questionnaire**
☐ **Retail investors**	☑ **Survey postcard enclosed in annual report**
☐ **Institutional investors/ sell- or buy-side analysts**	☑ **One-on-one telephone discussions or personal meetings**

Example: **Baseball club covers all its bases**

The professional baseball club was among the most successful franchises in the major leagues. Although it hasn't made the playoffs in several years, the team has strong fan support and was among the leaders in attendance during the past five years. Other teams with better winning percentages, in larger markets, have failed to do as well in attendance.

The club's owner and general manager are considered among the most innovative executives in sports. They have learned from other clubs' mistakes and don't seem to have the same types of major problems other teams fall victim to during the course of a year.

"What is the secret to your success?" the owner was asked by a reporter from one of the nation's most prestigious business publications.

"It's simple," the owner replied. "We ask a lot of questions. We always look for ways to do things better and try to determine any vulnerabilities we have at any given time. We seek opinions from all of our constituencies and measure their perception of our performance every six months. We carefully track satisfaction and pounce on a problem to fix it as soon as possible when it emerges through this process."

"Who do you consider your 'constituencies'?" the reporter asked.

"That's another one of the key factors in our success," said the owner. "We segment our publics, or constituencies, to a far greater degree than most businesses. We obtain opinions and measure attitudes from our season-ticket holders; those who attend less than five games a year; residents from our market area who attend only one or two games a year; those who used to attend our games but don't now; and, those who have never attended one of our games."

"Who else do you contact?" asked the reporter.

"We also survey our management team, corporate staff, stadium workers, part-time employees, our players and coaches, their spouses, the beat reporters who cover our team on a regular basis, other reporters who occasionally cover the team, media we'd like to cover the team but don't, people who live within a mile of the stadium, and businesses within a few blocks of the stadium," said the owner.

"How do you survey them?" asked the reporter.

"It depends," said the owner. "Some people are contacted directly by our management team or marketing representatives. Some receive a written questionnaire from us and others are contacted by an outside research firm."

"Gee, that must be extremely time intensive and costly. How can you justify it?" the reporter asked.

"It's actually quite easy to justify it," the owner said. "The time and money invested in the front end to do these things save us 20 times the time and money in the back end if we failed to do them. In dozens of cases throughout the past few years, this process has helped us reveal some warning signs that we took care of quickly. In some cases we even identified some ways to turn potential problems into great positives. Without this process, there's no doubt we would have suffered the same type of crises that other clubs face on a regular basis. It doesn't mean a crisis can't hit our organization, but the chances of one occurring is much less than if we didn't make the investment to stay in close and regular touch with those important to the success of our business."

Three lessons to learn

The example of the professional sports franchise helps reveal several important points:

1) **Conduct the analysis on a regular basis.** The real benefits of conducting vulnerabilities analyses emerge when they are done on a regular basis so the results can be tracked and measured over time. The occasional analysis, conducted perhaps every three or four years, may be an effective snapshot of current opinions but won't do much to identify trends or emerging problems. The baseball club conducted its analysis every six months. Your business should conduct one at least every year to ensure you will catch any potential warning signs in the early stages.

2) **Segment your publics.** Look at each of your publics as individual subgroups. Ask yourself if they are homogeneous. Are the questions you would ask the same you might ask others? How might you use the information gained from them? Will you want the ability to break out their thoughts to compare them with others? The baseball club segmented its publics 17 different ways. The methodology used to reach them and the questions asked might vary within those 17 ways. Your business may have five, 10, 15 or 30 different ways it can segment your publics. This is an important step to ensure you ask the right questions to a targeted group of people in the most appropriate ways.

3) **Keep it in perspective.** The baseball club owner had a confident glow about the organization's ability to identify warning signs and to prevent potential problems from igniting into crises. However, he also was realistic and knew that the analyses only helped reduce the risk – not eliminate it altogether. Analyses are outstanding management tools that are smart investments for all businesses. They should not be regarded as security blankets or panaceas that will protect the business from all crises. The smart executive keeps this in proper perspective and considers other ways to ensure the business survives – and perhaps even thrives – during a crisis.

◆

What questions would we ask our *employees*?

Consider asking a few or all of the following questions (which could be phrased in the form of multiple choice, yes/no or open-ended):

- What are your primary areas of responsibility?
- To whom do you report?
- What do you think our company does particularly well?
- What are some things we could be doing better?
- Would you say your work is closely monitored by your supervisor or is your department/area relatively autonomous?

- When you or others in your department/area signal a problem, is it usually handled immediately or does it take a while (and, if so, how long)?
- Has anything occurred in your department/area that might be considered a major problem or a crisis? If so, what happened?
- If a major problem or a crisis were to occur in your department/area, what do you think it would likely involve?
- What type of warning signs would likely arise that might signal a major problem or crisis could occur?
- Have those warning signs occurred in the past? If so, how were they handled?
- Are there problem areas you've mentioned in the past that still haven't been solved to your satisfaction?
- How well do you think your department/area would manage a crisis if one were to occur?
- What other vulnerabilities or potential crises do you think could occur in the company – outside of your department/area?
- Is there a serious problem or crisis that could occur in the company that wouldn't surprise you?
- How well do you think the company would manage a crisis if one were to occur?

What questions would we ask our *customers*?

Consider asking a few or all of the following questions of your key customers (which could be phrased in the form of multiple choice, yes/no or open-ended):

- How would you rate our company's relationship with you?
- Do we consistently meet or exceed your expectations?
- How would you rank the quality of our people? The quality of our products?

- Are there any services you wish we would provide?
- Have you ever experienced a serious problem with our company? If so, what was it?
- If you had a problem with our company, was it handled to your satisfaction?
- In your opinion, what do you think we could do better?
- If there were one thing you'd like to say to our CEO, what would that be?
- What other suggestions would you offer our company?

What questions would we ask *trade media* or *reporters* who closely cover our business?

Consider asking a few or all of the following questions of any reporter or editor who closely covers your company (which could be phrased in the form of multiple choice, yes/no or open-ended):

- How long have you followed our company?
- In your opinion, how well do you understand our industry/business?
- How well do you know our company?
- What are the greatest strengths of our organization?
- In your opinion, what are the most severe weaknesses or areas in our business we could improve?
- If our company were to experience a serious problem or crisis, what area would you expect that would involve?
- How well do you think we would manage such a crisis? Why?
- How could our company help you in your efforts to report about us?
- What other suggestions would you offer our company?

What questions would we ask our *suppliers/vendors*?

Consider asking a few or all of the following questions to select suppliers/vendors (which could be phrased in the form of multiple choice, yes/no or open-ended):

- How long have you worked with our company?
- In your opinion, how well do you know our company?
- What do you like the most about dealing with our organization?
- What you like least about working with us?
- Have you ever offered our company a suggestion – outside of the direct selling of your product/service? If so, what was it? How did we respond to the suggestion?
- In your opinion, what is the likelihood of our company experiencing a serious crisis? If we were, what area/department/division would it involve?
- If we were to experience a crisis, how well do you think we would manage it? Why?
- Which other companies do you know – within our industry or outside of it – that would do a particularly effective job of managing their crises? Why?
- What other suggestions would you offer our company?

Should we obtain input from any other publics/audiences?

You should obtain input from any publics that are important to the success of your business. After considering your own business, you might seek input from others such as:

- directors of the company's board
- former employees
- retirees

- regulatory officials
- community residents
- opinion leaders from your local community
- local, state and/or national political officials
- union leadership
- investors
- financial or industry analysts/ portfolio managers

So now we have a list of vulnerabilities. What should we do with them?

The list of vulnerabilities need to be ranked in priority order to help provide guidance as to which ones – considered as *potential* crisis situations – should be addressed immediately.

You should make two separate lists, dividing each list into three priority categories which will be color-coded red, yellow and green. The first list will be those vulnerabilities/crises ***most likely to occur***. The second list will feature those which – should they occur – would be ***most damaging to the business***. My definition of "most damaging" is its effect on the business' *reputation, credibility* and *goodwill.*

Then, each vulnerability/potential crisis should be listed in *priority* order.

Here's a look at the "Likelihood of Occurrence" list:

Potential Crises/ "Likelihood of Occurrence"

Highly likely to occur (Red)

1)
2)
3)
4)
5)

Could occur, but unlikely in the near term (Yellow)

1)
2)
3)
4)
5)

Is unlikely to occur (Green)

1)
2)
3)
4)
5)

Here's a look at the way to prioritize the vulnerabilities/potential crises in the order of "Most Damaging to the Business":

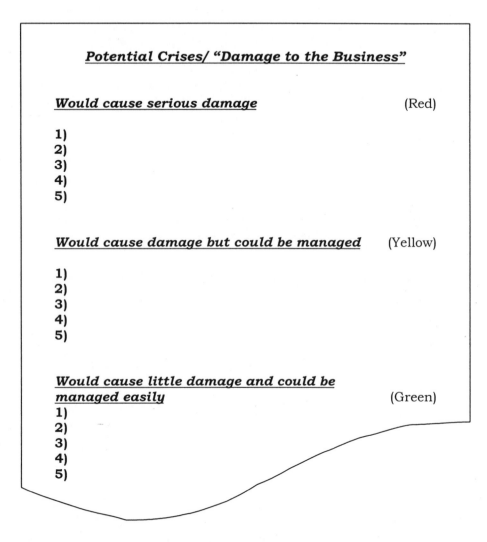

Potential Crises/ "Damage to the Business"

Would cause serious damage (Red)

1)
2)
3)
4)
5)

Would cause damage but could be managed (Yellow)

1)
2)
3)
4)
5)

Would cause little damage and could be managed easily (Green)

1)
2)
3)
4)
5)

What should we do after breaking out the vulnerabilities/potential crises on the two lists as you suggest?

The next step is to review both lists to make a *third* one. This list will be your guide on which vulnerabilities/potential crises are considered the "most likely to occur" and those which "would cause serious damage" to the business.

This list will begin with any vulnerabilities/potential crises which were "Red" on both lists, followed by those which were "Red" on one and "Yellow" on the other. Those to follow will be ones which were "Yellow" on both lists, and then "Yellow" and "Green." The lowest-priorities – "which were "Green" both lists – will be last on the list.

You now have a list of your business' vulnerabilities – based on significant input and research – which are in priority order. You now know which ones should be addressed, prevented and planned for. And, since you don't have the time to plan for all contingencies, you now have some excellent rationale for selecting the ones on which to focus.

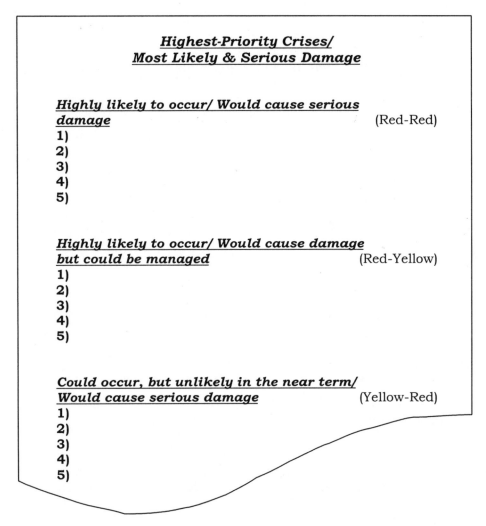

Highest-Priority Crises/
Most Likely & Serious Damage

Highly likely to occur/ Would cause serious damage (Red-Red)

1)
2)
3)
4)
5)

Highly likely to occur/ Would cause damage but could be managed (Red-Yellow)

1)
2)
3)
4)
5)

Could occur, but unlikely in the near term/ Would cause serious damage (Yellow-Red)

1)
2)
3)
4)
5)

Example: Glass manufacturer sets priorities

The privately held international manufacturer of consumer glass products is among the largest of its kind in the world. It operates manufacturing facilities in 15 different nations with its corporate headquarters based in New York.

Its VP-Corporate Communications and the Chief Operating Officer agreed that it should conduct a formal process to determine the crises which are most likely to occur and are among the most potentially dangerous. The purpose was to better set priorities to identify which crises the business should be best able to effectively manage.

The vulnerabilities analysis took six months to complete. The company selected a sample group of employees to survey from around the world. Those receiving written questionnaires to complete and forward back through internal mail included 150 senior-level managers, 200 employees from corporate headquarters, 500 employees from U.S. manufacturing operations, and 200 from its plants in the 14 other countries.

A research firm was retained to conduct five-minute telephone surveys with consumers in North America, Europe and the Asia-Pacific Rim countries. Approximately 1,500 interviews were conducted in each of the three world markets. Telephone surveys were conducted with 400 of its major distributors throughout the world. In addition, personal interviews were conducted with select politicians and regulators from each of their markets, and reporters and editors from the business and trade media that cover the company.

The survey data was analyzed and used to help improve the company's customer satisfaction, operations, marketing, public relations, investor relations and other areas. It also was used to help identify the corporation's most vulnerable areas that, if left unmanaged, could evolve into a crisis. This helped the company determine which crisis situations it should be best prepared to help prevent and manage.

The following are the results of the vulnerabilities analysis for the glass manufacturer.

Potential Crises/ "Likelihood of Occurrence"

Highly likely to occur

1) Glass chips or fragments injuring consumer

2) Negative rumors about quality of product seriously hurting sales

3) Slowness in manufacturing sufficient quantities of products, seriously damaging relationships with distributors

4) One of senior management leaving the company to join a competitor

5) Negative media coverage that causes a strong downturn in sales

Could occur, but unlikely in the near term (Yellow)

1) Sudden death of the chairman/CEO (who is currently 72-years old)

2) Fatality in one of the manufacturing plants

3) Political actions causing serious damage to the company and/or industry

4) Disgruntled current or former employee causes serious injury or fatality within the company

5) Major litigation against the company that significantly damages the company's reputation

Is unlikely to occur (Green)

1) Sudden plant closing

2) Massive layoffs of employees

3) Consumer death blamed on product

4) Shortage of minerals and other ingredients affecting ability to manufacture desired production levels

5) Unexpected resignation of chairman/CEO

Potential Crises/ "Damage to the Business"

Would cause serious damage (Red)

1) Consumer death blamed on product
2) Major litigation against the company that significantly damages the company's reputation
3) Negative media coverage that causes a strong downturn in sales
4) Unexpected resignation of the chairman/CEO
5) Glass chips or fragments injuring consumer

Would cause damage but could be managed (Yellow)

1) Negative rumors about quality of product seriously hurting sales
2) Sudden death of the chairman/CEO
3) Sudden plant closing
4) Fatality in one of the manufacturing plants
5) Disgruntled current or former employee causes serious injury or fatality within the company

Would cause little damage and could be managed easily (Green)

1) Shortage of minerals and other ingredients affecting ability to manufacture desired production levels
2) Political actions causing serious damage to the company and/or industry
3) Massive layoffs of employees
4) Slowness in manufacturing sufficient quantities of products, seriously damaging relationships with distributors
5) One of senior management leaving the company to join a competitor

Highest-priority Crises/ Most Likely & Serious Damage

Highly likely to occur/ Would cause serious damage (Red-Red)

1) Glass chips or fragments injuring consumer
2) Negative media coverage that causes a strong downturn in sales

Highly likely to occur/ Would cause damage but could be managed (Red-Yellow)

1) Negative rumors about quality of product seriously hurting sales

Could occur, but unlikely in the near term/ Would cause serious damage (Yellow-Red)

1) Major litigation against the company that significantly damages the company's reputation

Less likely to occur in the short term/ Would cause damage but could be managed (Yellow-Yellow)

1) Fatality in one of the manufacturing plants
2) Disgruntled current or former employee causes serious injury or fatality within the company
3) Sudden death of the chairman/CEO

The glass manufacturer determined these were the potential crisis situations that they should be most prepared to manage. The vulnerabilities analysis helped identify those areas the company should focus on to help prevent them from becoming major problems. This process also provides *focus* for the company's future crisis planning activities. Any future crisis-management plan for the glass manufacturer must adequately address these areas and be executable if any of these scenarios occurred.

Now that the company has established some benchmark data, in which future results can be measured against, it has agreed the next vulnerabilities analysis will begin in 12 months.

Three lessons to learn

The glass manufacturer's vulnerabilities analysis helps reinforce some key points:

1) **Be as comprehensive as time and budget will allow.** Most businesses won't need to invest the time or budget that the glass manufacturer did on its vulnerabilities analysis. They have a fewer number of publics, a smaller sample size is needed to adequately gauge their opinions, and they have less resources to devote to such a project. Remember this – any analysis is better than none at all. Determine how comprehensive your analysis should be and conduct the best analysis that is most appropriate for your business.

2) **Use the process to remain *focused.*** Recognize the real benefit of the vulnerabilities analysis is to become better focused on what's important. In this case, the glass manufacturer used the process to determine its top vulnerabilities: glass chips or fragments injuring a consumer; negative media coverage affecting sales; negative rumors about quality of product seriously hurting sales; major litigation damaging the company's reputation; a fatality in a manufacturing plant occurring; a disgruntled current or former employee injuring or killing someone in the company; and the sudden death of its elderly Chairman/CEO. This helps the company immediately focus on ways to prevent those crises from occurring, and plans that can be implemented to help manage them if they were to occur. The ability to stay focused on the most appropriate areas, and focus limited time and energies on what are most important, is at the essence of every successful business.

3) **Schedule the next one.** The analysis is finally done and the business is now focused on ways to ensure vulnerabilities are being addressed, crises are being averted, and future plans are most appropriate. Well done. But, before you move on to something else, mark your calendar to establish when the planning should begin for the next analysis. You've completed the most difficult part – establishing the core questions, methodology and process. You now have benchmark data that can be used to measure future performance. So, keep the momentum going by establishing two future dates – when you are committed to *beginning* and *completing* the next analysis.

◆

Should we hire an outside firm to help us with this or conduct the analysis with internal staff?

In most instances, it is usually more effective to have a third-party conduct the work. Internal-staff members are too close to the business to maintain their objectivity and have too many preconceived ideas themselves, which might interfere in the process. A consultant from outside the organization can also provide the third-party credibility that is important when trying to *sell* the findings to senior management.

But wouldn't people fail to be honest – hesitate to air dirty laundry – with an outsider?

Some people might be, but they are more likely to be open and talkative with an outsider who asks the right questions and acts curious about the organization.

What if we don't want to invest the time or the money to conduct such a *formal* analysis? What is a faster, less-expensive option we could consider?

If you want to limit the scope of the analysis, recognize that you can do as little or as much as you'd like. The minimum effort is to take a piece of paper and make a list of the organization's vulnerabilities/potential crises as you see them. This will represent only *your* thoughts, but a list coming from only you is better than no list at all.

Other quick snapshots can be obtained by meeting with a small group of employees, phoning a few customers or sending a questionnaire to a few suppliers/ vendors. Again, a *little* input is better than none at all.

These activities will help you develop a list of vulnerabilities that should be addressed. Unfortunately, the list won't reflect input from a reliable sample of your publics, and your confidence in the validity of the information will be substantially less than through the comprehensive analysis. However, it is far better than not doing anything.

Example: Waste-disposal company conserves funds

The waste-disposal company is a leading trash collector in its metropolitan area. It collects trash in 15 local suburban communities, and operates a landfill and industrial incinerator in the area.

"We have a worse reputation than lawyers," bemoaned the company's owner and founder, as he joked with his partner. "When was the last time you heard a kid say he wanted to be a trash collector when he grows up? He's more likely to want to be a proctologist."

"Ah, c'mon," said the partner. "It's not that bad. Hell, we're a waste-disposal company now. None of this trash collector stuff, okay?"

"But, people still have the same problems with our business that they had 25 years ago," the owner said. "We are still vulnerable to suffering a crisis every day we're in business."

"Y'know," said the partner, "it wouldn't hurt for us to make a list of the areas in which we are most vulnerable to a crisis. We can then plan ways to prevent them from turning into crises, and can decide how we will handle them if they do."

"Great idea," said the owner. "You develop the list and I'll tell you whether or not I agree with it."

"You're right, nothing ever changes," sighed the partner shaking his head. "But what about getting the input from others in the company, or from the communities that we serve, or anyone else?"

"Who's got the time or money for that?" the owner snarled. "Just tell me what you think and I'll tell you whether or not I agree. It's better than not doing it at all, isn't it?"

The partner developed two lists: **1)** vulnerabilities that could most likely erupt into crises; and, **2)** those which, if they *did* occur, would be most damaging to the business. His first list included 12 vulnerabilities and the second list included eight.

He then made a separate list of those which were on both lists. These were the areas, he said, called for immediate attention. They were: **1)** a major fire in the landfill or incinerator, causing significant community upheaval; **2)** a union strike or work stoppage; **3)** the local legislator renewing her efforts to rezone the district forcing them to move the incinerator to a different community; **4)** the death or major illness of either the owner or his partner (since they both had suffered heart attacks in the past); and, **5)** being unable to complete work on time and on budget due to a shortage of workers.

"This is one of the few times I agree with you," said the company's founder to his partner. "Now, what do we do with the list?"

"What if we tried this?" said the partner. "Let's share the list with our top 25 people and ask them to develop five ways we can help prevent each from turning into a crisis situation. And, we'll also ask them for five steps they think we could take if any did turn into a crisis. Then, we'll see how many of those could be done now."

"Great idea," said the owner. "Glad I thought of it."

Three lessons to learn

The waste-disposal example reinforces these three points:

1) **Doing even the crudest of vulnerabilities analyses is better than nothing.** If you don't have the time or budget to conduct a comprehensive vulnerabilities analysis, don't use it as an excuse to avoid it altogether. The process used by the waste-disposal company is a good example of the benefits derived by a minimal investment of time or money.

2) **Get others involved after the fact, even if you haven't before.** The approach taken by the waste-disposal company worked to develop a list of priorities on which to focus. However, it missed the opportunity to obtain the input, perspective and buy-in of others. Even if you choose not to get people involved in the *front* end, seek their feedback and solutions for the next step – determining how to prevent the vulnerabilities from turning into crises, and how the crises could be best managed if they evolve into crisis situations.

3) **Have a gameplan for using the information.** Don't make the mistake of collecting the information and failing to make the most of it. Use it as a way to meet with others in your business to obtain their thoughts and to determine specific action steps to address the vulnerabilities and plan for the future.

◆

How often should our business conduct some form of vulnerabilities analysis?

Some form of a vulnerabilities analysis should be conducted a minimum of once a year in most organizations. Tie it into the annual process of developing your business plan and budgets. Consider conducting a formal analysis more frequently, if your business meets several of the criteria mentioned earlier for those particularly vulnerable to a crisis. However, in most businesses, once a year should work well.

Continue to follow crisis-management philosophies – *between* formal analyses – which include being aware of warning signs and considering whether to do something about them. By doing so, you can better determine your business' special needs in this area.

Closing thoughts

It sounds easy. You've been taught it since you were a child. Keep your eyes and ears open. However, that becomes increasingly difficult in business when so many things are competing for your attention and diverting your focus. It's like the scuba diver watching the schools of colorful fish and playful dolphins, totally unaware that a hammerhead shark is fast approaching from behind. It's simply too easy to get caught up in meeting day-to-day demands, oblivious to vulnerabilities circling and eager to eat away at your business.

Every successful business needs a formal process to provide a radar-like discipline that identifies and analyzes vulnerabilities on a regular basis. These vulnerabilities, as discussed in this chapter, are the warning signs that can erupt into crises if left unattended. The first step to preventing crises is to identify the vulnerabilities and recognize what can be done to ensure they don't cause unnecessary damage to the business.

Consider how you and your business will benefit from an increased discipline in this area – formally, on an annual basis, and through an ongoing, enhanced awareness. Move forward with a strong commitment to initiate this in your business – beginning today.

Tips to consider

- **Recognize that *every* business – including yours – has vulnerabilities that can grow into crises.**

- **Determine whether your business is particularly *crisis-prone*** (based on the criteria listed earlier in this chapter).

- **Conduct annual *vulnerabilities analysis* in your department/ business.**

- **Obtain regular input from your key publics.**

- **Break out your key publics (i.e., employees, customers, suppliers, community residents, media) as specifically as possible to determine the methodology to use for obtaining their input, and who to tap to obtain it.**

- **Determine a small group of *priority* vulnerabilities that need to be addressed.**

- **Encourage employees, suppliers and others to point out warning signs to your business when they emerge.**

- **Empower employees to do something to fix the vulnerabilities in their areas so they don't escalate into crises.**

- **Talk with others in your business about vulnerabilities, potential crisis situations and *The Crisis Counselor* mindset.**

- **Retain the services of a public relations firm and/or research firm to help plan and conduct the vulnerabilities analysis.**

- **Begin to make this happen in your business – beginning *today*.**

CHAPTER 3

Preventing crises in your business

Will a preventive approach work at my business?

Take a few minutes to assess the level of crisis prevention practiced at your company:

1) Has anyone in your business listed its specific areas of vulnerability?

2) Does your business make a concentrated effort to prevent the vulnerabilities from becoming crises?

3) Is *decisive* action usually taken when a potential problem is identified in your business?

4) Does the leader of your business or department encourage an open exchange of new ideas?

5) Are employees empowered to make decisions appropriate for their levels?

6) Are you satisfied that your concerns and questions are addressed sufficiently in the company?

7) Is the quality of your products at a consistently high level?

8) Are there specific problems or vulnerabilities in the business that wouldn't surprise you if they escalated someday into a crisis?

9) Does your business have an organized safety program?

10) Do each of your employees follow the policies and procedures set forth by the business?

Evaluation:

0 - 3 "no" answers	Your business is doing more than most to prevent crises from occurring. Keep up the good work.
4 - 6 "no" answers	You could be doing much more to help prevent a problem from damaging your company's reputation.
7 - 10 "no" answers	This chapter will help you review action steps to consider for immediate implementation at your business.

First of all, let's dispel any false hopes that all crises can be prevented. Even the most crisis-prepared business under the best of circumstances can incur a crisis that couldn't have been avoided. As mentioned earlier in *The Crisis Counselor*, most crises are preceded by one or more warning signs that tip-off the advent of a crisis. Other times, crises are like the despised brother-in-law who shows up unexpectedly on your front porch with his suitcases and growling stomach to stay for a couple of weeks. No warning and no mercy.

However, in the majority of cases, crises can be prevented by identifying warning signs and fixing problems before they grow into crisis monsters. But, how can problems be fixed and crises prevented? This is accomplished, in large part, by having the discipline to prevent *minor* problems from turning into *major* ones – and not simply letting the problem go as if it will somehow magically disappear and everything will be right again.

This chapter describes ways to actually prevent crises from occurring in most businesses.

How can businesses prevent crises from occurring?

A business has the best opportunity to prevent crises in one of two ways:

1) Avoid problems from occurring altogether.

2) Identify existing problem areas and implement actions to solve them altogether or to minimize the potential damage if they grow into crisis situations.

How can my business "avoid problems from occurring altogether"?

Your business can create the best environment for avoiding problems from occurring through the following ways:

- **A strong base of goodwill with each of your key publics.** Work hard to establish a loyal and trusting workforce, a supportive customer base, objective and fair media covering your business and goodwill with others who are important to the success of your business. Problems are less likely to occur if the business is seen as credible, honest and respected. (This is referred to in *The Crisis Counselor* as "insulating the business" and is discussed further in Chapter 8.)

- **Open, two-way communications between employees and senior management.** Problems are less likely to occur in a business where employees have a healthy, ongoing dialogue with senior managers. The dialogue empowers employees to identify vulnerabilities and fix them whenever possible. It's the organization with employees who are scared to mention problems to their supervisors that inadvertently nurture landmines in a business.

- **A positive reputation for quality work.** People will give your business the benefit of the doubt in most cases if you have a reputation for being successful and producing quality work. And, your employees will likely work hard to prevent problems if the business has a strong reputation that they must uphold. Employees will not care as much if mistakes are being made all the time, and another one won't seem to matter much. It is the business that makes *few* mistakes that has employees who don't want to contribute to the aberration.

- **Business plans to cover the next one-, three- and five-year periods.** Problems can be avoided and addressed proactively through simple business planning. This process forces a business to step back from day-to-day operations to consider strategies, goals, tactics and other areas that identify opportunities to seize and potential weaknesses to correct. The successful business has both short- and long-term business plans.

- **Annual *vulnerabilities analyses.*** The essence of preventing problems from occurring are: **1)** performing at high quality standards and **2)** identifying vulnerabilities and working to ensure they don't become full-fledged problems and crises. The *vulnerabilities analysis,* described in Chapter 2, helps ensure a formal process for identifying weak spots that can turn into crises.

- **A comprehensive crisis-management plan.** A comprehensive crisis-management plan, integrated in a business and used as guidance in a crisis, will help ensure manageable crises don't turn into unnecessary strings of problems. (This is reviewed in detail in Chapter 4.)

- **Annual crisis-simulation practice.** This, as in the crisis plan, will help ensure a crisis is managed most effectively so it doesn't inadvertently turn into a greater number of crises. (This is discussed in Chapter 4 as well.)

- **Easy-to-understand company policies and policy handbooks.** Sometimes problems and crises evolve in a business due to unclear or unspecified policies. This has occurred in recent years more frequently with changing interpretations of discrimination and harassment policies. Clear and concise company policies, and specifics on how they are enforced will help avoid some problems in a business.

- **Comprehensive new-employee orientation.** Problems in a business often arise from new employees who lack the training and experience to avoid needless mistakes and problems. A comprehensive employee orientation and training program can help prevent some problems from occurring.
- **A culture of following counsel from highly regarded and competent professionals.** This includes those in the areas of law, accounting, taxes, public relations and advertising/ marketing. They have the experience and knowledge that most businesses are without, and can help prevent some problems from occurring in a business.

The Crisis Counselor mindset

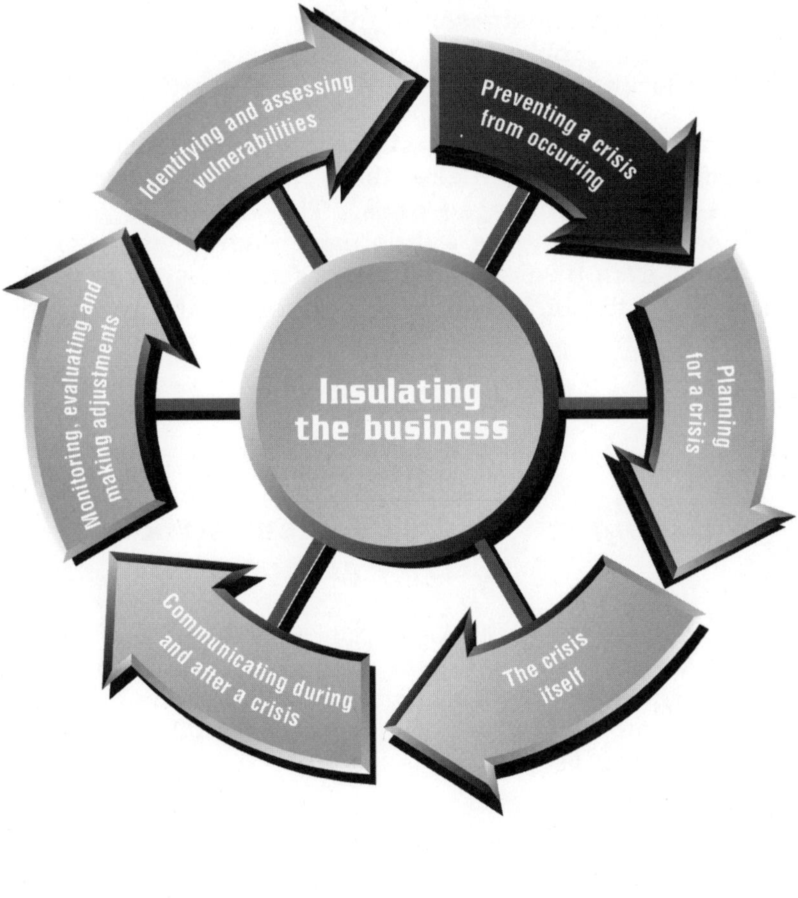

How do these help prevent a potential crisis?

They help to achieve:

- **A checks-and-balances system that makes it difficult for problems to go unnoticed.** A business has to have more than one way to notice a vulnerability and catch a problem before it's too late. These help create a checks-and-balances system that provides several ways to ensure problems are identified and managed effectively.

- **A "family" and "team" culture that helps encourage a supportive, empowering and loyal organization.** The successful business establishes a culture of strong support and teamwork between staff and management, the company and its customers, and the business and the communities in which it operates.

- **A well-managed business.** In this type of business, vulnerabilities are identified, problems are fixed and crises are averted. With this working for the business, it can't help being a winner.

- **A bank of *goodwill* and support that helps avert problems altogether and can make the difference between damaging crises and well-managed ones.** The amount of goodwill earned with each of its publics will do more than anything to help small problems from turning into crises. You and your business will be more likely to obtain the benefit of the doubt and be presumed innocent.

Example: Embezzlement strikes charity group

The East Coast nonprofit organization provides community-based services for needy families. It is perennially among the state's top fundraisers and most popular charity groups. It has an outstanding reputation for providing high-quality services for the needy by keeping administrative costs low.

The organization never experienced a major crisis in its 30-year history. The President/CEO said that was due, in large part, to the culture established in the business.

"I credit our fine reputation and ability to maintain our high credibility to the internal culture we've established and the strong goodwill we've earned with the community," the President/CEO said. "That sure came in handy a few years ago when our comptroller tried to embezzle more than $200,000 from us.

"She began by seeking reimbursement for false expense reports. It took us a while to catch on to that, but it didn't take us long to notice how the cash donations from our Christmas program were not being accurately reported," he said.

"How were you able to nab her?" someone asked.

"We had a checks-and-balances system led by our board's Treasurer, who is attuned to looking for such things," said the President/CEO. "Every quarter we conduct a mini-internal audit to ensure any warning signs are addressed. Most of the time they are problems or innocent mistakes that are easily handled. In this case, it was a serious problem that could have been a disaster to the organization and our hard-earned reputation. We would have lost the trust of our contributors and the community if this proved the organization is unable to effectively manage its funds. This would have taken years from which to recover."

"How was the situation settled?" the President/CEO was asked.

"We confronted her and she eventually admitted guilt," he said. "We fired her and decided not to press charges if the funds were returned in full – which they were. Luckily, she had embezzled only a few hundred dollars, and we caught her before she was on her way to stealing more than $200,000 from us and our contributors."

"What did you learn from that situation?" asked the visitor.

"We learned the importance of a culture that identifies vulnerabilities on a regular basis, and takes warning signs very seriously," the President/CEO said. "We learned that we need to screen our employees better and have made some changes in our hiring policies and procedures. We learned our board of directors is extremely supportive of the organization and will go to great lengths to preserve our integrity, credibility and fine reputation."

Three lessons to learn

The charity embezzlement example reinforces a few key points:

1) **The *prevention* of a crisis is always far less costly than a crisis itself.** The price of a crisis for a business is a costly one. A damaged reputation. Lower credibility. Diminished loyalty and trust. Suspicion is raised. It's far better to take the time and effort to prevent a crisis than to suffer the consequences of one that is potentially preventable.

2) **Build crisis prevention into the *culture* of your business.** This nonprofit organization recognized the importance of identifying risk and vulnerabilities, and building that into the culture and procedures of the business. It had a board structure and quarterly audit schedule to ensure this was done on a regular basis. If this is considered an ad-hoc activity, it will likely be done on an irregular, inconsistent and inferior basis. Determine a structured way it can be integrated in your business.

3) **Recognize the value of your company's reputation and work hard to protect and preserve it.** Nothing is more important than your reputation, credibility and trust. Poor grades in those areas will affect your ability to attract and retain high-quality employees. Revenue and profits will suffer. And, you'll likely be unable to remain in business for long. One of the best ways to protect and preserve your reputation is to prevent everyday problems from turning into full-blown crises. Ensure your business can adequately do that on a consistent basis.

◆

Is it possible to actually *prevent* crises from occurring?

Yes, most crises can be prevented by careful planning, positive relationships with key publics, along with ways to identify vulnerabilities, heed warning signals and fix them altogether.

It's not possible to prevent most crises, is it? Don't most strike out of nowhere?

No, actually *most* crises are preceded by warning signs. The volatile employee who causes damage at the workplace almost always starts with derogatory comments to a fellow worker, threats to a supervisor, or other unusual behavior. Massive downsizing in an organization is almost always preceded by several quarters of unsatisfactory financial performance. Product recalls are always preceded by substantial numbers of customer complaints, warranty claims or unsatisfactory safety tests. Lawsuits are usually preceded by unresolved conflicts.

Does it always mean crises can be prevented just because warning signs are identified and something is done about them?

Certainly not. Business would be much easier if that's all that was needed to enjoy success and avoid crises. But, you'll stand a much better chance of avoiding the major crises by having a *management discipline* that considers the potential damage of organizational warning signs and does something about them.

How do warning signs turn into crises?

Warning signs turn into crises when they are ignored. In most cases, either the problem that arises is either not *fixed* satisfactorily or insufficient communications causes a breakdown between the business and one or more of its publics. The ignored problem often creates the dreaded *downhill-snowball effect* which, if not heeded before it picks up speed, can avalanche an organization into a serious crisis.

Example: Cowboy boot manufacturer misses warning signs

The manufacturer of cowboy boots was having a particularly difficult year. Prices of leather had escalated to all-time highs. Employee morale had never been lower, since it was the first year that employees would not receive year-end bonuses. And, a few product-quality problems had caused negative media coverage in the trade magazines.

The Executive Vice President-Marketing of the company was a 55-year old, butterball at a hefty 325 pounds. He had the energy of a teenager and the intensity of a middle linebacker. He was known as "Big Red," an appropriate nickname for someone whose face turned the color of a tomato when he became upset at a vendor or employee. Despite his shortcomings, "Big Red" was the star performer in the company. He had relationships with large-store buyers and retailers that were built on extraordinary customer service and trust. His customers represented 75 percent of the company's annual revenues.

"I'll tell ya," said one customer, "'Big Red' would walk through a cage of rattlesnakes if that's what it took to deliver what he promised. He's a helluva guy and – although the quality of the company's products aren't what they used to be – we hang in there with them because of ole 'Big Red.'"

Another customer said, "I wish the company would make a better boot, at a more competitive price, but we still carry more of their boots than any others because of 'Big Red.' I can tell you one thing, if something ever happened to 'Big Red' we would probably stop carrying their products altogether."

Unfortunately, "Big Red" was a one-man band and wouldn't let others in the company contact "his" customers. He found it simply slowed him down, and he never really had the patience to put up with someone's questions or mistakes.

The company's management team recognized the firm control "Big Red" had with his customers and viewed it as a strong positive.

"We sure are lucky to have 'Big Red,'" said one senior officer. "Some of these customers wouldn't still be with us if it weren't for him. I just wish he would take better care of himself, and let others in on his customer relationships."

One day, the president of the boot company received a phone call from the West Coast customer that "Big Red" was visiting to take next fall's orders. It was unusual for the customer to be calling the president, who – when told the customer was on the line – knew something was wrong. "Big Red," according to the customer, collapsed in their office from an apparent heart attack and never regained consciousness.

The management team at the boot manufacturer was deeply saddened about the loss of "Big Red" and extremely worried about keeping its customers satisfied. It wasn't sure how best to communicate the news to their customers, and it took them up to four days to contact all of them through letters or phone calls. Many of the customers had already heard the news before the company reached them.

Three months later, new orders for the boot manufacturer were down 70 percent over the previous year. Customers were complaining more fiercely about the quality of its products, and mistakes on orders were being made with regular frequency.

"We are in a real crisis," said the founder and president. "We've learned several lessons from this experience. I just hope we can recover from this situation, but it will take a long time to do it."

Three lessons to learn

The boot manufacturer learned three important lessons:

1) **Pay attention to warning signs.** The boot company had several warning signs begging for attention. They included: **1)** deteriorating product quality that was severely affecting customer confidence; **2)** an overweight and overstressed senior executive, highly vulnerable to a heart attack or other health problem; and **3)** 75 percent of its business was controlled by one person, who wouldn't allow others to share in the relationships.

2) **Most crises are preventable.** The company's management team learned it could have prevented the crisis by recognizing the warning signs as serious vulnerabilities that needed fixing immediately. Perhaps "Big Red" would have suffered a heart attack, *despite* preventive actions, but the negative impact on the business could have been seriously diminished. What could have been done to prevent the crisis? You may have your own ideas, but here are just a few: **1)** find the heart of the quality problem and fix it; **2)** review product-testing procedures and determine if a greater investment should be made in that area; **3)** establish a customer advisory panel to test new products, and offer input and suggestions for the future; **4)** insist that all executives have a yearly medical physical, and follow doctor's orders to lose weight and lower blood pressure; **5)** establish incentives for employees like "Big Red" to meet better health standards; **6)** create a company policy that makes it mandatory for a minimum of two people to be working with each customer; and **7)** establish and enforce disincentives for employees who don't follow company policies and procedures.

3) **Plan for the future.** Don't put off planning for the future. The boot company wished it had a succession plan for the position held by "Big Red." Examine each position in your business and ask yourself what would happen if the person holding the job were to suddenly depart. Who would step in to fill the position? Is she properly trained? How long would the transition take? What damage to the business would occur? What can be done now to prevent the problem from occurring? In addition to succession planning, determine steps to take in communicating the crisis itself. In the case of the boot manufacturer, the challenge was how to communicate to customers the unfortunate news about "Big Red" in a fast and effective manner. It took the company far too long to complete the job, in many cases well after customers learned about it elsewhere, and it further weakened its already fragile relationship with specific customers.

◆

Even if we determined that our company or department is vulnerable to one or more crises, what should we do about it?

In practicing *The Crisis Counselor* mindset – the crisis-management philosophy of management and leadership – your business would consider the following to help prevent the crisis from occurring:

1) **Stop to recognize the issue or situation as a possible warning sign.** Make a point to consider vulnerabilities in your business and take them seriously.

2) **Consider its potential to escalate into a more serious problem.** Determine whether the situation has potential to escalate into something more damaging. Consider the *worst case* and determine if you could live with it.

3) **Determine the various publics affected by the problem.** Consider which of your publics are affected by the problem and how they would be affected if it escalated into a crisis. The answer to this may convince you to take immediate action to correct the problem or, in some cases, may persuade you to move on without any corrective action.

4) **Consider the steps that could be taken to help prevent it from turning into a crisis.** This should be done initially without concern about possible costs, investment of time or any other short-term negatives. If it's a serious problem and has potential to be extremely damaging to the business, you'll be best served by incurring substantial short-term negatives to avoid even greater long-term consequences.

5) **Evaluate whether the potential damage in a worst-case scenario exceeds the negatives (i.e., costs, time) of attempting to immediately solve the problem.** Determine the long-term consequences and assess whether those could exceed the short-term investment to correct it. If it does, you will want to move quickly to correct the problem. If it doesn't, you might focus your attention on something else.

6) **Take the time to solve the problem or, if it's not possible to solve it completely, to help minimize the potential damage from it.** Try to correct the problem. In the event that the problem can't be averted, attempt to reduce the potential damage from it by taking decisive action anyhow. Don't

consider it a lost cause because it can't be averted altogether. Consider what corrective action can be taken and move on it as soon as possible.

Can you offer some examples of what can be done to help prevent *potential* problems from becoming *real* problems?

Here are some potential problems and examples of proactive preventive measures and reactive action steps that could be taken to address them:

Potential problem	*Preventive measures*	*Reactive action steps*
Disgruntled employee	Semi-annual employee reviews and monthly forums to obtain employee input and answer questions	Face-to-face meeting(s) to discuss problems and answer questions
Disappointing financial performance	Set realistic and achievable expectations with investors, analysts and directors, and listen to your existing and potential customers through meetings and research	Communicate honestly and directly with the key publics affected by the news
Customer complaints	Establish easy ways to obtain input from customers (e.g., toll free phone lines, surveys, focus groups, face-to-face meetings)	Answer them quickly and do what the customer wants, if possible
Environmental citations	Establish strong environmental policies, implement strict assessment practices and environmental audits	Plan and implement remediation activities and communicate and cooperate with regulators

Can you give a real-life example of a business that identified warning signs and helped prevent additional problems from occurring?

ViaGrafix Corp., a computer software company that makes interactive CD-ROM tutorials and publishes DesignCAD, experienced a situation that many growing companies face at one time or another.

The company, which had grown from 10 to 120 people in three years, made a presentation on its new line of CD-ROM interactive tutorials to Microsoft in June 1995. One of the Microsoft executives in attendance at the presentation called a ViaGrafix employee responsible for supplying product information to Microsoft customers. Unfortunately, this was a new employee who was unaware of the new product line, and who couldn't answer any questions as a result.

The client from Microsoft was concerned but the problem was quickly defused by a ViaGrafix apology and explanation. However, the situation was a clear *warning sign* that some communications procedures should be adjusted to ensure the problem doesn't recur with Microsoft or any other customer.

Doug McCabe, ViaGrafix's communications director, said: "The situation showed us we had to communicate new-product information to *all* of our employees. Our rapid growth had made it difficult to keep up with the basics – making sure everyone was kept up-to-date and aware of company and product changes.

"We designated two people in the organization who are now responsible for ensuring information is posted on bulletin boards, and e-mailed to all employees with e-mail addresses, so people see the new product and company information as soon as possible," said McCabe. "We also added information on product and company changes in employee's paycheck envelopes. And, we do a better job of managing inquiries on the telephone. We established a dedicated telephone-answering crew which is trained to answer customer questions in an effective and professional manner."

ViaGrafix, based in Pryor, Oklahoma, recognized a *warning sign* and made adjustments to prevent a customer-relations crisis from igniting. Other businesses can learn from ViaGrafix's experience.

How much time, effort and money should my business invest to prevent potential problems from occurring?

It depends on your business' propensity for crises and vulnerabilities. As described in Chapter 2, some companies in specific industries are more susceptible to suffering a crisis. Those businesses should invest the time and budget necessary to conduct vulnerabilities analyses, implement preventive measures and react swiftly to potential problems when they arise.

The excessive costs and investment of time necessary to rebound from a crisis far exceeds the investment made to prevent a crisis from occurring. Only businesses with few inherent risk factors can afford to invest limited funds and time in preventing possible crises.

If crises can be prevented, why is it necessary to learn about the entire scope of crisis management?

Since not all crises can be prevented, it is important to be prepared to successfully manage crisis situations when they do occur. This means planning for worse-case scenarios and being ready to act decisively and confidently. The other elements of crisis management are described through the remainder of *The Crisis Counselor.*

Closing thoughts

Preventing a crisis in your business is like preventing a fire in your home. To do so, you consider how a fire could be started and how you can avoid that from happening. Specific precautions can be taken. Keep matches and lighters away from children. Don't smoke in bed. Keep a fire extinguisher handy. Have your furnace and chimney cleaned each year.

It's the same in business. Think about the types of crisis situations to which your business is most vulnerable. Look at your business with an objective eye. What are the weak spots? If we were to face a crisis, what would it likely involve? How can we prevent the crisis from occurring altogether? If we can't prevent it, what can be done to help ensure it is managed properly to reduce the amount of damage it could cause?

The previous chapter discussed identifying vulnerabilities in a business. That process is a waste of time when the vulnerabilities are ignored. Consider how to heed the warning signs and turn around the vulnerabilities by taking immediate action to prevent them from igniting into individual blazes. Fires have a way of destroying businesses just as quickly as they consume homes. Follow through today in your business to hide the matches, find the fire extinguishers and clean your operations in an effort to reduce the likelihood of a crisis.

Tips to consider

- **Attempt to avoid problems altogether by doing quality work, and establishing and maintaining outstanding relationships with your key publics.**

- **Conduct *vulnerabilities analyses* at least once per year.**

- **Retain and follow the advice of highly regarded, competent attorneys, accountants, tax consultants, public relations professionals and advertising/ marketing specialists.**

- **Look for organizational warning signs and take the time to consider what can be done about them.**

- **Consider both *preventive measures* and *reactive action steps* to challenges that exist within your organization.**

- **Invest the time and budget necessary to identify vulnerabilities and work to prevent crises from occurring.**

- **Plan for the future on issues related to succession, crisis management, and strategic planning.**

- **Don't overestimate the effectiveness of attempting to prevent crises from occurring – even with the best of planning, some crises may still occur, and many can't be totally prevented.**

- **Continue learning about the crisis-management process and establishing the management discipline within your business.**

- **Discuss with your supervisor, partners or employees how the items covered in this chapter relate to your business.**

- **Read the next chapter on planning for the inevitable crisis.**

CHAPTER 4

How to plan for a crisis

Has my business planned sufficiently for a crisis?

Take a few minutes to answer the following questions:

1) Does your business or department have a crisis-management plan?

2) Has your business or department conducted a simulated crisis/training exercise during the past 12 months?

3) Have information materials been developed for use in the event of a crisis?

4) Has a crisis-management team been established at the company?

5) Is it understood in your business who would be he company's spokesperson during a crisis?

6) Have your spokespersons received training during the past 12 months on dealing with the news media during a crisis?

7) Do you agree with this statement, "It is quite unlikely that our organization would ever experience a crisis situation"?

8) Would your business adequately survive a crisis if no advance planning were conducted and it simply had to improvise?

9) Do you understand what should be done to sufficiently prepare your organization for a crisis?

10) In your opinion, is your business prepared to effectively manage a crisis?

Evaluation:

0 - 3 "no" answers	Your business is well prepared for a crisis.
4 - 6 "no" answers	You could be better prepared for a crisis, and your business may suffer needless damage due to a lack of preparation.
7 - 10 "no" answers	The business is unprepared for a crisis and is risking significant damage to its reputation. You'll be glad you read this chapter and followed the advice.

A distaste for planning of any type is inherent in nearly everyone. Isn't it easier and more gratifying to take care of *today's* needs than to plan for those that may or may not occur in the future? Who has the time to plan for the uncertainties of tomorrow when managing today's problems are difficult enough?

These and other questions are the stark reality of today's business executive. However, the smart executive weighs taking care of today's needs with the problems that could arise from ignoring future needs. The successful executive – with *The Crisis Counselor* mindset – recognizes that every business will face a crisis, and it is those who are best prepared that will survive and perhaps even thrive from the crisis.

This chapter discusses what should be done by a business well in advance of a crisis. Consider the effect to your business if you ignore this type of advance planning. And, think about how the steps described here can be implemented immediately in your business.

What do you mean by planning for a crisis?

Businesses of all types, and in all types of industry or service, need to plan and prepare for the inevitable problems and crises that naturally occur in an organization. The key to success in business is the ability to effectively navigate through the gauntlet of various problems and crises that occur as the organization evolves. Those businesses that are most successful are almost always those which planned for the inevitable crisis and managed the bumpy road with aplomb. The extremely successful organizations are those that, through planning and ability, manage to turn *negative* problems into *positive* opportunities.

Do most businesses conduct advance planning for a crisis?

No, actually most don't. Estimates of *Fortune* 1000 companies of the early '90s with formal crisis-management plans have ranged from about 5-10 percent. However, more and more businesses are becoming increasingly sophisticated in crisis planning. Hopefully, after reading this book, the percentage will increase significantly.

The Crisis Counselor mindset

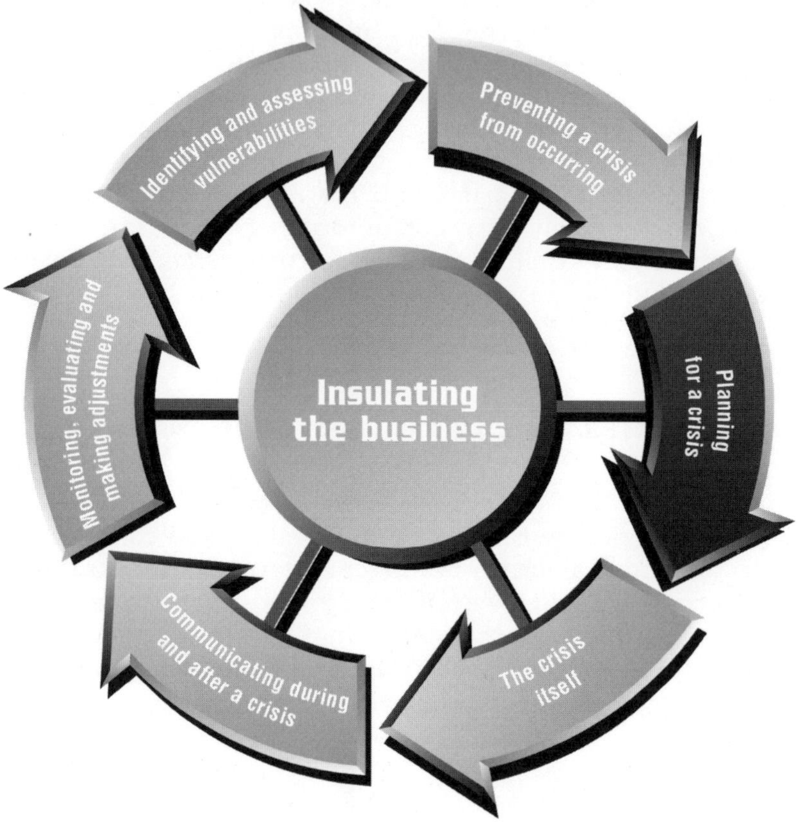

Why don't more organizations plan for crises?

Their rationale for failing to plan in advance for a crisis usually includes one or more of the following:

- **"A crisis would *never* hit our company."** Many business owners and executives think about crises as only the large, debilitating ones you read about in the newspapers (i.e., plane crashes, deaths). They quickly brush off the possibility that a crisis could affect their businesses, and forget about the more typical crises that nearly every business faces at one time or another (i.e., those involving problems with product quality, client relationships, employees, senior executives).

- **"We have a well-managed business and could manage our way through a crisis without a plan."** Planning for a crisis involves a recognition that, despite your outstanding management abilities and leadership skills, you still may be unable to prevent a crisis from occurring. Then, if that wasn't enough, you need to admit you'd be better served by planning in advance, as opposed to winging it when the situation arises.

- **"We don't have time to develop plans for something that might never occur."** Most people are great procrastinators. They put off until tomorrow what should be done today. But, many of those things aren't done tomorrow either. Crisis planning is often shoved to the bottom of the priority list when day-to-day demands seem to bury any possibility of planning for the future.

- **"Crises just don't happen in our industry/field."** You might recognize that crises occur in other industries – such as environmental, chemical, transportation, and others – but you've convinced yourself it just doesn't happen in your line of business. The truth is that problems happen in every business and, when they are mishandled, they turn into full-fledged crises. Although some crises may occur more often in some industries than others, crisis situations affect every type of business in every kind of industry.

- **"Every crisis is different. It's impossible to plan for them."** Yes, every crisis has varying dynamics that affect every business in different ways. However, as discussed earlier in *The Crisis Counselor*, it is possible to determine the types of crises your business are most likely to face – and then to ensure you are best prepared to manage those. It is both possible and necessary to plan for crises.

- **"We have a great, ongoing public relations program. We don't need to do anything more to plan in advance for a crisis."** A successful public relations program, coupled with credible and respected performance by your business, will help ensure you have a strong base of goodwill heading into a crisis. This is the most important factor in your ability to survive a crisis. However, take advantage of this by teaming it with advance crisis planning. Then, you'll be best prepared to manage the crisis.

- **"We don't have anyone on staff that knows anything about crisis planning."** If this is true in your business, you have two choices: **1)** Identify someone to follow the advice and steps provided in *The Crisis Counselor* to conduct the planning activities. You have everything here to conduct it yourself. **2)** Hire a crisis-management or public relations firm to conduct it for you. The objective, third-party perspective of an experienced counselor in this area will be helpful, and it will ensure the project is completed and doesn't get pushed aside.

- **"Our business can't afford to hire someone to help us conduct crisis planning."** First, recognize the cost of hiring someone to conduct the planning project can range greatly depending on your market, the experience of the firm you are hiring and the assignment. You also can determine if you want the consulting firm to simply lead the project, with others internally helping to implement it, or to conduct the entire project from beginning to end.

- **"We've never done crisis planning before, and we've managed to be very successful without it."** The success of the past is today's security blanket in many organizations. Unfortunately, the blanket can easily suffocate a business by convincing it that – because it's survived well up to this point – a crisis isn't likely to hurt the company in any way. Consider the vulnerabilities of today and the future – not the past – when assessing the impact of a crisis on your business. Then, plan for the inevitable crisis visitor to knock on your company's door.

Why is it necessary to plan in advance for a crisis?

Here are a few reasons why businesses need to plan in advance for crisis situations:

- Crisis situations occur in every organization.

- Many crises can be prevented or greatly minimized – well before they cause severe damage.

- A properly prepared business is more likely to be better focused and more decisive and effective after a crisis occurs.

- Many decisions need to be made, actions need to be taken and materials need to be produced when a crisis occurs – a surprisingly high number of these can be made *in advance.*
- It's easier to make smart decisions when you don't feel the pressure of a guillotine hovering over your head.
- The input of others can be obtained more effectively when obtained in advance.

Example: Secretary of State's office unprepared for crisis

The Secretary of State department is responsible for issuing drivers' licenses and license plates in this large western state. It has approximately 200 offices throughout the state. Most of the offices are understaffed and often receive harsh criticism from customers who don't appreciate waiting in line for 20 or more minutes.

The employees are almost always grumbling and snipping at each other. They frequently treat customers rudely and have little sympathy for those waiting in line or taking the written exam to renew their licenses. The employees' treatment of customers is a direct reflection of how they are treated by their supervisors, who appear heartless and insensitive to employee needs or concerns.

"Just get back to work and stop complaining. Don't expect any sympathy from me," was the common response from the supervisors.

Unfortunately, as stress and distrust boiled up like a whistling teapot, the risk of a crisis erupting increased in intensity. Finally, a worst-case situation occurred. An employee, who had worked there for 10 years and couldn't take it any more, stormed into a supervisor's office shortly after lunch and began screaming at him.

"What do you think we are? Your slaves?" yelled the angry employee, who had been drinking heavily during lunch. "Well, here's something to remember me by."

At that point, the employee took out a small pistol and shot the supervisor three times in the chest. Other employees were screaming and running out of the office. A few yelled to customers: "He has a gun. Get the hell out of here."

The employee then took the pistol and shot himself in the head, to die in the slain supervisor's office as well.

The Secretary of State was stunned and distraught by the situation, and was admittedly unprepared for such a crisis. The Secretary and his Office was criticized harshly by the media for allowing such pent-up pressures to continue building. Most employees didn't want to return to work, and several felt their best interests still weren't being considered. Customers were reluctant to visit their branch offices.

"I really never thought this type of thing would happen to us," the Secretary said. "We should have anticipated such a worst-case situation and determined in advance what we would do if our worst nightmares became reality. Now, we have three issues to address: **1)** Fix the damage caused from this situation; **2)** Ensure this won't occur again; and **3)** Prepare us to manage such a crisis better in the future."

"We learned some valuable lessons," said the Secretary of State. "I just hope we will be better prepared if there's ever a next time."

Three lessons to learn

The Secretary of State learned several important lessons from the tragic shooting incident. Here are three of the lessons related to planning for a crisis:

1) **Make crisis *planning* a priority.** Planning for a crisis just doesn't happen in a business. It needs to be a major priority. The Secretary of State wished his Office had considered possible vulnerabilities – some of which could have been resolved – and planned ways to manage crises when they occur.

2) **Obtain input and buy-in on the planning process.** Include the input of supervisors, employees and others in the crisis planning process. This will help uncover simmering vulnerabilities before they boil over into crises, and will establish their support of the process itself. Crisis planning can't be done in a vacuum or through some ivory-tower overview. The most effective planning is done by obtaining broad perspectives and input.

3) **Recognize the potential fallout from failing to plan.** Consider the potential risk and damage caused by failing to conduct crisis planning. The investment of time and effort in the front end is small and inconsequential compared to the price to be paid after a bungled crisis. The Secretary of State surely would have conducted considerable crisis planning if he would have recognized the damage the incident was to cause his Office.

◆

What is the best way to *plan* for a crisis?

The most effective way is to do the following:

- **Make it clear which executive is responsible.** It won't get done unless someone is clearly named as the person responsible to make it happen.
- **Establish a dedicated budget.** Although planning for a crisis doesn't have to be expensive (see Chapter 2), it will involve an investment of time and some budget. It will make things much easier, faster and less complicated if a dedicated budget is established in advance.
- **Include crisis management in your annual business plan.** Crisis planning and crisis management should be an important element of your annual business plan. It should be a major priority, with someone being held responsible and accountable for its implementation and results.

- **Establish a crisis-management team within the organization.** A specific team of executives should be established to help in the planning of a crisis and the implementation of the communications. (This is discussed in greater detail later in this chapter.)

- **Conduct a vulnerabilities analysis in the organization at least once a year.** As mentioned in Chapter 2, a vulnerabilities analysis will help identify which crises are most likely to occur and help focus your planning efforts.

- **Prepare worst-case scenarios for the five highest-priority crises that could occur in the business and develop plans to prevent and manage them.** Consider those crises most likely to occur and to cause serious damage to your company's reputation, and determine ways to minimize the potential damage.

- **Develop or update your crisis-management plan once a year.** Keep your crisis-management plan fresh and pertinent. Otherwise, it won't be useful when you need it.

- **Prepare, and update annually, individual crisis-response manuals for those from your organization who will help manage your crisis.** The individuals responsible for managing the crisis will need to know exactly what they should do when a crisis occurs. Crisis-response manuals, tailored specifically for each of them, should be developed and updated regularly. (This is discussed in greater detail later in this chapter.)

- **Develop drafts of any fact sheets, backgrounders, memoranda, letters and core messages that can be revised quickly in the event of a crisis.** Consider what you might need in the event of a crisis. You may be surprised as to how many of those items can be developed now – before the crisis occurs. Although the materials will undoubtedly need revising, once you know the specifics of the crisis at hand, developing them in advance will save considerable time and confusion.

- **Obtain the involvement and counsel from key advisors outside your organization, including those in the practices of law and crisis management.** Consider retaining the input and assistance of legal counsel and crisis-management specialists to help plan for the inevitable crisis. They can help ensure you are prepared to effectively manage the crises you've identified as most likely to occur and cause the most damage.

- **Plan and participate in *crisis-simulation training* at least once a year.** Conduct a crisis-simulation training session at least once a year with those executives most likely to be involved in managing your company's crisis. Select a potential crisis and improve your preparation based on the results of the training. It is better to make mistakes during the training session than an actual crisis. (This is discussed later in this chapter.)

- **Participate in *media training* at least once a year.** Conduct a training session once a year with those most likely to represent your business in media interviews. The sessions will help ensure your spokespersons know the most effective ways to answer routine and difficult questions, and feel comfortable being interviewed. (This is discussed in this chapter as well.)

What is a crisis-management team?

A crisis-management team is a small group of people assembled to help plan for and manage a crisis. Members of a crisis-management team are those whose input is important when planning for a potential crisis, and will be critical when a crisis occurs.

Why is a crisis-management team important?

A crisis-management team helps an organization achieve the following:

- Valuable input from executives with different areas of expertise.

- Ownership and commitment from a wide range of executives to integrate crisis management in the business.

- Additional resources to help identify vulnerabilities, and develop plans to prevent and manage them.

- Assistance in developing materials that are prepared in advance.

- Third-party involvement and counsel from those outside your organization.

Who should be on a crisis-management team?

This will change from organization to organization, depending on the positions in your company and the size and structure of it. Nevertheless, your crisis-management team will likely include two or more of the following:

- Chief Executive Officer
- Chief Operating Officer
- Senior public relations official
- Senior marketing official
- Human resources director
- Heads of any company divisions
- Quality-assurance director
- Manufacturing or plant manager(s)
- Chief Financial Officer
- Chief legal counsel
- Attorney from the company's legal counsel
- Senior counselor from a respected public relations or crisis-management firm
- A senior administrative assistant to document discussions during the meeting and to take minutes

What is the optimum number of people on a crisis-management team?

The group should be large enough to obtain a sufficient amount of input and involvement for the size and complexity of your business. However, the team size shouldn't be so large that it stifles the input and exchange of ideas and concerns. Therefore, the number of people on your crisis-management team is likely to be between five and 10 – and possibly even *fewer* at a smaller company.

Is it always necessary to have the CEO on the crisis-management team?

Not necessarily. The CEO's involvement does help underscore the organization's commitment to crisis management. In many cases, the CEO's active participation is important to ensure major strategic decisions are made and specific responsibilities are assigned. However, in larger corporations, this can be accomplished in a surrogate manner through the participation of the organization's No. 2 person or another senior officer.

If the CEO is not involved as a regular member of the team, he/she should be a guest at the crisis-management meetings at least once a year to review and approve the group's plans. In addition, the CEO should receive copies of the minutes from and decisions made at the meetings.

Who should lead the crisis-management team? The CEO or someone else?

It could be anyone on the team who is responsible, committed to crisis management and respected among peers. It could be the CEO in some organizations, but is the person who has the responsibility for crisis-management in the organization – most likely a Vice President or Senior Vice President of Public Relations, or the individual responsible for public relations in the organization.

How can the crisis-management team help in the planning area?

The crisis-management team can help in the following areas:

- Determine crisis-management objectives, strategies and tactics for the organization.
- Discuss vulnerabilities and help establish priorities.
- Make decisions, assign responsibilities and establish deadlines.

- Review, revise and approve the business' crisis-management plan and crisis-response manuals.
- Identify the company's spokespersons.
- Ensure that crisis management is a priority area that deserves ongoing attention.
- Provide input, feedback and counsel to the CEO, the board and other senior executives.

Example: Cement manufacturer organizes crisis team

The cement company operates one of the state's largest cement kilns and manufacturing facilities. The owner has seen the damage caused in competitors' businesses by bungled crises of all types. One competitor was indicted for tax evasion after a two-year probe into the business and the CEO's personal finances. Another competitor lost two employees in a tragic incident involving an explosion in the kiln. And, another business is rumored to be facing unprecedented penalties for failing to comply with strict environmental air-quality standards.

The owner of the cement company has seen the damage caused by poorly managed crises and wants to ensure his business is well prepared to survive such a crisis.

"I've been reading about the idea of establishing a crisis team," said the owner to his management team. "The team helps identify where we are most vulnerable to a crisis, and then ranks them in priority order. It also helps determine what can be done to prevent the vulnerabilities from growing into problems for us, how we can avoid crises from occurring, and what can be done now to prepare for best managing a crisis."

"It makes sense to me," said one officer. "But, we hardly have enough time to get our current work done. How are we supposed to do all that as well?"

"We just have to find the time," the owner said. "Otherwise, after a crisis occurs, we'll wish we had done it."

"Okay, so who would be part of our team?" the officer said.

"Well, let's figure out who would be dragged into a situation like that if a crisis occurred," said the owner. "Besides you and me, who would that be?

The officer and owner identified the following: the plant manager, the Director of Operations, the VP-Sales and Marketing, the Chief Financial Officer and the Director of Human Resources. In addition, they placed on the crisis team the attorney from the law firm working with the cement company on a regular basis and the senior officer from the local public relations firm they use. They also assigned the owner's executive assistant to be on the crisis team as well to take minutes at the meetings, and help facilitate and document future action.

"I will be the leader of the crisis team," said the owner, "and you will be the alternate leader if I'm not around when needed. Let's set our first meeting and we can discuss what we'll do first."

Three lessons to learn

The discussions at the cement company on its crisis team reinforces several key points:

1) **Learn from others.** Be perceptive about the type and severity of problems occurring in your industry and market. Take some action so you don't inadvertently make the same mistakes. Make crisis planning a major priority in your business.

2) **Establish a broad but manageable crisis team.** Identify who would most likely be called in to help in a crisis situation, and consider naming a select group of people to special crisis team. Keep the team to no more than 10 in number, if possible, and ensure they cover most of the areas where immediate action and quick decisions will be needed.

3) **Identify a leader and alternate, and get moving.** Determine both a leader and alternate leader for the crisis team, and conduct the first meeting to get things moving. The team's initial responsibility will be to develop a process for identifying the company's vulnerabilities and how those could be prevented. Other steps will be to help determine what items may be needed in the event of a crisis; what materials can be developed in advance; who the spokespersons would be in a crisis; which messages will be communicated; and other areas discussed in this chapter.

◆

When and how often should a crisis-management team meet?

The crisis-management team should meet as frequently as necessary, based on the extent to which its areas of responsibility have been covered, discussed and planned. In its first year of existence, a typical company's crisis-management team will meet about six times – if a *real* crisis doesn't occur and make it necessary to meet more frequently.

After the first year or two, the crisis-management team will meet three or four times a year.

What is a crisis-management plan?

A crisis-management plan basically describes the steps the business will take to effectively manage a crisis situation and establishes specific staff responsibilities for each area. Special emphasis is placed on reporting and communications to help ensure the company's key people know their roles and responsibilities. It also includes the organization's most important publics and describes the manner with which each will be communicated.

How important is a crisis-management plan?

A crisis-management plan, if used properly in an organization, is important to accomplish the following:

- Establishes a gameplan that can be reviewed and absorbed by several different people in the organization.
- Restates the highest-priority crisis situations that could potentially affect the organization and describes how they would be managed effectively.
- Assigns specific roles and responsibilities.
- Obtains pre-approval on several items – before a crisis occurs – so the business can act swiftly and confidently during an actual crisis.

- Helps remind an organization which publics need to be addressed – and in which ways – during a crisis situation.
- Includes phone, fax and pager numbers for important executives, departments, divisions, news media, and police and fire departments for quick reference during a crisis.

What are the components of an effective crisis-management plan?

Most crisis-management plans differ in content, format and style; however, many of them include several of the following:

- The organization's crisis-management philosophy and importance of the plan – perhaps in a memoranda or letter from the CEO in the plan's preface/introduction.
- A definition of an event, issue or a problem the business would consider a "crisis" (and that would ignite the implementation of the crisis plan).
- A list of potential crisis situations that could affect the business.
- The types of potential crises the business could face in the future.
- The overall goal and crisis-management objectives of the organization.
- The reporting structure for notification and coordination of a crisis.
- A list of the crisis-management team members (with phone, fax and pager numbers).
- Emergency procedures – including interaction with all appropriate police, fire and other community officials (including phone numbers).
- News media to be contacted in the event of an emergency (including updated names, titles, and phone and fax numbers).
- List of the organization's primary and secondary spokespersons, and a strong statement prohibiting others to discuss the situation with the news media or other groups.

- Immediate, priority steps to take in the event of a crisis (i.e., who should be contacted, where the crisis-management team should meet).
- Updated fact sheets, backgrounders and other information on the business that may be needed during and after a crisis.
- Reporting forms to complete for documentation of phone calls from the news media and others.
- Updated lists of employees (or only key directors/managers, if the list otherwise would be too lengthy); major customer contacts; suppliers/vendors; stock-exchange contacts (if you have a publicly held company) and, local political, civic, business and opinion leaders – all with addresses and phone numbers.
- Lists of community, social, minority and industry activist groups that are appropriate to your business and its issues.
- Lists of key market and industry analysts.
- Other information that may be needed for your organization in the event of a crisis.

You mentioned previously if the crisis-management plan "is used properly in the organization." What did you mean by that?

In many organizations, a crisis-management plan is developed, and the senior executives feel a great sense of accomplishment and security for having done so. Unfortunately, in too many cases, the crisis-management plan gets placed on a bookshelf or shoved in a file drawer and is rarely considered again. In fact, some organizations develop a crisis-management plan and found – after an actual crisis – that it was never used.

So, either a crisis-management plan is a waste of time and effort, or something needs to be done to ensure it is used as intended. Which one?

I assure you that a well-conceived and dedicated plan to help your business prepare in advance for a crisis isn't "a waste of time and effort." It will be one of the most important documents your business ever produces. However, even if the plan is never used in a crisis, the preparation and discussion that went into developing the plan will help greatly in your ability to effectively manage the crisis.

How can you ensure a crisis-management plan is used properly and doesn't just get filed somewhere, never to be seen again?

Once a crisis-management plan is developed and approved, consider the following:

- Assign one individual in the company to be responsible for integrating the plan in the business and for updating the plan as necessary – make this an important part of the executive's job responsibilities and performance evaluation.
- Place the document in a three-ring binder, so it easily can updated and revised.
- Conduct orientation sessions for middle- to senior-management employees to review the plan and discuss their roles during a crisis.
- Distribute the plan to all appropriate middle- to senior-management employees.
- Schedule one-on-one meetings with all those who received the plan to seek their input and suggestions for improvement.
- Ensure that your crisis-management team reviews the plan and discusses any necessary updates and revisions at its meetings.

- Prepare a *crisis-response manual* – tailored for each individual who has responsibilities in the crisis-management plan – to provide specific step-by-step guidance on actions to take during a crisis situation.
- Conduct *crisis-simulation training* once a year for a core group of those most likely to help manage a crisis in your business.

Why are crisis-response manuals needed?

The crisis-management plan has a *macro*-perspective that provides overall guidance and direction for the business to take in event of a crisis. It's an important, necessary document for the entire organization. However, individual crisis-response manuals are necessary to give each individual – who will have responsibilities during a crisis – a step-by-step checklist of his/her specific actions to be taken. The more specific and relevant the manuals are for each individual, the more likely they are to use it as a critical reference tool.

What should be included in the crisis-response manuals?

The crisis-response manuals should include only the information that you want each individual to use. For instance, those who are not company spokespersons should not receive information on news media to contact. Those who are not members of the crisis-management team shouldn't receive information on where and when the crisis-management team should meet during a crisis.

The objective of the crisis-response manuals is to simplify and streamline the crisis-management plan, and to make it abundantly clear the specific steps to be taken by the individual receiving the plan.

In addition to including information from the crisis-management plan that is specifically relevant and pertinent to the respective individuals, each *crisis-response manual* should include the following:

- A list of crisis situations that could affect the individual's department, division or function.
- Step-by-step checklists on who to contact, and what steps to take, when a crisis occurs.
- A reporting-tree chart to show the flow of communication from the respective individual to another during a crisis.
- Reporting forms to document phone calls and other inquiries received – along with specific instructions on what to do with the completed information.
- Phone, fax and pager numbers the individual needs to complete his/her responsibilities during a crisis.

How many crisis-response manuals should we produce?

It depends on the number of people in your business who would have specific roles and responsibilities in a crisis. It could be as few as two or three, to many times that amount.

Crisis-response manuals should be developed for the following:

- The chief executive officer
- All senior-management members (defined as direct reports to the CEO)
- Members of the crisis-management team
- Any others who will have specific leadership responsibilities during a crisis

How often should we update the crisis-management plan and crisis-response manuals?

They should be updated as frequently as necessary to ensure they are accurate, relevant and useful. If significant changes are occurring at the company, they may need to be updated regularly throughout the year. Otherwise, maintain a regular schedule for review and update them when necessary.

You mentioned *crisis-simulation training* a few times in this chapter. What is that?

Crisis-simulation training is an important practice drill that establishes a crisis scenario and assesses the crisis-preparedness of an organization through role playing and critique. It helps ensure the organization's crisis-management plan and the individuals' crisis-response manuals are utilized as intended, and that everyone stays focused and ready for battle.

What would be an example of *crisis-simulation* training?

Most everyone is familiar with the type of simulation training conducted – usually twice a year – by hospital and healthcare systems to maintain their accreditation credentials. They will simulate an unexpected crisis that could affect their emergency room, and medical and administrative staffs. Written critiques and suggested improvements follow the simulations.

Unfortunately, a much-smaller list of hospitals and health-care systems include sufficient crisis-management components in their training. For instance, the effectiveness of the training would be increased significantly by including the role of the news media, a media briefing or news conference, videotaped interviews, and calls coming into the hospital and its public relations department.

I understand how crisis-simulation training would work for a hospital, but in which way could it be used in a regular business? Can you offer an example of that?

Any business can conduct crisis-simulation training. It doesn't have to be as expansive as that conducted for a hospital; however, it can help meet the same objective – to ensure the organization is prepared to manage a crisis situation as effectively as possible.

A trucking company, for instance, could conduct crisis-simulation training during a three-hour period on a weekend or a slow period for them. The company could inform its employees that a crisis scenario will be presented to them, but without giving them details about the specific situation. A mock phone call would be placed to the company that would inform them that one of their trucks – carrying flammable gases – was in a horrible accident and exploded on the west side of town. It appears the driver is killed and several other people are seriously injured. Deadly gases are spreading throughout the neighborhood and the local police officers are already coordinating evacuation procedures for community residents.

What are you doing about the situation? Why did it happen? Who is the driver? What was his/her driving-safety record? Could this occur with any of your other trucks? This scenario would certainly test the company's crisis-management procedures, and help evaluate the level of its crisis readiness.

Staff members from an outside public relations/crisis-management firm could pretend to be print, television and radio news reporters. Video crews could be hired to simulate television-camera crews and to also help document the session for subsequent critique.

Obviously, the events would be greatly condensed to fit into the three-hour time frame of the crisis simulation; however, the session would significantly help prepare and fine-tune the company for a possible, *actual* crisis in the future. If mistakes are made during the session, it will be reassuring to know they were made during a practice session and that they can be corrected before an actual crisis occurs.

This type of training will be among the most valuable time to be invested in your business.

Example: The sporting goods store practices like a team

The sporting goods retail outlet is a single-store business that goes head-to-head against the major superstores in the market area. Although it can't beat the superstores' prices or offer their array of merchandise, the sporting goods store relies on its outstanding customer service and friendly employees to win over shoppers.

The store tries to make shopping there a fun, helpful and no-pressure experience. The atmosphere includes large, television screens showing live or taped sporting events. Employees are dressed in various sports or cheerleader uniforms. Customers are invited to eat small bags of popcorn or munch on cotton candy, while sipping on a sports drink while shopping – all at no charge.

The store's owner believes in training her employees to be well prepared for worst-case situations. Orientation for new employees includes how to handle specific crisis events should they occur in the store. Each employee understands ways to ensure problems are effectively managed, and disruption to business and customers is kept to a minimum.

"I believe every business, no matter how well managed, will face a crisis of some type," said the store's owner. "The difference between the most successful businesses and those which aren't so successful is often based on how well they've managed problems – either turning into major crises or just fizzling out."

She also said, "All of my employees need to understand the principles of helping to prevent a crisis and how to manage one. We talk a lot about how we could do things better and about our vulnerabilities. I also believe in conducting simulated crisis training. Because we often have new employees or those only working during specific seasons, we conduct our simulated crisis training every six months."

Once every six months, the sporting goods store pays its employees to come into the store 90 minutes before the store opens on a Saturday for a training session. Other employees who work nights are paid to stay an extra 90 minutes after the store closes. The employees are aware that a simulated crisis will occur, but will not know the nature of the crisis. On one occasion the crisis was a loud and obnoxious customer who refused to leave the store. On another simulation an employee suffered a heart attack. And, on another, a mock television crew entered the store to determine why a customer didn't receive a refund.

All simulated crisis sessions are followed by a friendly critique in which the employees discuss how they did and what could be improved for the next time. The sessions end with a raffle that gives all participating employees an opportunity to win one of three prizes – usually something like a team jacket, an expensive golf bag, or a gift certificate for merchandise.

"Every time we hold one of these everyone laughs and says 'Gee, I'm sure glad this was just practice and not the real thing'," said the owner. "We always find ways we can do things better, and are more confident in ourselves that we can handle a real crisis when it happens. We've been fortunate so far not to have experienced a real crisis, but we will be ready when we do."

Three lessons to learn

The sporting goods store example reinforces several key points on simulated crisis training for a business:

1) **Invest the time and effort to be prepared.** Commit your business to be prepared for the inevitable crisis situation. It has to be a priority activity within your company, and a strong commitment of time and energy is needed to do it properly. The owner of the sporting goods store made it a priority to conduct the crisis training twice a year, and determined a way to ensure all employees could participate. Consider how your business could make crisis training a priority.

2) **Get people involved.** Consider who in your business would be involved in managing a crisis if one were to occur. Then, determine how many of those people could be involved in your crisis training. The sporting goods store determined a way to involve all its employees in the training. Determine how to get the participation of your key people in the training.

3) **Make it fun.** Consider how you could make your training enjoyable, perhaps with something fun after the session – similar to the raffle conducted by the sporting goods store. Ensure the actual training session is taken very seriously, but work in something fun at the close of the session so people might look forward to the next training event.

◆

What are the components of successful crisis-simulation training?

Successful crisis-simulation training includes the following:

- The participation of those most likely to be involved in managing an actual crisis in your business.
- Sufficient time to conduct an effective session (a minimum of three hours).
- A crisis scenario that could actually occur and is consistent with one of the vulnerabilities identified as "high priority".
- An appropriately complex scenario to involve several people from the business – which would likely be the case in an actual crisis.
- The involvement of people role playing several publics (e.g., employees, customers, political officials and the news media).
- Active involvement by "news media" that show significant interest in the crisis.
- Media interviews.
- A video crew to monitor and record the situation for subsequent review and discussion.
- People assigned to observe and evaluate the management of the crisis, and to offer subsequent suggestions for improvement.
- Specific evaluation forms – developed in advance to ensure consistency with the company's crisis-management objectives – that can be completed by the observers/evaluators.

How often should we conduct *crisis-simulation training* in our business?

This type of training should be conducted once a year. Additional training sessions should be scheduled if the business is particularly vulnerable to a crisis, or if significant changes in senior-management personnel have occurred throughout the year.

What is *media training* and how could that help our business prepare for a crisis?

Media training is the focused effort to train a company's spokespersons on effectively communicating with and through the news media. Most businesses have little experience dealing with the news media and how to communicate their messages most effectively when briefing or being interviewed by the news media.

Media training can be particularly effective and useful when a crisis situation catapults a business into the spotlight. During a crisis situation, particular attention is paid to the messages communicated, the tone and emotion conveyed, and the perceived competency of the company's spokespersons. These all play a major part in shaping the company's reputation, trust, credibility and goodwill – which often can take major positive or negative swings during and after a crisis has occurred.

What are the components of an effective media-training session?

An effective media-training session should include the following:

- A discussion of the news media, and the inherent differences between print, television and radio media, and general-interest, business and trade reporters.
- A review of core messages to be communicated.
- Answers to routine and difficult questions that could arise.
- A discussion of tips and techniques to communicate effectively (i.e., overcoming fears and nerves, and proper body language, eye contact and attire).
- Videotaped (or audiotaped for radio training) rehearsal of news conference or media briefing – or, stand-up interview or talk-show appearance conducted by an experienced interviewer.
- A positive, motivating critique with helpful tips on ways to improve communications with the media.
- A written binder/manual of reminders for easy reference at a later time.

Example: Paper manufacturer uses media training

A manufacturer of paper goods – including facial tissue, toilet paper and paper towels – is among the largest in its industry. Selection of an appropriate spokesperson for the company is made based on several criteria including the specific issues to be discussed, the media outlets involved, and the priorities placed on the situation.

"We have several people who might speak on behalf of our company," said the President and CEO. "So, we need to make sure each of them are well prepared and able to most effectively represent our business. We put our people through media training at least once a year and more frequently when needed."

Spokespersons for the paper-goods manufacturer include the Chairman, the President/CEO, the Executive Vice President and Chief Operating Officer, the Vice President of Sales, the Vice President of Public Relations, the Director of Operations, its 10 plant managers across the country and the company's Director of Media Relations.

The manufacturing company hires a local public relations firm that specializes in media training businesses of all kinds. Each session for the company is approximately four hours in length. It includes a review of the company's core messages, along with how to answer both routine and difficult questions. The messages and Q&A are reviewed and discussed during the first two hours, and the final two hours are devoted to conducting simulated interviews of the spokespersons – so they can practice ways to effectively communicate the information. Those interviews are videotaped and critiqued by the consultants together with the participants.

Some of the questions covered asked of the spokespersons at the company's most recent training session included: What makes your products better than those from your competitors? How does your company in its manufacturing process demonstrate its concern with the environment? How would you describe the profile of your typical consumer? Why have your sales flattened during the past two quarters? What is the outlook for your company's stock during the next six months? Why don't you have more women and minorities on your management team and board of directors?

The media training sessions are conducted usually by three people from the public relations firm – two senior-level trainers/consultants and one person to operate the camera and to help take notes. Typically, no more than three of the company's spokespersons are trained during the same session. Those trained together usually include the Chairman with the President/CEO; the Executive VP/COO with the Vice President of Sales; the Vice President of Public Relations with the Director of Media Relations; and the Director of Operations with one or two plant managers. The plant managers are usually trained in groups of three.

"I always look forward to the training sessions," said the Vice President of Sales. "Heck, I'd rather make a mistake I can just laugh off in a training session than to make the same mistake when it really counts and it's no laughing matter."

Three lessons to learn

The example of the paper manufacturer helps underscore the following points:

1) **Build the training into your schedules.** Make media training a priority for your spokespersons. Train all those who will likely represent your business on which messages to communicate, how to answer routine and difficult questions, and tips on communicating effectively and confidently.

2) **Focus on the *messages*, not solely on *delivery*.** Many media training companies focus too much attention on how to deliver the information and not enough on the content of the information itself. They spend too much time working with someone on hand gestures, posture, body language and eye contact, and insufficient time is spent on understanding the information itself. The paper manufacturer spent the first two hours of each four-hour session reviewing and discussing content, before it began the actual simulated interviews. Many media training companies prefer to jump too quickly into the interview portion of the training without first adequately covering the messages.

3) **Hire professionals to help with it.** This is an area where you most likely will be better served hiring an outside consulting firm to conduct the training. This might be a public relations firm, as used by the paper-goods manufacturer, or – in larger markets – consultants who specialize only in solid training. In either case, the trainers likely will be former reporters who have a news instincts and judgment, and can best reflect what your spokespersons may face in front of real-life reporters. Another reason to hire an outside firm for the work is its ability to provide third-party perspective and constructive criticism, which may be more easily accepted than if delivered by someone internally.

◆

How often should media training be conducted for our company's spokespersons?

It depends on the effectiveness of the spokesperson and the frequency in which your key messages and answers to questions need to be revised. In most cases, once every 9-12 months should be sufficient.

Is it possible to *over*-train a spokesperson?

Yes. Someone can be provided so much information and tips to consider that he can't think clearly about the communications itself. It's like the golfer who is told to keep his right elbow tucked near his hip, his right shoulder tipped, his backswing slow, his wrists cocked, his heels on the ground and his eyes looking at the ball. If too many swing thoughts occur during the swing, the golfer will most certainly do one or more things wrong.

It's no different when, for example, someone is being trained to appear on a television talk show. Smile. Nod your head. Cross your legs. Sit up straight. Use lots of hand gestures. Make sure you say this. Don't say that. Stay relaxed. Look at the host. Don't look at the camera. Maintain good eye contact. Don't shift your eyes when answering a question. A typical media training session might include another two or three dozen tips. If you think about all or most of those during a media interview, you will likely forget about what you are there to talk about.

The best benefit of an effective training session is to: **1)** assimilate the core messages and answers to questions and **2)** build your confidence about interview opportunities so you can look confident and act natural. Remember, the best actors and actresses are those who just look and act natural. They don't over-do their hand gestures, offer fake smiles or have unnatural motions – they just act like they are having a conversation with someone.

Some media trainers actually damage confidence and inadvertently make those they are trying to improve *less* effective. This most frequently occurs in simulated interviews when the trainer tries to prove to the trainee how totally inept they are at being an effective communicator (reinforcing why the training is needed in the first place).

This tact may work well for someone who is pompously over-confident and doesn't see any need for participating in the training. However, in most cases, the trainers' job is to help the spokespersons become confident and relaxed to ensure they can remember the content and communicate the information naturally and effectively.

Over-training or improper training is worse than no training at all. It can turn someone into a stiff robot or a babbling spokesperson who is unfocused and unsure.

What else should our business do in advance to help plan for a crisis?

Other steps to consider include the following:

- Update and revise your company's emergency policies and manual once a year.
- Ensure your mainframe and client/server data are copied on a regular basis and stored off-site.

- Install a toll-free phone line with a separate number that can be communicated and used if necessary to answer questions or obtain feedback during a crisis.
- Consider automating the delivery of voice and fax documents to your key publics. These documents can be loaded into a talking tele-computer accessed from any phone or any fax in real time. This automation of message delivery can ensure consistent messages are being communicated and can help take pressure off your spokesperson during a crisis.
- Determine ways to enhance your company's relationships with its key publics (e.g., employees, customers, community leaders, news media) and implement public relations activities to improve the relationships.
- Review your company's list of vulnerabilities and consider again the steps to help prevent them from occurring.
- Develop any written materials that can be quickly updated and revised during a crisis.

What written materials can be developed in advance of a crisis?

Consider the types of information and materials your business may need in the event of a crisis. You might be surprised by the number of items that can be developed now and updated and revised later. These include:

- Fact sheets and backgrounders on the company and its products/ services.
- Brief biographies and photos of key executives.
- Answers to frequently asked questions about the company.
- A draft memorandum reminding your employees to refer any news media inquiries to the company's primary spokesperson.
- A draft letter to your most important customers informing them about the situation (even though you don't know what it is at this time), thanking them for their support and asking them to call you with any questions.

- A draft letter to your key suppliers/vendors that will be similar to the customer letter.
- Any other item you feel could save time during a crisis if developed (or, at least, *started*) at this time.

Isn't it a waste of time and effort to develop the materials now when they'll need to be revised anyhow?

No. Most of the materials will be needed immediately, and it will save you considerable time if only minor revisions are required. You won't have the luxury of focused concentration and sufficient time to develop all the materials from scratch once a crisis situation occurs. Take them as far as possible now – you'll be glad you did.

How can interactive voice response help during a crisis?

Computers can be programmed to talk to people through the telephone, fax and/or e-mail. Artificial intelligence programming allows computers to interact with people, take information, process that data and send out the appropriate responses as either a voice file or hard copy document.

- Voice files on any subject matter can be created over the phone and stored for retrieval by interested parties.
- Fax copies of responses, statements, position papers and other literature can be retrieved in seconds from any phone to any fax.
- In today's global business environment, multi-lingual communications are a must. Consider making your voice and fax files in the languages of your customers.
- Interactive tele-computers can take information from callers on any particular situation and automatically create management or user reports.

To learn more about automating your company's message delivery system, you might consider calling the Fourth Wave Group at (313) 343-9577 or send them an e-mail message or question to: mindglue@ix.netcom.com.

How prepared does our business need to be? How much is *too* much?

You and others in your organization will need to make that assessment. The amount of preparation needed in your business will be based on the vulnerabilities present, the company's recent history of crises and the likelihood of a crisis occurring. If these factors indicate the business should be well prepared, then make sure you heed the warning and invest the time, effort and cost to do so.

What's the best way to get others to buy into the idea of crisis planning?

The most effective ways to get others to support the concept of planning in advance for a crisis include the following:

- Involve others in the process – perhaps through the vulnerabilities analysis, the crisis-management team, crisis-simulation training or other ways.
- Remind senior management about the vulnerabilities and potential crisis situations – recommend ways to help prevent and manage them.
- Share with others examples of mismanaged crises – particularly those in your industry or field.
- Give *The Crisis Counselor* to your boss as a birthday present!

Closing thoughts

Advance planning can improve the chances of surviving a crisis. A number of options exist when considering steps your business can take to plan in advance for a crisis – formation of a crisis team, preparation of written plans and manuals, training sessions, background information and materials, and the like.

It is too easy to put off advance planning. Too many other ways exist to spend time and resources than to invest it in advance planning. However, can your business survive the consequences of failing to plan for a crisis? It is likely you can quickly think of three to five ways in which your business could experience a crisis. Take a few minutes to use this chapter as a guide to consider how some advance planning can occur in your business to help reduce the likely damage from one of those crises.

Then, plan for the planning process. Establish a budget. Determine the timing. And, make it happen in your business. You'll be glad you did.

Tips to consider

- **Make a commitment to plan in advance for crisis situations.**
- **Identify an individual in the business to be responsible for crisis planning and other aspects of crisis management.**
- **Establish a dedicated budget for crisis planning.**
- **Conduct a vulnerabilities analysis at least once a year.**
- **Establish a crisis-management team within your organization.**
- **Prepare worst-case scenarios for the company's five highest-priority crises.**
- **Develop a crisis management plan and update it at least once a year.**
- **Prepare individual crisis-response manuals for those who will help manage a crisis in your company.**
- **Develop any possible written materials in advance.**
- **Plan and participate in crisis-simulation training at least once a year.**
- **Conduct media training for your spokespersons at least once a year.**

CHAPTER 5

The crisis itself

What is there to know about a crisis? Isn't it enough to know that a crisis is a problem or situation you don't want to face?

Please take a few minutes to consider whether you think the are true or false:

1) Specific factors can make some crises easier to manage than others.

2) The *cause* of the crisis can affect its potential longevity and impact on an organization.

3) Some crises escalate in intensity.

4) A problem turns into a crisis when the news media finds out about it.

5) It is always apparent when warning signs turn into crises.

6) Your employees should be among your highest-priority audiences during a crisis.

7) It's best not to involve the police or fire department immediately after a crisis until you address other priorities.

8) Don't do anything in a crisis without first consulting your attorney.

9) A *publicly held* company often faces greater scrutiny in a crisis than private enterprises.

10) The CEO of your business should always be on site at the crisis to prove that he/she cares about the situation.

Answers:

1) **T;** 2) **T;** 3) **T;** 4) **F;** 5) **F;** 6) **T;** 7) **F;** 8) **F;** 9) **T;** 10) **F**

Evaluation:

0 - 4 correct answers	You have the wrong idea about crises. Cuddle up with *The Crisis* Counselor and read this chapter with great care.
5 - 7 correct answers	You have a good feel for crises and the management of them. This chapter will help round out your knowledge on the subject.
8 - 10 correct answers	You have an excellent foundation heading into this chapter. A few of the questions and answers might appeal to you, and then you're ready for the next chapter: "Communicating during a crisis."

If you've made it this far in the book, you are now well-grounded in some basic principles about crises in business:

1) Crisis situations occur in every type of business.

2) Crises that affect most businesses are not the high-profile, headline-grabbing variety commonly labeled as business crises – such as plane crashes, shootings, oil-tanker accidents and product tamperings. More common crises are negative media coverage, quality problems, employee layoffs, plant or office closings, sudden death of a senior executive, government probes, recalls, boycotts, pickets and the like.

3) Most crisis situations are preceded by one or more warning signs.

4) The level of advance planning and preparation has a direct impact on the ability to effectively manage a crisis and reduce its negative impact on your business.

5) It is necessary to move swiftly and confidently after a crisis has occurred.

These principles help establish a solid foundation for this chapter which describes the evolution of a crisis; how to identify the crisis itself; and first steps to consider when a crisis occurs in your business.

How will our business know when a crisis has occurred?

The situation will likely possess most or all of the following *characteristics*:

- It will be something unusual or out of the norm that has occurred in the business.
- It will force your senior-management team to make several difficult decisions.
- It has the potential to negatively affect the company's reputation – and sales, productivity, and market share – by the decisions that are or aren't made.
- It will be an event or situation that the news media will find newsworthy and of significant interest.
- It will encourage your key publics – such as employees, customers, community leaders and suppliers – to have increased expectations for information and answers to questions.
- It takes a business off its regular, course-of-business focus.

The Crisis Counselor mindset

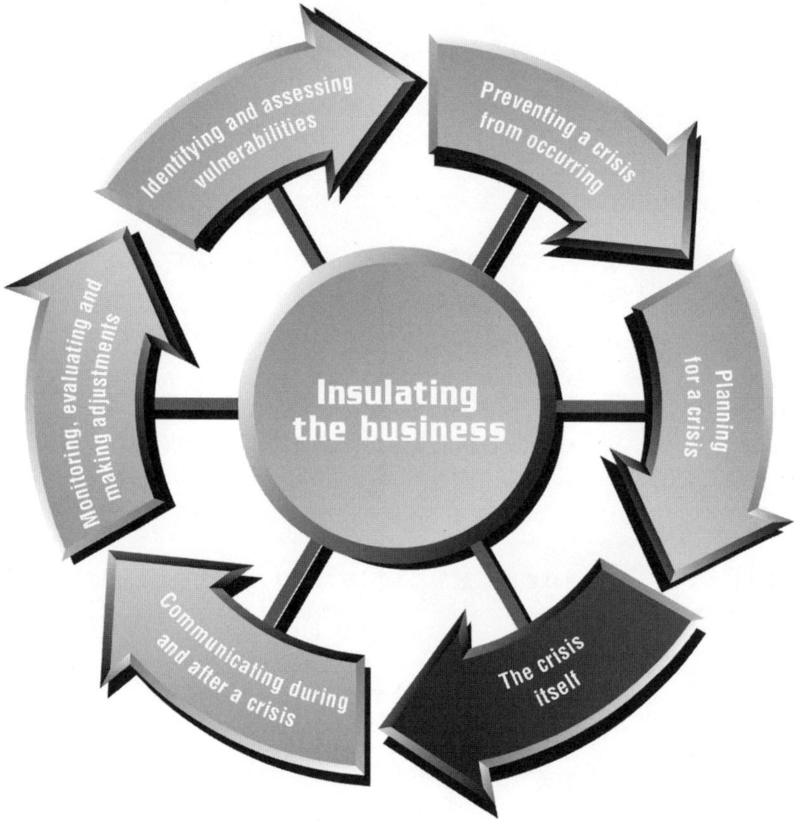

How can you tell whether a problem is a *warning sign* or an actual *crisis*?

Don't concern yourself too much with the act of *identifying* it. Crises can be disguised momentarily as *warning signs*. And, warning signs can shift swiftly to become crises before you can even say the words. Therefore, don't worry as much about *labeling* the situation as following through to conduct the first two steps of the crisis-management process: identify the problem and attempt to prevent it from occurring or growing in intensity or severity.

If the situation can't be prevented and becomes a significant problem or crisis, consider it as such and manage the situation through steps described in *The Crisis Counselor.* Then, monitor and evaluate the situation and make any necessary adjustments.

Finally, check the characteristics described in the previous question. If the situation meets most of those characteristics, go ahead and consider it a *crisis* – then implement what you've learned here about managing it.

How quickly do crises occur and how much time will we have to react once they begin?

It depends on the crisis. Some crisis situations occur in seconds – a plant accident, sudden death of a senior executive, notification of a government investigation, and a chemical spill. Other crises occur and evolve over a much-longer period of time – hostile takeovers, labor unrest, a boycott, corporate embezzlement and vandalism.

The length of time you'll have to react to a crisis is directly related to its perceived impact on the business and your key publics. To what extreme will the crisis affect the success of – and your focus on – the business? Does it affect your employees? Will the news media be interested in it? How will your customers react to the situation?

Example: The newspaper with the columnist's foot in mouth

The daily newspaper was among the nation's largest for a major metropolitan market. It had enjoyed an impressive growth in circulation throughout the past few years and had earned tremendous reader loyalty from being the primary source for written news in the community for the past 50 years.

One of the city's most popular celebrities was the newspaper's general-interest columnist. She had the freedom to write about anything she found noteworthy, funny, interesting or controversial. The friends and admirers she made from her column far outweighed any critics or enemies she made.

"I'm the luckiest person alive," she would say. "I can write about anything I want, as long as I keep it to 400 words or less."

One day, however, she wrote on a subject she would later regret. The column was about how she is tired of people always complaining and blaming other people for their lack of achievements in life. The subject matter would have been okay until she said it is her perspective that these attitudes stem from specific racial and ethnic groups. She generalized that two such groups are inherent complainers and are dragging "the rest of society down with them."

As you might expect, her prejudicial remarks sparked a significant public backlash. It first began with a few phone calls to the newspaper's managing editor shortly after the newspaper was delivered to homes and newsstands.

"I thought she went a bit too far with that column," said the managing editor after hanging up the telephone. "I probably should have talked with her about it before it ran. I sure hope others aren't too offended by it."

By midday, they were told by one religious and two ethnic groups that they will recommend to their members immediate cancellation of their subscriptions. Each group said they will boycott the newspaper and its advertisers.

"What can we do about this?" asked the frustrated managing editor to whoever was nearby.

"It's too late now," said another editor. "The damage is already done. We just need to sit back and take our medicine."

By day's end, the columnist and managing editor had received more than 100 phone calls – which included a bomb threat and two death threats.

"I'm sorry I caused all this trouble," said the columnist to the managing editor. "Maybe I should just leave town for a while until all this blows over. People will forget about it in a few days."

Three lessons to learn

The crisis experienced by the newspaper helps reinforce some points about how crises often begin and grow in intensity. Here are some lessons to learn from this incident:

1) **Identify the crisis and begin planning as soon as possible.** The newspaper's managing editor and columnist failed to identify the problem as a crisis at its earliest stage. At the least, they should have started to discuss what could be done to help reduce the negative fallout from the column.

2) **Be decisive before it's too late.** It was clear that the newspaper's management had not previously prepared for such a public backlash. This type of situation was certainly a vulnerability that could have been considered well in advance. The lack of preparation forced the newspaper to simply sit back, accept the criticism and hope it all just goes away.

3) **Take some action.** Advance planning makes it possible to think and act quickly during the first few hours of a crisis – well before being placed in a reactive, defensive hole from which is difficult to climb out. The newspaper could have taken some immediate action if it were better prepared. The columnist could have written another column for the next day, apologizing for the interpretation of her previous column and clarifying her position. The management and columnist would agree on the messages to be communicated. The managing editor could include a brief letter from him on the front page of the newspaper, expressing the newspaper's position on the previous day's column. And, the managing editor and columnist could show their initiative by placing phone calls and letters to racial and religious groups in the area.

◆

Are some crises more difficult to manage than others?

It depends on the *cause* of the crisis. The difficulty in managing a crisis is often based on the amount of goodwill, trust and understanding the company possesses before, during and immediately after a crisis. If this goodwill erodes, based on a mistake it made or a perceived management deficiency, a crisis can be very difficult to manage effectively and quickly.

For example, if a company is perceived to be the *victim* of circumstances of a situation over which it had no control, its publics usually give it the benefit of the doubt. Therefore, the business has much more leniency in the management of its crisis. This is seen when a company faces a natural disaster – such as a flood or tornado – or when a product tampering was clearly not the fault of the business.

However, if the crisis is perceived to be a mistake that the company could or should have avoided, then it can be more difficult to manage. This is particularly the case if the crisis is borne from a management mistake, misjudgment or oversight. The company quickly loses goodwill, credibility and trust, and is often vaulted into a defensive, reactive posture. Crises become extremely difficult to manage under these circumstances. Examples include embezzlement, age-discrimination accusations, a severe manufacturing error or a chemical spill.

What stages typically occur over the life of a crisis?

A crisis typically (but not always) evolves in the following way:

1) **Warning sign –** the signals that usually precede a crisis.
2) **Actual crisis event** – the situation which rears its head and necessitates immediate action.
3) **The turning point** – the crisis is either neutralized, abolished or escalates in intensity at this stage.
4) **Protracted crisis aftermath** – the ghost of the crisis event which lingers on affects the company's ongoing strategies and plans.

When does a crisis evolve in a *different* way?

As mentioned previously in *The Crisis Counselor*, occasionally a crisis strikes quickly without even a hint of a warning. Examples of this include a tanker explosion, a train derailment, a terrorist threat or a virus wiping out the files in your computer system. And, under very fortunate circumstances, a crisis is managed so well that it drifts away quickly into oblivion – never making its way into the "protracted crisis aftermath" stage.

Can a crisis actually *escalate* in intensity? If so, how?

A crisis can definitely escalate in intensity if the company's publics feel the situation is not properly managed. This is particularly true if they feel the company has not clearly recognized that a problem exists, committed itself to fixing the problem and shown the appropriate amount of remorse. Frustrations, criticisms and damaging rumors are side effects caused by failing to meet the *communications* expectations of the company's key publics. This means that problems identified as "crises" can – and often do – escalate in intensity when the communications are mismanaged and fall short of the expectations of the news media, key customers, employees, regulatory officials and the like.

Example: The bus company with an employee crisis

The manufacturer of school buses was a strong regional leader in the industry. Its reputation for producing quality buses helped it increase sales and market share over the past five years. However, one of its major competitors has found a way to produce a high-quality bus, with more accessories as standard equipment, for a lower price.

"We just aren't able to sell our products as swiftly and easily as in the past," said the sales manager from the bus manufacturer. "Even our loyal customers who have bought from us during the past 10 years are telling us they are forced to buy from our competition."

This downturn forced the company to cut its payroll from 1,100 employees to 900. It was the first time in the company's 25-year history that it was forced to terminate such a high number of employees at one time. The employee layoff of 12 years ago, the largest previous termination, was only 25 people.

"This is devastating to our company," said the sales manager, who had his sales staff trimmed from 35 to 15 executives. "I've never seen morale this low. The employees want to be told why we had to cut so deep, and want to be assured their jobs are safe in the future."

The employees weren't told much. Since the company had never experienced this type of situation, it bungled the execution of it. Employees learned about the 200-person layoff from their supervisors, and from what those who were terminated told them between their curses and tears. No general announcement was made, no employee memo was distributed, and no outplacement-service company was retained to help with it.

Employee morale and productivity dipped even more during the next several weeks. Rumors were circulating that sales were continuing to fall, and another round of layoffs was imminent.

"Ahh, don't worry about it," said one supervisor. "They would have told us supervisors if another layoff might happen. Heck, they cut 200 people from the payroll. How much more muscle can you take out of the system before you hit bone?"

Unfortunately, the rumors came true, and management announced another round of devastating layoffs. One-hundred additional employees were terminated immediately and without notice. This time a staff memo was distributed and posted in coffee rooms and bulletin boards. But, otherwise, it was handled in much the same way as the previous layoffs.

"How can this happen, and we aren't even given an explanation?" asked the same supervisor. "How do we know this won't happen again? I don't care if they are counting on me to stay or not, but I'm going to put together my resume and start looking for another job right away."

Another manager said: "I didn't think things could get worse around here after the first layoffs, but this second round – particularly the way both were handled – has wrecked this company. I want no part of a company like this."

The company lost many of those it considered the "top stars," who were recruited heavily by the competing company with the growing sales and market share. Six months later, the bus company filed for bankruptcy to reorganize the company and its debt.

Three lessons to learn

The school-bus manufacturer should have learned several important lessons from their situation. Here are three of them:

1) **Recognize how crises *intensify* when mismanaged.** The bus company should have better communicated a realistic view of the sales downturn it was experiencing, and why it was necessary to make such a deep cut in its payroll. The company learned that things *can* and *do* get worse when crises are mismanaged.

2) **Crises call for *increased* communications.** The natural tendency during a crisis is to bury your head in the sand or to run away from the problems. Unfortunately, that strategy only makes the situation worse. During times of crises, a greater number of questions are being asked, frustrations are boiling over and rumors are circulating. These need to be managed and controlled, and often communicating specific messages in a timely way to targeted audiences can help accomplish that. Failure to communicate almost always leads to a failure in managing the crisis.

3) **When possible, pool all the negative action/news together.** If you have some bad news to communicate, don't try to soft-peddle it by communicating it in bits and pieces. You're almost always better off pooling all the bad news together and getting it all out at once. A deep cut in a company's reputation is easier to manage than a superficial one that can't heal because of new negatives that tear open its scab periodically. In the case of the bus company, it would have been far better off by being more open and honest about its current and impending financial condition. And, it should have tried to avoid a second set of layoffs by cutting deeper than it thought it had to in the initial round. By doing so, it might have avoided the second layoff, which played a part in the destruction of the company.

◆

What should be our "thought process" immediately after identifying the situation as a crisis?

The "thought process" should be to gather as much information as possible – as swiftly as possible. You need to identify the problem first. Try to solve the problem and consider which of your company's publics are affected, in some way, by the situation. Determine the core messages that should be communicated about the crisis, who should be the company's spokesperson(s), what form the communications should take and which activities should be implemented and when.

These decisions should be made decisively and confidently. The more prepared you are for a potential crisis, the more likely you'll be to have an effective and focused "thought process."

What is typically the *objective* during a crisis?

Although the objectives differ depending on the nature of the crisis, the primary objective is usually focused on minimizing the potential damage to the company's reputation. In some cases, the objective may be to even turn any potential negatives associated with the crisis into *positives* for the organization.

What should be our *strategy* in a crisis?

Strategies from one crisis to another are almost always different and unique. However, the strategies for most crises have common elements. In most cases, the strategy focuses on planning and preparing materials in advance, identifying and segmenting the organization's key publics and communicating three to five key messages to help convey the sense of honesty, openness, sincerity, confidence and credibility.

What should be the first few action steps to consider after identifying the situation as a crisis?

Again, it all depends on the crisis and the amount of time you have to conduct advance planning or whether you are immediately thrust into the *reactive* mode. For instance, if you've uncovered a possible case of embezzlement in your company and it's necessary to increase your investigation and eventually inform a law-enforcement agency, you'll have significantly more time for advance planning than if you've just learned three people have been killed by an explosion in your company's major manufacturing plant.

Nonetheless, here is a checklist of 10 steps to consider when first learning of a situation that is – or could potentially become – a crisis situation for your business:

1) Identify the problem.
2) Learn as much as you can about the situation.
3) If necessary, contact the local police, fire department or hospital if imminent danger exists or safety is a concern.
4) Attempt to solve the problem.
5) Contact the appropriate senior managers/officers in your company to notify them of the problem and to discuss solutions and communications steps.
6) Identify the publics who are most affected by the situation.
7) Determine core messages to communicate and think through appropriate answers to questions likely to be asked.
8) Place in priority order the planning and communications steps necessary to implement in the short term.
9) Ensure your spokespersons are briefed and can effectively represent the company during the crisis.
10) Implement the short-term tactics and communicate with your key publics in a manner that conveys honesty, accessibility, credibility and confidence.

Closing thoughts

So, what's the big deal about identifying when a crisis actually occurs? Isn't it like asking, "When will I know when someone has punched me in the face?"

It would be nice if identifying a crisis in a business were that easy. Many businesses suffer substantial damage from a crisis, when much of it could have been avoided by addressing it earlier.

Depending on the nature of the crisis, the time period available to make a judgment on what to do and when to do it could range from minutes to hours to days. Failure to move quickly enough can put your business in a defensive hole – significantly damaging your credibility and reputation – of which can take years to pull yourself out.

We discussed in previous chapters how adequate preparation allows you to be decisive and most effective when time is of the essence. In this chapter, we covered the importance of recognizing the crisis situation and taking smart action as quickly as possible. The manner in which the first few steps are managed is often the difference between a crisis is relatively unnoticed and one that etches an ugly tattoo right on the forehead of a business.

Recognize the importance of identifying crisis signs and moving quickly to take the important first steps in whisking away the unwanted visitor. The next chapter offers some thoughts on how to communicate effectively once the crisis has occurred. You should find it most helpful in your pursuit down the road to most effectively manage crises in your business. Best of luck.

Tips to consider

- **Plan as much as possible for an eventual crisis (particularly if you sense specific vulnerabilities in the organization that have the potential to ignite into a crisis).**

- **Quickly identify the problem and move onto solving it, if possible.**

- **Identify the publics that will be affected and consider how they will feel about the situation (i.e., questions they will ask, information they will expect to be told).**

- **Determine the objectives, strategies and tactics to consider, and be decisive on all decisions.**

- **Implement tactics with confidence.**

- **Make adjustments as necessary.**

CHAPTER 6

What should we say and do?

How do you know what to say and do during a crisis?

Please take a few minutes to consider whether you think the following statements are true or false:

1) In *some* crises, communication doesn't play any role in the act of managing them.

2) The rule of thumb in a crisis is to communicate everything you know about the situation to every possible public/audience.

3) The window of opportunity is usually *less* than 48 hours for your communications to be credible and effective.

4) Communications should be limited solely to direct, face-to-face contact when a serious crisis arises.

5) Communication through *electronic mail* should be avoided altogether during a crisis.

6) Only the organization's CEO should be used as a spokesperson during a serious crisis.

7) Employees usually know what's happening in a crisis. You're better off focusing your time and energies in communicating with your external publics.

8) News media will report on what they see and hear regardless of your efforts during a crisis.

9) Customers and prospects should be the only audiences on whom your communications efforts should focus during a crisis.

10) Usually it's necessary to conduct proactive communication during the first day of a crisis.

Answers: **The correct answer is *false* to every question, except for question #3 which is *true*.**

Evaluation:

6 or less correct answers	Hopefully, you'll read this chapter before experiencing your first crisis. You should have a greater appreciation for the *Crisis Counselor* process in communicating during a crisis. Read carefully.
7 - 8 correct answers	You now can see that communicating during a crisis is not nearly as cut and dry as you might have thought initially.
9 - 10 correct answers	You understand most of the fundamentals about communicating during a crisis. You might further expand your *Crisis Counselor* mindset as you read this chapter.

Despite the best efforts to prevent a crisis from occurring in your business, the odds eventually catch up to every organization and a crisis erupts. Your business can be the innocent victim of a crisis –

perhaps suffering the effects of a tornado or a malicious product tampering. Or the crisis may have ignited through an unfortunate oversight by your management team or a sloppy error by one of your sales managers.

Nevertheless, crises of varying degrees of intensity affect every business at one time or another. When they do, more questions arise than answers. What should we do? Who should we notify? How can we best manage the situation? How can we ensure the crisis won't cause major damage to our business? Where's that *Crisis Counselor* book you told me about?

The tricky part of communicating during and after a crisis is that every situation is different. Some crisis events in an organization dictate the need for strong and aggressive communication with employees, customers, prospects, suppliers, government officials and other important publics. Failure to do so could turn a problem in your business into a crisis and eventually into a disaster for the organization. However, some crises don't necessarily mean you need to communicate the problem to all your primary and secondary publics. In fact, doing so could turn a manageable problem into an out-of-control crisis – if you're not careful.

The strategic decision on ways to communicate before and after a crisis is one of the most important decisions you will make in managing a crisis. Setting and agreeing on a strategy for communications – and doing it quickly after a crisis occurs – can make the difference between a crisis that is forgotten about in a few days and one that lingers around to haunt an organization for years.

This is the one area that many businesses do seek the immediate assistance from an experienced crisis-management professional or public relations firm. Unfortunately, the majority wait until the crisis has already erupted to establish a relationship with these experts. Valuable time is wasted orienting the firm about not only the crisis itself, but the company, its people, culture, products, services and other information needed for a professional to provide insight and counsel on the situation.

This chapter takes you through the thought process in setting strategy for communicating during and after a crisis, and includes the steps you'll want to consider if a crisis erupts in your business. Plenty of examples are included to make the concepts easier to understand, and to demonstrate the distinctions between different scenarios occurring in varying types of businesses.

How communicative should we be during a crisis?

The level of communications necessary in a crisis is directly commensurate with the complexity of the crisis and the publics it affects. The easiest way to determine the necessary level of communication is to consider this question as it relates to each of your key publics, **"If I were them, would I have questions about the situation and become frustrated or upset if I didn't receive any information?"** If the answer is "yes," you need to continue – or increase – the communications.

What do you mean by being communicative? Are you saying we need to reveal *everything* about the crisis?

No, being *communicative* doesn't necessarily mean telling everything you know about the situation. In fact, doing so might actually make the problem worse. But, not communicating at all usually exacerbates the problem.

Example: How much to communicate

A local dry cleaners has had 10 complaints from those who picked up their dry cleaning two days ago. All 10 complaints involve the customers experiencing skin irritation and hives after wearing the newly cleaned garments. The owner and manager checked the cleaning solution used during the past two days and realized a new employee inadvertently mixed the wrong combination of chemicals to make the solution.

"What should we do?" asked the manager. "Should we call all our customers to tell them about this?"

"We don't need to alarm those who haven't been in during the past two days," said the owner. "Let's first change the chemical solution to ensure we don't use the wrong solutions on any other garments. Then, let's call all the customers who had garments dry cleaned during the past two days to apologize for the problem. Tell them we will re-clean their garments for free and will give them a coupon for another cleaning free of charge. Let's be honest about the mistake and tell them it has been corrected, and that it won't happen again."

Three lessons to learn

The dry cleaners' example helps reinforce the following:

1) **Fix the problem first and then consider how to communicate about it.** The dry cleaners identified the problem as the chemical solution and quickly changed the solution before it was used on any other garments. They decided to contact customers with affected garments, and quickly considered how to explain the mistake to them and other customers. They also decided the best way to avoid losing the customer was to re-clean the existing garment for free and then to provide a coupon for a free cleaning of their next garment.

2) **You can be selective with whom and what you communicate.** Consider who your crisis affects and *how* they are potentially affected. Communicate with them in a manner that specifically addresses their concerns and needs.

3) **Identify a small number of core messages to communicate and do so with repetition.** The dry cleaners selected the following messages to communicate: **1)** We made a mistake by using the wrong combination of chemicals in our cleaning solution on a few garments that were cleaned during the past two days. **2)** We apologize for our mistake and invite you to bring in the affected garments so we can dry clean them again – for no charge, of course. **3)** Your garments have not been damaged in any way, but they should be re-cleaned to avoid any possible irritation to your skin. **4)** We also will provide you with a coupon for a free dry cleaning of your *next* garment. **5)** We are sorry for the inconvenience to you.

◆

Should the crisis-management team we established at our company make some of these decisions?

The crisis-management team should meet on a regular basis to ensure the decision makers are equipped with all the information needed to make informed and effective decisions. (See Chapter 4 for information on who would be part of a crisis-management team.) The crisis-management team should help quickly analyze the situation and discuss various options for solving the problem and communicating to the company's key publics. However, don't let the meeting process unnecessarily slow you down, and make sure someone is clearly in charge to make the final decisions (particularly when disagreements arise between team members). If you've identified a Chief Crisis Officer (see Chapter 1), put that person in charge.

The Crisis Counselor mindset

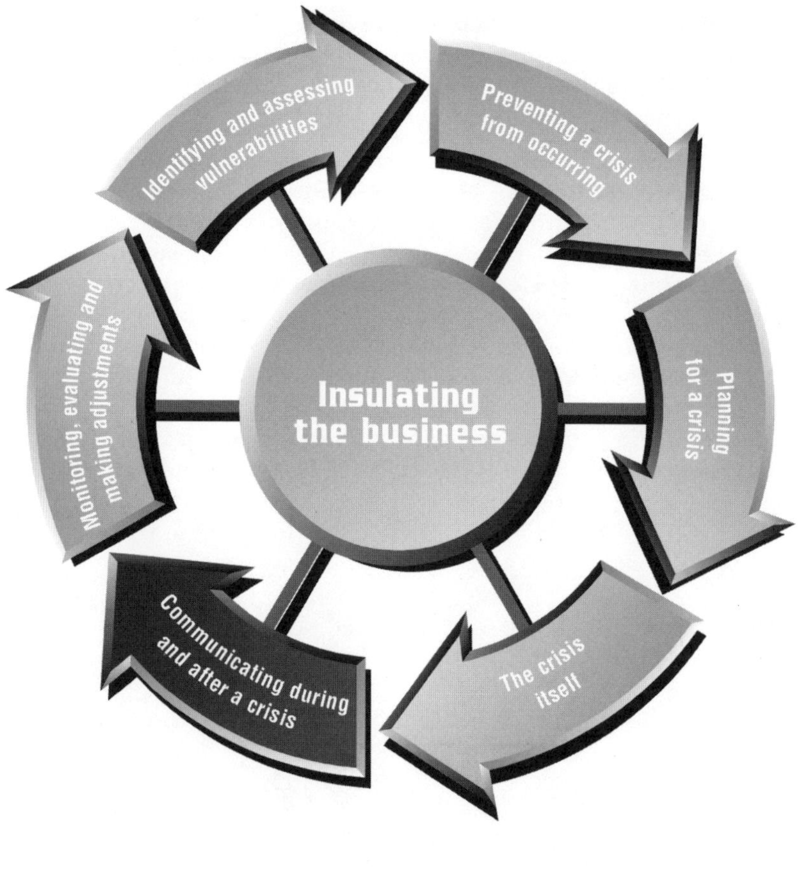

What are some general tips for communicating during a crisis?

You should have *The Crisis Counselor* mindset and consider the following when communicating during a crisis:

- **Identify all the various publics who may be affected by – or expect to be informed about – the crisis.** Remember, we discussed in Chapter 1 how to segment your company's publics to ensure an understanding about the differences between them. Are the messages to be communicated different? How can we best reach them? Who should be the spokesperson or deliverer of the messages? In what priority should we communicate with them?

- **Prove you have identified the problem and are doing something about it.** Your employees, customers and other publics will be extremely frustrated and perhaps hostile if they don't feel you have identified the problem as a serious one. They will often beat on you and your staff until they feel you recognize the problem. After all, they know you can't fix a problem until you admit one exists.

- **Communicate a small number of core messages to the appropriate publics.** It is extremely important early on to identify a small number of core messages to communicate with repetition. Then, develop the most appropriate ways to communicate them to your publics in an easy-to-understand manner.

- **Communicate only those things that can be confirmed with absolute certainty.** Fight the temptation to speculate on anything. It is far better to explain why you are able to confirm only a few points than to speculate on others and seriously damage your credibility if proved wrong in the future. The points that can be confirmed and communicated with absolute certainty should be done so confidently and effectively. Avoid doing so with other, less-certain points.

- **Don't lie about anything.** In addition to avoiding speculation, make sure you are never dishonest. One little white lie often turns into a string of them, when you find it necessary to cover your original twist of the truth. This is the worst mistake any business can make as it attempts to protect and preserve its reputation during a crisis. Getting caught in a lie is the worst and most damaging of all business mistakes.

- **Don't comment on hypothetical situations.** The news media often asks for comments on hypothetical situations. "What would you do if ______ occurred?" "If _____ happens, how will your business react to that?" Discipline yourself not to comment on hypothetical situations.

- **Convey a strong sense you'll be accessible and communicative.** In many crises, there is often little that can be confirmed and discussed immediately after the crisis occurs. In that situation, it is important to explain what can and can't be communicated at this time and to convey a strong sense of honesty, openness and accessibility. This is among the most important factors in effectively managing a crisis.

- **Be decisive.** The window to prove to your publics that the crisis is being managed as effectively as possible is usually only a few hours long (depending on the specific crisis, of course). A crisis forces a business and its senior management to be quick on their feet and fast in making informed decisions. If the business is well prepared for the crisis, you will be in the best position to be decisive, confident and organized. It is important in the early stages of a crisis to prove your competency and control over the situation. You'll have a difficult time establishing this once you get placed in a *defensive* mode.

- **Keep your cool.** Don't become upset at anyone or give the impression you are panicking. It's important to convey a sense that the situation is being effectively managed and hasn't totally consumed the organization.

- **Don't say "no comment" to the news media or anyone else.** Several ways exist to say *nothing* but to still convey a sense of control, accessibility, honesty and credibility. Saying "no comment" is a sign you are an *amateur* who has never managed a crisis.

- **Communicate all the bad news at one time.** If possible, communicate the bad news together; take your lumps and move on with things. This is almost always more effective than allowing your business to rupture each time bad news is communicated or speculated.

- **Include ways to obtain feedback and input from your publics.** Don't think that simply providing information will be sufficient. It is important to consider feedback, suggestions and ideas from your employees, customers, vendors and other publics. Failure to have sufficient two-way communication in a crisis almost always leads to a disconnect in relationships.

- **Document for the record.** Make sure you document phone calls received, meetings held and communications conducted during a crisis. Your legal counsel, public relations folks and others will need the information to refer to in the future. Who was that community resident who threatened us? What was the name of that television reporter who interviewed you? Who did we notify and when?

- **Monitor and evaluate the situation.** How are the communications being received? What messages are getting across? What types of questions are we receiving? The answers to these and other questions will help determine the adjustments that are necessary to make in communications.

- **Don't stop communicating.** Many businesses make this mistake. They are relieved to get by the initial day or two of the crisis, and feel their publics don't need any further communications. Although it may be unnecessary to continue communicating about the crisis itself, it is almost always a mistake to stop communicating altogether with your publics. The crisis may have given you an excuse to be in strong contact with your key publics. Continue the momentum and look for ways to further enhance your relationships.

What if we actually made a mistake? Is there a way to talk our way out of it or are we better off just fessing up to it?

In most cases, people will be more willing to forgive and support your business if you admit to a mistake. Frustrations rise when they feel the company doesn't recognize the mistake or its impact on others. In that situation, customers and others emerge as angry and vindictive – unless you prove to them specific steps are being taken to solve the problem. Examples of mistakes to fess up to include a quality problem due to an unfortunate oversight; an error in a delivery schedule that led to a serious problem for your customer; or a poor decision or comment that inadvertently hurt one of your key publics. In this type of situation, you're almost always better off doing the following:

- **Admit the mistake.** In most cases, if the business made a mistake (or you did individually), it is usually quite apparent who is to blame. One of the best, most disarming moves you can make in these cases is to admit the mistake and confidently move forward to repair the damage. This alone can often cool off an irate customer or frustrated employee.

- **Apologize, if appropriate.** If you or the business made a mistake that negatively affected others, apologize for the error and (if appropriate) shoulder the responsibility for it. Most people will forgive a mistake if someone admits the error and apologizes for it.

- **Show your displeasure and disappointment over the situation.** Even though *you* may have been the one who caused the problem, show that you are more displeased and disappointed about the situation than anyone else.

- **Describe steps taken to solve the problem quickly and effectively.** Many of your publics will keep beating on you until they are convinced you are solving the problem. In many cases, they will want to hear what you've done to solve the situation so they can decide for themselves whether the problem has been sufficiently addressed.

- **Explain steps taken to ensure it doesn't occur again.** Your publics will expect to hear what steps you are taking to ensure the problem doesn't happen again. These can include changes in policies, procedures or personnel. They want to hear how you are fixing this problem and working to avoid future ones.

- **Mention how you plan to keep them informed on the progress.** Your publics also will want to know that this isn't the last time they will hear about the situation (depending on its severity). They will want to know when they will learn more.

- **Reinforce your appreciation of them.** It is important to thank your employees, customers, vendors and other publics for their support and cooperation during your difficult situation. Mention to them the importance of their support and that you appreciate their understanding while the situation is being resolved.

Example: Taking the medicine

The international robotics company had experienced 40-percent growth in each of the past four years. Its founder and CEO was seen as a superstar on a meteoric rise in the robotics industry. The company's initial public offering was extremely successful, and its share price had tripled during the past two years – primarily on the success of its newest product, XL-550, the powerhouse of all robots being used in more than 750 manufacturing plants worldwide.

Despite the recent success, the company has had a growing number of complaints about the durability of the XL-550. It seems the base of the robot is prematurely wearing out and is becoming unstable during high-production times – particularly as the heat in a plant rises above 80 degrees.

The company's testing facility has determined that an inferior alloy was used in the base of the XL-550. Although the alloy was tested in the laboratory, sufficient time didn't exist to properly test it in the field. The problem could be fixed by the robotics company replacing the base of the 750 products currently in operation. The cost to do so is expected to be more than $15 million, and the Chairman and CEO fears customers and shareholders will lose confidence in the company – resulting in a far greater loss.

Customer complaints are increasing in number and volatility, sparking industry rumors that the XL-550 is a disappointing and failing product. The company's share price begins to suffer as market analysts change their "buy" recommendations to "sell."

After considerable discussion in the company, a proactive communications strategy is established by the VP-Public Relations, VP-Operations, General Counsel and the President and COO. The Chairman and CEO agrees to present it to the board of directors, and it is agreed the company will change the inferior base in all XL-550s – at no cost to the customers – and will include the new and improved alloy in all future XL-550s.

The company admits the mistake, apologizes for the error and explains how it has been resolved for the future. The communications program includes notifying all customers, prospects, market and industry analysts, local and trade media, the robotics trade association, regulatory officials and select vendors. The company increases its communication to ensure all questions are being answered and that it conveys a strong sense of responsibility and forthrightness. After an initial drop in the company's share price, the stock rebounds nicely and sales of the new-and-improved XL-550 increase again.

Three lessons to learn

The robotics company learned a few important lessons from its crisis:

1) **Identify your vulnerabilities and heed the warning signs.** Although the alloy was tested in the laboratory, sufficient time didn't exist to properly test it in the field. The robotics company was vulnerable to a problem with its marquee product. It also had several warning signs leading up to the final decision to pull the XL-550. A barrage of customer complaints failed to persuade the company to identify the situation as a problem and to replace the product. It finally did so, but only after it began to generate negative publicity, resulting in a serious drop in the company's stock price.

2) **Move quickly.** If a problem arises in your business and warning signs are flashing, the chances are remote they will go away on their own. Show strong leadership and move quickly to fix the situation before it grows into a crisis, and control the crisis before it becomes even worse. The key is to be decisive and move quickly. The robotics company suffered some needless damage to its reputation and share price that, perhaps, could have been avoided if the problem with the XL-550 had been proactively fixed by the company in the early stage.

3) **If you make a mistake, admit it, apologize and work to fix it.** The company learned that it should have said, much earlier, that the base of the XL-550 isn't measuring up to the company's high standards and it will replace all of them. They could have addressed it in that way, admitted the error, apologized for any inconvenience and fixed it in a fashion that surely would have drawn far less negative attention. It waited too long to step up to the problem, and it became a crisis that didn't need to occur.

◆

If we get contradictory advice from our attorney and public relations people, who should we listen to during a crisis?

You should listen to both, but you may find yourself with a common problem that arises in many crisis: **"Do you risk significant *financial* damages in the court of law or long-term *reputation* and *credibility* damages in the court of public opinion?"**

In most cases, this isn't an all-or-nothing proposition. It usually involves a compromise after analyzing the situation with experienced legal and public relations counselors who are objective and recognize the need to be flexible. Don't make the mistake of intentionally keeping one side out of the input process, in order to avoid conflict and confusion. If you are fortunate enough to have both an attorney and a senior-level public relations counselor as resources, bring both professionals in at the outset.

Can you offer some general tips for analyzing the communications possibilities during a crisis?

Sure. Here are some tips:

- **Ensure you have first identified the problem, segmented your publics and know what you're trying to achieve.** These all sound pretty basic, but it's easy in a crisis to jump to the implementation of specific tactics before first laying the proper foundation. This involves identifying the problem as specifically as possible; segmenting your publics and consider how each is or will be affected by the problem; and writing down specific objectives for the communications effort. These don't need to take more than a few minutes, but it's a mistake to move onto the next step without addressing those points first.

- **Fight the temptation to speculate about the problem and how to fix it.** Don't make the problem worse by taking an educated guess about what you think might have caused the problem or how to fix it. Think before you talk, and recognize the problem will be made worse if false information is communicated.

- **Identify three or four options or alternative ways to approach the problem.** Fight the easy, knee-jerk reaction to quickly identify ways to address the problem. Consider all the most feasible options and, after quickly weighing the pros and cons, make the best decision possible and move forward confidently.

- **Determine the core messages to communicate to each group of publics.** As mentioned previously, your core messages might be slightly different from one public to another. For instance, if your manufacturing plant is moving to Mexico, your current employees will be most interested in their jobs, future opportunities and severance packages. Local community leaders and politicians will be most interested in the effect it will have on local employment, the tax base and similar issues. The news media may be most focused on what led to the decision to move to Mexico and what could have been done to prevent it. Consider all your publics and develop no more than five messages to communicate to each of them with confidence.

- **Identify your spokesperson(s).** Who will speak on behalf of your business? You should identify the specific person who is authorized to communicate the organization's official position on the situation. This may be more than one person but, if it is, make sure each person's role is clearly identified. And, ensure that the spokespersons are well trained with specific messages to communicate and answers to the questions likely to arise.

- **Determine the specific communications tactics to use.** You will need to quickly determine the best ways to communicate to your various publics (i.e., customers, employees, vendors, news media, community leaders, regulators, politicians). Tactics to consider could include personal and group meetings, letters or memos, phone calls, e-mail messages, newsletters, flyers, brochures and newspaper ads.

- **Make the decision on when implementation will begin.** Weigh all the options, settle on a plan and decide when to begin implementation of the communications activities. Make this decision quickly, but only after first completing the previous steps described here.

- **Monitor and evaluate the results of the communications.** How will you monitor the situation to evaluate the success of the communications activities? This might be done through a toll-free phone line, focus groups, a telephone survey, one-on-one interviews or an advisory panel. Consider the feedback, ideas and suggestions and adjust the communications as necessary.

Communicating with your *employees*

Too many businesses take their employees for granted. It's easy to assume they are well informed, loyal and positively motivated to help the business succeed in any way possible. This is often true, but many times it's not.

Employees are often the most complex and sensitive of all publics. They believe they have *earned* the right – through hard work and loyalty – to be communicated with on a regular and ongoing basis. They have developed a strong sense of "ownership" by working at the business and, therefore, feel they have the right to be particularly critical of all decisions made (which, by the way, they can almost always make better than their bosses).

Employees also look at everything as it relates to them *personally*. They worry about job security. They are concerned about morale and teamwork. They fear staff layoffs and pay reductions. And, most of all, they think about how all of these could affect their careers, quality of life, paychecks and family obligations.

Almost all of these are communications issues – managing expectations, keeping employees focused, allying fears and concerns, and maintaining a sense of excitement and confidence in an organization. You see, employees can be an organization's strongest *allies* or its greatest *opponents*. And communications can play a major role in which way they will go.

Here are some issues to consider when cultivating your employees as company *ambassadors* as opposed to *town critics*.

Why is it important to communicate with my employees during a crisis? Wouldn't they already know what's occurring?

The effective Crisis Counselor recognizes that employees should be your company's first line of communication in a crisis. They can be your most credible allies or most damaging antagonists during a crisis. You may sense that they are aware of the situation and, therefore, you shouldn't need to communicate with them. However, even without communicating with them, employees know just enough about a crisis situation to be either tremendously helpful or extremely damaging.

Wouldn't employees be the most likely group to be supportive of the organization in a crisis?

You might think so, but they also can be the most *critical* and *negative* of any of your publics. They are like family members who often don't appreciate their parents and are bothered by the smallest faults of their brothers or sisters. Like children in a family, employees need to feel like you care about them and appreciate their contribution to the family. Failure to meet their expectations for this type of reinforcement almost always leads to employee morale problems and a crisis which can increase in complexity and difficulty.

Example: Winning employee support

The hospital's President & CEO had earned the trust and confidence of her employees since she became the chief executive five years ago. She was known best for her knowledge of the healthcare business, her outstanding judgment and particularly the warmth and sensitivity she showed all hospital employees. She established three employee advisory panels where she sought suggestions, and she would often walk the hospital floors to ask how things were going with the employees and medical staff. Her staff memos and e-mail messages were extremely popular by their level of candor, honesty and humor.

Unfortunately, the President's Assistant had difficulty meeting the CEO's high standards and eventually was terminated. The disgruntled employee contacted the local, daily newspaper and accused the CEO of embezzlement, harassment and discrimination. A campaign was conducted by the disgruntled employee to seek the termination of the CEO through community and board action.

The CEO took a temporary leave of absence while an investigation was conducted by the board of directors. In the meantime, a group of first-shift employees met after work to plan its own campaign to show its strong support for the CEO. More than 80 percent of the employees and medical staff signed a "show of support" form for the CEO, and a rally was conducted in the parking lot.

The hospital's Executive Vice President and COO, who was named the interim CEO during the investigation, kept employees and medical staff informed about the situation through memos and e-mail messages. Employees were self-motivated to write letters to the editor of the local newspaper and sought additional support from local political officials.

The investigation soon ended. The CEO was reinstated and the community gained a better appreciation for the strong support she had earned as the CEO. She is now in great demand as a speaker on management, leadership and employee communication, and is widely recruited for other CEO positions within the healthcare industry.

Three lessons to learn

We can learn the following three lessons from the hospital's crisis:

1) **Work hard to establish goodwill with your employees *before* a crisis occurs.** The hospital's President & CEO survived the false accusations and potential damage by previously establishing a high amount of goodwill with her employees. It was reinforced that the most important factor in surviving a crisis is the level of goodwill you've earned with your key publics before the crisis occurs. If the hospital CEO hadn't previously earned her strong base of support, she would have likely been terminated by the hospital's board.

2) **All businesses are vulnerable to negative actions by current and former employees.** Every business shares the same vulnerability – the potential that some current and former employees could become disgruntled, frustrated and dangerous. Therefore, all businesses should plan for this eventuality, so they can anticipate and react to these problems before they turn into serious crises.

3) **Communicate openly and honestly with employees during a crisis.** The hospital's Executive Vice President and COO, who was named the interim CEO during the investigation, kept employees and medical staff informed about the situation through memos and e-mail messages. The hospital didn't attempt to hide the problem under the rug, hoping people would forget about it and keep doing their jobs. The communications even helped encourage some employees to take it upon themselves to organize an effective letter-writing campaign, which showed board members that the hospital CEO had plenty of support.

◆

Example: Failing to win employee support

The flood waters rose at an unexpectedly rapid pace. The 50-person law firm, in its large Victorian mansion setting next to the lake's borders, saw its front porch quickly immersed by water, and the first-floor carpeting soon became soggy and smelly. Evacuation was likely to be necessary within the next few hours, as the forecast called for inch-an-hour rains for the next 10 hours.

Employee morale has been poor at the firm for the past three years. The Managing Partner is unpopular with his puffing on cigars in the office, with little concern for others, and his generous use of four-letter words in even the most serene discussions. Employees complain of never being informed about important issues at the firm and often feel they are being "used" by the partners. Employee benefits were reduced last year after the firm lost four major clients, and rumors of impending across-the-board salary cuts have circulated the past few weeks.

Now, the firm really needs employee participation and teamwork. The partners are concerned client work won't get completed during the flood. Depositions can't be rescheduled, and court dates are as inflexible as some of the judges they will face. They need a small group of employees to weather the flood by slopping through the first floor to work on the second and third floors. They have obtained temporary office space 45 minutes away, so the remaining employees can continue working there.

The Managing Partner sent a cold, forceful memo to the staff informing them which people have been assigned to each station. He said, due to client demands, "no flexibility will be considered."

The partners were surprised when five people said they felt ill and were leaving early. And, only 15 of the 50 staff members came in the next day to fill their respective roles. The others either called saying they were sick or simply didn't show up.

The Managing Partner said: "What the hell is wrong with them? After all we've done for our employees, they can't manage to do us a favor when we need them most?"

Three lessons to learn

The law firm, and its obstinate Managing Partner, could have benefited from these three points:

1) **Employees have long memories.** Just as the hospital's employees in the previous example were supportive of their CEO because they were treated well, the behavior of the law firm's employees was greatly affected by the treatment from the Managing Partner. Unfortunately, for the law firm, its employees had only animosity and negative feelings toward their heartless boss. A time will come when you will need your employees' help. Start working today to enhance your goodwill with them.

2) **In a crisis, *ask* for assistance – don't just *expect* it.** Have you ever stubbornly held back help for someone simply on the grounds that you felt it was taken for granted and that they didn't appreciate it? It is important to remember that your business will sorely need the support and cooperation of your employees in a crisis. When a crisis does occur, don't take their assistance for granted. *Ask* them for help, *inform* them why it is so important and *thank* them for their teamwork. When the crisis is over and things are back to normal, consider holding a thank-you party or doing something else to express your gratitude to them. After all, as the law firm found out, employees may not always be there when you need them most.

3) **Think about the best way to communicate something.** The law firm made a mistake when the Managing Partner sent a cold, forceful memo to the staff informing them which people have been assigned to each station. Remember, his memo said, "due to client demands, no flexibility will be considered." An impersonal memo was simply the wrong communications vehicle to use in a situation like this. He would have improved his chances for cooperation by meeting personally with the employees in a staff or smaller-group meetings. And, of course, he would have had to nicely explain why their help was greatly needed and how much he appreciated their teamwork and dedication during this difficult time. Perhaps not everyone would have stepped up to help, but he surely would have had greater participation using this communications approach.

◆

How can communications make employees "helpful" to our company in a crisis?

Employees who have sufficient information and feel the company has met their level of expectation in communicating with them are more likely to:

- **Be supportive of the company's position.** Employees who feel they are treated well are more likely to be strong supporters of the business. A sense of family loyalty is established in supportive businesses, and employees in those organizations are like the big brothers protecting their kid sisters. But, they won't be loyal unless strong support is first given to them – most of which is built on communication.

- **Avoid spreading rumors about the situation.** Supportive employees, who feel they are communicated with effectively, are less likely to spread damaging rumors about the business or its problem. They will avoid doing anything they feel might hurt the company, particularly while the business is in a vulnerable state during a crisis.

- **Feel the company's senior executives are managing the situation as effectively as possible.** When morale slips in a business, it is often because employees have lost confidence in the leaders of the organization. Sometimes this occurs based on decisions made by senior management, other times it is simply because employees don't like the way they are being treated. You need employees to feel confident in their organization's leadership during a crisis. They are most likely to be supportive if the level and manner of communications meet their expectations.

- **Help reinforce your core messages to fellow employees and other publics.** You need the cooperation of employees to understand and help communicate the organization's core messages during a crisis. Those who are supportive are more likely to do so.

- **Maintain focus on their day-to-day responsibilities.** They are less likely to be distracted and overwhelmed with the crisis – speculating about the company's future plans and second-guessing management decisions.

- **Keep a positive attitude with customers, suppliers and other employees.** You will need them more than ever during a crisis to be your company's goodwill ambassadors. If they are supportive, they are most likely to have a positive attitude that can help persuade customers, suppliers and other employees to do the same.

What are the keys to communicating effectively with employees?

The following are a few keys to communicating effectively with employees during a crisis:

- **Communicate to employees quickly after a crisis has occurred.** Employees feel they have earned, through hard work and loyalty, the right to be told about anything affecting the business before they learn about it elsewhere. This is among the most important factors in a well-managed crisis. Anticipate employee questions and communicate with them openly and honestly about the situation.

- **Clearly state your *core messages* and reinforce them.** Make it clear to the employees what messages will be communicated by the organization. Ask for their help to communicate the messages.

- **Maintain a regular level of communication.** By maintaining a regular pace of communication, you will reinforce to employees their importance to the business and improve the likelihood of keeping their support. This also reinforces to them that you have a strong control over the situation and are competently managing the crisis.

- **Tell them as much as you feel is appropriate to communicate.** It's important to show employees they are trusted and important to the business. They want to know as much as possible and are more likely to be supportive if they feel they are getting the whole picture in an honest, non-manipulative manner.

- **If you feel they want to know something you consider to be confidential, mention to them why you feel it can't be discussed.** If an area exists where you simply can't level with them, explain to the employees why you are unable to talk about it at this time. They will appreciate the honesty and the fact you've even considered them.

- **Convey to them some *factors* that went into arriving at any major decision.** One of the biggest mistakes most companies make is simply telling employees what was decided and leave it at that. Employees are more discerning and judgmental than that. They not only want to hear about the decision made, but also the factors that went into making the decision. Give them a feel for the rationale and thought processes that were used in arriving at the decision.

- **If difficult decisions are announced, such as employee downsizing or plant closings, do so in a fair and compassionate manner.** In these type of cases, the employees often remember most about how they were treated – even beyond what they were told. Be extra careful to communicate to them in a fair and compassionate way.

- **Provide more than one opportunity for the employees to ask questions, offer feedback, make suggestions and express concerns.** Employees need opportunities during and after a crisis to ask questions, vent frustrations and work through issues with supervisors and others. Give them opportunities to do so through ways such as one-on-one, department, group and company-wide meetings; employee town-hall meetings; special employee phone lines; intranet bulletin boards; e-mail messages; and employee surveys.

- **Treat them the way you would want to be treated.** This is a good guiding principle to follow in all of your communications. Put yourself in their shoes and determine what, if you were them, you'd like to know. What would you feel the company should be obligated to tell you? In what ways would you want to receive information? How often would you want to know?

- **Ensure all employees are informed about important news at approximately the same time.** This is important to ensure consistency of the message and to avoid someone first hearing about it from someone else. This is easy to do in a smaller organization, but gets increasingly complex in large companies operating over several time zones or in different shifts throughout the day.

- **Communicate with them in an appropriate manner.** Consider whether the most effective vehicle is a staff meeting, one-on-one meetings, employee memo, letter sent to the home, a mention in an employee newsletter or some other means. This depends on the message to be communicated and whether everyone in the business is hearing the same thing. For instance, if 10 employees are being terminated because their product line has been eliminated, they will likely be informed in a group meeting – followed by subsequent one-on-one meetings. Other employees may be told in a staff meeting or through a memorandum – perhaps with an accompanying questions-and-answers document to give them more detail.

- **Use an appropriate and effective spokesperson.** Consider what is being communicated and who, in the business, is the most appropriate and effective person to communicate it. Should it come from the CEO, or is it more appropriate to emanate from someone else more directly involved in the decision? Who is the most credible person to make the announcement? Who will likely be the most effective spokesperson? Should there be more than one spokesperson?

- **Inform employees you will continue to update them as events dictate, and follow through with your promise.** It is important to remind your employees they will receive communications as new information is available and as events change. Reinforce to them that they are a top priority, and then make sure you follow through to prove it to them.

- **Give them a "call to action."** Employees want to be clear on what you are asking them to do. Encourage them to do something. In a crisis, this might be to help communicate your core messages, remain focused on their jobs, maintain confidence in the company and refrain from spreading rumors.

In what ways can we communicate with our employees during a crisis?

Many ways exist to communicate with employees. Here are a few ways to consider communicating during a crisis, with some suggestions on when each might be most appropriate:

- **Staff meetings.** A staff meeting usually works best when the company's number of employees is small enough to get everyone in the same room or at multiple sites via video teleconference. This should be considered when the announcement will greatly impact the organization, and everyone needs to hear the same messages communicated by the same person at the same time. Plenty of time should be left to answer employee questions and listen to their comments and suggestions.

- **Departmental meetings.** Meetings at the departmental level are most appropriate when the announcement is less critical or when the company is too large to conduct a meeting with the entire staff. Departmental meetings work best when the information affects some departments or functions in a company more than others. After being briefed by the CEO or other senior officials, managers of each department can put the announcement in perspective for their area, and convey their support and confidence in the company's actions. As in the staff meetings, it is important to leave sufficient time for answering questions and listening to employee concerns and comments.

- **One-on-one meetings.** These meetings are most effective when an announcement only affects a *few* employees, and it is important they understand the decision and its impact on them. One-on-one meetings should be held when particularly sensitive and serious information is communicated. This would include notification of layoffs and terminations, government or company investigations, quality problems, and lawsuits affecting the employee.

- **Memo to employees at work.** This can be done either through electronic mail or an actual paper copy (or both). Employee memos should be considered to help reinforce key points after staff or department meetings or to provide information that doesn't warrant one or more meetings.

- **Letter to employees at home.** Letters should be considered when an announcement is of sufficient importance that spouses and significant others will be greatly interested in learning about the company's official position on the matter.

- **Q&A document.** As mentioned previously, it is more effective to *anticipate* employee questions and answer them before you are put on the defensive. A document with answers to likely questions could accompany the memos or letters. The Q&A provides opportunities to reinforce your key messages and suggests ways to answer questions when they are addressed to the employees.

- **Telephone calls.** Phone calls should be considered when communicating news that dictates fast notification but isn't so personal that the employee will be offended by the impersonal nature of a phone call. Although it sounds ridiculous, some employees are notified of their terminations by telephone in the most antiquated of organizations. Phone calls work best when only a few people need to be informed, and they don't involve the coordination and timing of several managers calling multiple employees simultaneously. An audio-only teleconference involving several people, however, can be an effective tool when groups of employees from different sites need to be informed about news quickly and with opportunities to ask questions and offer feedback.

- **Toll-free phone line.** A toll-free phone line can be useful when employees total into the thousands and are dispersed into several geographic areas. The phone line can be used to provide answers to employee questions, or obtain questions that can be answered through some other vehicle such as e-mail, voice-mail or a company newsletter. The most effective phone lines are those that use real people – not machines – to answer the calls, if the phone attendants are trained properly.

- **Employee newsletter or special bulletin.** Newsletters can be effective communications vehicles to reinforce key messages and remind employees about company information and actions. However, most company newsletters are published on a monthly or quarterly basis and, because of that, are of limited benefit during a crisis. Many organizations produce a special-edition bulletin-type newsletter to help communicate more timely information – but in a less-formal manner than an employee memo or letter.

- **Bulletin-board notice.** Most companies have bulletin boards in or near employee-gathering locations in the office where notices and memos are displayed. These are useful in maintaining a longer life for important information, but shouldn't be used as the sole means to inform employees about critical, sensitive items. Many organizations have electronic bulletin boards that can be accessed on-line or through the system's local area network.

- **Paycheck stuffers.** Key messages can be reinforced in memo or notice form and placed inside employee payroll envelopes. This can be an effective way to reinforce previously communicated messages but shouldn't be used to convey important news about policies or decisions that have never before been communicated to employees.

- **Videotape presentation.** A video backgrounder can be useful when the information conveyed involves seeing or touring something that is impractical for all employees to view in person. The video medium can be used to convey a "personal" message from the CEO to employees, with copies of the video distributed to each department or sent to employee homes. This can be useful to help reinforce key points, to explain something complex, and to convey from the CEO a sense of concern and empathy.

- **An intranet.** Some large corporations have intranets for communications. These are *internal* websites on the Internet that are accessible only through previosly approved company servers and/or by using confidential domain names or specific passwords known only by employees. The internal website is used to update employees about important information, provide details on new pricing and policies, to include Q&A interviews, and to seek input and questions from employees. This is another effective way to reinforce key messages and to convey a strong sense of proactive communication; however, its effectiveness is limited because it is necessary for employees to access the information themselves.

Example: **Tactics to implement**

The privately owned automotive supplier has just been notified that the National Highway Traffic Safety Administration (NHTSA) is conducting an investigation that has the potential of escalating to a full recall of more than 400,000 of its battery cables. It seems that more than 300 complaints have been filed from car owners who have said the battery cables are overheating the battery and – on occasion – have caused engine fires. The problem stems from an inferior installation process the company used to attach the copper to the tubing during a two-year period four years ago. All 300 complaints are on automobiles produced during this two-year period. No complaints have occurred on the *new* product.

Since the company has an immaculate record devoid of serious quality problems in its entire 50-year history, its leadership feels it should notify employees before they read about it in next week's automotive trade publications or the local newspaper. After considerable discussion, it is decided to inform the employees about NHTSA's investigation and to use the opportunity to reinforce the company's high-quality standards.

The VP-Corporate Communications, with the assistance of the company's public relations firm, developed a plan to notify the employees through letters to their homes, and bulletin-board notices in coffee rooms. In addition, the company newsletter will discuss quality processes, reinforce the success of the new manufacturing process and include answers to possible questions on the minds of employees. A special insert will be included in the next paycheck envelope the employees receive, and small-group meetings with key executives are scheduled at the individual plant and office sites. A toll-free phone line has been established so employees can call to ask any questions related to the investigation.

As the investigation evolves and new information becomes available, the company plans to keep employees informed about the situation – which will include answers to questions being asked on the toll-free phone line.

Three lessons to learn

The automotive supplier learned three important lessons from their crisis:

1) **Don't hide the bad news from employees.** Most companies are pretty good about telling employees about positive news. It becomes a more difficult decision for most businesses when bad news has struck. The automotive supplier informed its employees about NHTSA's investigation, before they read or heard about it elsewhere, and used the opportunity to reinforce the company's high-quality standards. Your credibility and trust will be enhanced with employees if you are forthright and honest about the company's blemishes as well as its accolades.

2) **Use a variety of communications vehicles to reach employees.** The automotive supplier recognized the benefits of communicating with employees through a variety of ways. They notified employees through letters to their homes and bulletin-board notices in coffee rooms. The company newsletter discussed quality processes, reinforced the success of the new manufacturing process and included answers to possible questions on the minds of employees. A special insert was included in employee paycheck envelopes, and small-group meetings with key executives were held at the individual plant and office sites. And a toll-free phone line was established so employees can call to ask questions related to the investigation. Some people prefer receiving information in writing, where others like to be explained things in person. Use a variety of vehicles to ensure you reach everyone, and reinforce your core messages through repetition in the process.

3) **Keep employees informed and updated on the crisis.** The automotive supplier knew they should continue to keep its employees updated and informed about the situation. The company realized some employees will worry about the problem, others will question how the company is handling it, while others may feel it will cause irreparable damage to the business – perhaps even leading toward bankruptcy. It is important to keep employees informed through a regular stream of communications, which can be done by a staff memo, letters sent to the home, newsletter articles, an employee video, staff or group meetings and special voice or e-mail messages.

◆

Do you have any other advice about the various ways to communicate with employees?

Yes, here are a few other tips to consider:

- **Segment your employees and determine the key messages for each group and who would be the most appropriate contact with them.** Many types of employees exist, and several are sufficiently different to justify the consideration of a differing communications approach, core messages and even a spokesperson. These might include senior management, plant workers, union membership, corporate-headquarters staff and branch employees.

- **Recognize that sometimes even *internal* documents get into the wrong hands.** Write everything with the sensitivity and care you would if it was going to appear on the front page of your daily newspaper. This includes letters and memos distributed to employees, but also e-mail notes that can inadvertently be sent to the wrong address (or be forwarded to several people with little effort).

- **Don't be flippant, sarcastic or cute – someone will surely misinterpret what you've said.** If you are communicating something as serious as a crisis, avoid the temptation to be funny or sarcastic. It almost always will be misinterpreted by someone and may make the situation worse.

- **Reinforce your core messages – as the old line goes, "*Tell them what you're going to tell them ... tell them ... and then tell them what you've told them.*"** Clarity and repetition are the keys to effective communications. Keep your core messages simple and deliver them in a clear and easy-to-understand manner.

- **Provide sufficient opportunities to *listen* to employees, seek their suggestions and answer their questions.** Give them opportunities to share their ideas and vent any frustrations. Consider the suggestions and use them where appropriate.

- **And, remember the best advice of all: "*Communicate with employees the way you would want if you were in their shoes.*"** You will almost always do well if you follow this guiding principle.

Communicating with your *customers*

No one needs to be told customers are important. However, when a crisis occurs in a business, one thing isn't always so clear: "Do we need to tell our customers?"

Then, the questions get even more complex: "What are the consequences if we don't tell them? How will they react when we do tell them? Who should we contact? Are there some customers who should be notified and others who don't necessarily need to be? *What* do we tell them? *When* should we tell them?"

In some cases, your customers may know about your problem even before *you* do. In other instances, you may decide that the crisis doesn't affect or relate in any way to your customers. And, at other times, you may inform only your largest customers and may determine not to inform others about it.

In all cases, you need to carefully – but quickly – assess the situation and the customers' role in your problem. This section will help you make this determination.

How do you know when to notify customers about a problem or crisis – particularly if you'd rather not let them know you're having a problem?

These two questions should guide your strategy:

1) "Are they likely to learn about the situation even if we don't tell them?"

2) "If I were the customer, would I want to be told about the problem from the company before learning about it elsewhere?"

No one likes to admit to a mistake or a problem, but you're almost always better off showing the initiative and positioning it the way you want. You would much rather have them learn about the situation from *you* and not through the morning newspaper or a discussion with a supplier or competitor. Otherwise, your customers may wonder why you didn't think it was necessary to tell them. And, they may wonder if *other* problems exist that you haven't told them about.

Example: When do you tell?

The fish market is the premier source of fresh fish for area restaurants and walk-in customers, many of whom have been loyal customers for more than 20 years. The family business has purchased its fish from the same core group of fisheries since it has been in business. However, for the first time in 30 years, it recently added a new supplier to its vendor list.

The owner/manager of the fish market didn't feel it was necessary to inform the restaurants and walk-in customers that they were receiving product from a new supplier. However, the owner was just notified by the fishery that a recent investigation showed that the fish delivered last week to the fish market contained a 50-percent higher than normal concentration of mercury.

The fishery's sales contact said, "No one will notice, and it won't hurt anyone who is eating a small amount of the fish each day. I don't think you need to worry about it, or inform your restaurants and other customers, but we felt you should know. From now on, you won't receive any fish unless their mercury levels are at or below health standards."

The owner and his family discussed whether they should inform their customers. After all, they don't even know the market is buying its fish from a new fishery.

After considerable discussion, the owner and family decided to do what they felt was morally correct. They terminated their business relationship with the new fishery.

The store owner and his family sat down to agree on what they would tell their customers. They agreed to communicate the following core messages:

1) One of our fisheries sold us some fish, which you bought from us, that had higher than acceptable levels of mercury. We are very sorry. This was a new fishery, and we have decided to no longer do business with them.

2) If your fish hasn't already been sold, please return it for a *double* refund. We will provide you with new fish, and also give you a coupon for a free order equal to the amount of your original order.

3) We stand behind our products and are as disappointed as you are that one of our fisheries let both of us down. Please accept our apologies and assurance we will no longer buy from that fishery.

The owner informed the restaurants who received fish obtained from the fishery, and the family members helped contact the walk-in customers who could be reached by telephone. All the customers were upset about the high levels of mercury in the fish they served or ate, but admired the way the fish store handled the problem.

"You bet I'm mad it happened," said one walk-in customer. "I certainly don't need high concentrations of mercury in my body. But, I'll tell ya, I appreciate the way the store's owner was honest about it. I think they learned their lesson, and I got a coupon for some free fish which we are grilling tonight. They haven't lost me as a loyal customer, I'll tell you that much."

Three lessons to learn

The fish market owner and his family went through that unpleasant experience and can now learn these three points that emerged from that situation:

1) **You'll never do wrong by doing the right thing.** The fish market was faced with an ethical dilemma. Should it tell its customers about the mercury-laden fish and the new fishery it had used without previously informing them? The owner and his family concluded that doing so was the right thing to do. If they were customers of the fish market, they would have wanted to know. Customers want to do business, and have long relationships, with suppliers that have high ethics and strong values. Doing the right thing will always serve you well with customers.

2) **Identify the problem and then communicate about it.** The fish market owner had to ensure he understood the problem before he could fix it, and he wanted to fix the problem before he notified his customers. It is not always possible to completely fix a problem

before customers are notified. Sometimes you need to inform customers about a problem to ensure it doesn't turn into a crisis. He felt he should discontinue doing business with the fishery. And then, he developed specific messages with his family to communicate immediately to customers.

3) **Isolate the crisis.** The owner isolated the problem to one fishery and a bad batch of fish that was purchased and then sold by the fish market within a two-day period. This strategy to "isolate the crisis" was extremely important to the fish market, so its customers didn't feel that *all* of its fish were contaminated (only a relatively small pool purchased from the new fishery). Work to keep your crisis in perspective for all those who will want to generalize about its effect and sensationalize the potential damage it will cause your business.

◆

What should we attempt to convey to customers during a crisis?

You should communicate a small handful of core messages to them. These would likely include those with the following themes:

- **The specific problem or crisis that has occurred.** What is the problem? How damaging is it? How are customers affected?
- **How the problem occurred.** What exactly happened? How serious is it?
- **The impact of the crisis in your business.** What effect will the crisis have in fulfilling the responsibilities to your customers (i.e., service, products, commitments, deadlines)? How will it affect your business as a whole?
- **Steps being taken to ensure the problem doesn't occur again.** What is being done to avoid a recurrence? What steps will affect the customers?

- **A strong sense that the situation is being managed well by you and others at the company.** What other steps are being taken by the business to show the situation is well under control?

- **Your accessibility and willingness to answer questions or discuss with them any concerns.** Who should they call with questions or comments? If they want to help, how should they go about offering it? Can they reach the person in charge if necessary?

- **They will be notified if the situation changes substantially.** When will they hear from you again? In what manner will you communicate with them in the future? How will you determine when it's most appropriate to contact them again?

- **A possible "call to action."** What are you asking them to do? When should it be completed?

- **You appreciate their continued support and loyalty.** Have you thanked them for their support? Can you do anything to lessen the negative impact of your crisis on them?

Should *all* customers be treated equally during a crisis?

It depends upon the business. If you own a pizza shop that caters specifically to local residents, then you should treat them all the same way. If you own a computer software company and five, large clients equal more than half your total business, then you'll want to treat those five clients with special communication plans. Some customers will deserve special, personal attention while others may not need to be contacted at all during a crisis. Think about the way your customers are – or can be – segmented and how that might influence the manner and frequency of your communication along with who should be your company contact to them. Customers can be segmented in a number of ways, including:

- By volume of business

- Customers most likely to be affected by the problem

- Those likely to be contacted by news media for comments
- Customers located in the market being most affected by the crisis
- Those who could be *allies* for your organization
- Customers likely to be *critical* of your company

In what ways can we communicate with our customers during a crisis?

The most effective ways to communicate with your customers during a crisis include:

- **Personal meetings.** If sufficient time exists to do so, and the crisis may have a serious affect on key customers, personal meetings should be considered to individually explain the situation and answer questions.
- **Telephone calls.** Due to time limitations and the number of customers that must be contacted, phone calls may be necessary to communicate with your most-important customers during a crisis,.
- **Customer letters.** Letters should be considered to inform customers who are important to your business but don't fall in the higher-priority group who deserve personal meetings or phone calls. The letters should be faxed, rather than mailed, if time limitations dictate the need to do so.
- **Customer newsletter or special bulletin.** Newsletters can be effective communication vehicles to reinforce key messages to customers during a crisis. However, most company newsletters are published on a monthly or quarterly basis and, because of that, are of limited benefit during a crisis. Many organizations produce a *special-edition* bulletin-type newsletter to help communicate more timely information – but in a less-formal manner than a customer letter.

- **Electronic mail.** You should have the *e-mail* addresses to your most-important customers as part of your crisis-planning initiatives. As a greater number of customers depend on electronic mail in communicating with other businesses, sending e-mail messages to your key customers would be an effective way to notify them about your crisis.

- **Internet website.** If your company has a website, the information should be updated with facts, analyses and answers to questions about the crisis. Your most-active customers will likely search your home site to determine your position and perspective on the crisis.

- **Q&A document.** As mentioned previously, it is more effective to *anticipate* customer questions and answer them before you are put on the defensive. A document with answers to likely questions could accompany your correspondence to them. The Q&A provides opportunities to reinforce your key messages and would be an effective leave-behind piece when meeting with priority customers.

- **Customer hotline.** It's important to give your customers an easy way to obtain answers to questions and to provide input, feedback and suggestions to your company. It may be appropriate to establish a toll-free customer hotline. (Remember back in the "crisis planning" chapter when I suggested you obtain a toll-free phone number for use when a situation like this arises?) The hotline can be staffed by some of your senior managers or – in higher-volume cases – by a telemarketing staff trained to stick within a script of answers to most-likely asked questions. An interactive voice-response program can be established to inform customers of important information or to determine their opionions on a number of questions. Notify customers of the hotline number and encourage them to call if they have questions or concerns.

Example: Tactics to implement

The 45,000-square-ft. Superstore is the community's largest and most popular retail outlet for meat, bakery goods, flowers, household supplies and casual clothes. It is one of several thousand nationwide and is one of the largest employers in this small town.

Unfortunately, the Superstore was damaged by a huge lightning and wind storm that blew through the community. A bolt of lightning struck the east side of the store and approximately 5,000 sq. ft. was damaged by fire and the water needed to extinguish it. The store is temporarily closed while clean up continues, and several hundred customers each day are left to find other options, uncertain when the store will re-open.

The Superstore wants to keep loyal customers informed about its situation and ensure they return as ongoing customers when the store re-opens. In an effort to do so, the retail outlet conducted the following activities:

1) Notified the local news media about its situation.
2) Had a spokesperson accessible for media interviews and customer inquiries.
3) The store's manager and assistant managers took turns stationed in front of the Superstore to answer questions and encourage customers to return when it reopens.
4) Published large ads in the local newspaper, and commercials on the radio, to inform customers about their planned re-opening date.
5) Activated a toll-free phone line with a recording to update customers.
6) Special cards sent to the homes of local residents that will make all customer coupons worth three times their value (for the first two months after the store re-opens).
7) A re-opening celebration with proceeds for that day going to the local volunteer fire department.

Three lessons to learn

The Superstore's situation brings to mind these three thoughts:

1) **Use a variety of ways to communicate with your customers.** Customers, particularly retail consumers, need to be reached through a number of communications vehicles. The Superstore didn't just rely on the news media to communicate its messages. It ran newspaper ads, sent direct-mail pieces to the home and established a toll-free phone line to keep people updated as well. Don't limit your efforts to only one medium when you need to make a real impact with your customers.

2) **Be open and accessible for your customers.** The Superstore went out of its way to be available and accessible to its customers – even when it wasn't open for business. It recognized it shared a special bond with its customers and didn't want the temporary shutdown to affect the hard-earned relationship. The store's manager and assistant managers took turns stationed in front of the Superstore to answer questions and encourage customers to return when it reopens. A company spokesperson was available for regular updates to the local media about the store's re-opening. If a crisis occurs for your business, remain as open and accessible as possible to your customers.

3) **Give your customers another reason for staying with you.** You should hope that sufficient customer goodwill has been earned by your business before a crisis occurs. However, even with a reservoir of goodwill, a major crisis can quickly deplete it and place the relationship at risk. If a problem occurs that affects customers, give them an extra incentive to remain with you. The Superstore provided customers with a special card making all coupons worth three times their original value for the first two months after its grand re-opening.

◆

How will we know if we are being successful in communicating with our customers?

Believe me, you'll know. Usually customers aren't shy about communicating their concerns, questions and reservations. However, if you still aren't sure, here are some other signs to gauge your level of success in communicating with your customers:

- Are your customers continuing to ask the same questions, even though you've been *attempting* to answer them?
- Do you sense your customers have lost confidence and faith in your company?
- Have your sales declined with no sign of rebounding in the short term?
- Are you hearing rumors about customer dissatisfaction from your suppliers who also deal with your customers?
- Is the customer hotline receiving a large volume of calls that are escalating in numbers each day?
- Are you receiving virtually *no* calls on the hotline, yet sales have decreased substantially?

Do you have any other tips about communicating with customers during a crisis?

Here are some additional tips to consider when communicating with customers during a crisis:

- **Tell your customers about the crisis quickly.** If a possibility exists they'll learn about the crisis elsewhere, contact them proactively to notify them about it. It will give you an opportunity to frame it from your perspective and ensure you've given them an opportunity to ask questions.
- **Don't ever lie to your customers.** They are likely to excuse a problem or crisis you are address forthrightly, but aren't likely to give you a second chance if you're caught in a lie.

- **If you have bad news to tell them, reveal it all at one time.** Don't let bad news leak out. Tell them everything you know about the situation and deal with it at that time.

- **Keep reinforcing your core messages.** Continue to communicate the core messages so they clearly understand your perspectives on the crisis. To accomplish this, the messages will need to be communicated with great repetition.

- **Identify your best customer allies.** Recognize that some news media might contact a few of your top customers for their comments about your crisis. Identify your strongest allies and steer the media toward them if they are seeking thoughts from a few customers.

- **Move swiftly.** Keep to a minimum the time spent in a *defensive* mode. Make decisions quickly and move on in a confident and effective manner.

- **Don't forget the news media.** You might feel your customers are the only thing you care about and "To hell with the media." If that's the case, remind yourself that your customers read the newspaper, watch television news and listen to the radio as well. All of your positive, personal efforts with the customers could evaporate in one negative newspaper story if it contradicts something you mentioned to your customer earlier. Cooperate with the media and ensure your messages to them are consistent with those communicated to your customers.

Communicating with the *news media*

The news media: Reporters. Editors. Photographers. Television crews. Talk-show hosts. Radio personalities. On-line commentators.

Their reporting of your crisis can either help or hinder your ability to manage the problem. We are referring to the editorial (or news-gathering) side of the media here, as opposed to the advertising side. Except for extremely rare cases with small trade publications or small-circulation newspapers, the editorial side of the media cannot be controlled or forced to cover (or not cover) something according to the wishes of a specific business. Threats to pull advertising, refusing to talk with reporters or other actions will not dissuade credible journalists from covering an event or activity as they feel it should be reported.

Many business people, particularly chief executive officers and entrepreneurs, who are used to getting their own way, have difficulty dealing with the uncertainty and loss of control in working with the news media. It can be a difficult and tenuous task for many businesses and executives, and often they seek help from a public relations firm to assist in this area.

This section offers advice and suggestions to help you work in the most effective way with the media that covers your business and industry. Your ability to do so could be the difference between a crisis for which you are heralded for managing with exquisite skill to one where your personal reputation – and that of the business – receives irreparable damage that may take decades to overcome.

What should we know about the news media as it relates to the management of a crisis?

You should recognize the following about the news media:

- **They are very competitive and want to be the first to report information.** This is why they are often very aggressive during a crisis. They would like to uncover something their competitor hasn't, and will work hard to ensure they are the first to report it.

- **They make a lot of judgments during crises to determine the newsworthiness of a crisis.** Are you returning their calls promptly? Do you sound honest and trustworthy? Do you appear defensive or scared? Are you being cooperative with their requests? Is there something more here than you're telling me?

- **Many reporters and editors are skeptical of businesses.** Most reporters have an instinctive distrust of businesses. Many have difficulty trusting that you're telling the truth and not hiding anything. Therefore, they will often check other sources and dig into a crisis from a variety of angles.

- **They want to make sure you *get it*.** News media want to ensure you understand the problem, how it was caused and what is being done to avoid it occurring again. They want you to step up and take appropriate responsibility for it. Many reporters will keep pressing the issue – through questions or negative stories – until they feel you understand the seriousness of the situation.

- **Don't assume they know your business or industry.** Most news and business reporters don't know as much about your product, company or industry as you might think – unless they cover your company and/or industry as a regular "beat." Therefore, you need to make it easy for them to learn quickly and effectively. If you don't help them understand it, they may likely misinterpret something or inadvertently make an error.

- **They are interested in fresh, timely news.** If they sense it no longer exists in your crisis, they will likely move on to something else. The sooner they recognize the story is no longer newsworthy, they will move on to something else.

- **It is extremely difficult to win a battle with the news media.** Do whatever you can to cooperate with them and to avoid a no-win situation with them. Getting into a scrap with a reporter or media outlet almost always hurts a business. You might win a battle against them, but you will surely lose the war over the long term.

Example: **Working well with the media**

The multinational pharmaceutical company markets a number of successful but somewhat controversial prescription drugs. Due to the nature of the business, it finds itself in somewhat benign litigation on a regular basis from consumers who may have used the drug inappropriately. In this particular case, the pharmaceutical company is faced with a small, but potentially damaging, class-action suit about one of its products – a drug to help relieve tennis-elbow pain. The lawsuit has drawn significant media attention because it claims the company didn't sufficiently warn of the potential side effects: decreased sexual drive in otherwise physically active adults.

The pharmaceutical company claims that some minor side-effects can occur in some people – including stomach irritation and diarrhea – but a decrease in sexual drive cannot be related to the drug in any way.

News media of all types – including local newspapers, trade journals, television magazine shows and the like – are all interested in this story. The pharmaceutical company is faced with the choice of cooperating with media requests, and drawing negative attention to the company, or avoiding all media inquiries and taking their chances that the story will die a fast death.

The company enjoys a remarkably positive relationship with the news media. This is based primarily on the availability of its senior executives for media interviews and their lengthy history of investing the time to help teach reporters and editors about the industry, company and products. Time has shown that the background sessions with media have resulted in objective – albeit not always positive reporting – and fair treatment of its company.

Therefore, in this case, the company decides to conduct a briefing session with all interested media to provide them in-depth background information on the drug. Written background information on the drug and company is provided in a two-pocket folder. The objective is to show them that the connection between the drug and a reduced libido is coincidental. It is the company's hope that its credibility with the news media will help convince them that this is only someone's fabrication and certainly not newsworthy.

The case was dismissed by the court for lack of evidence, and the news media agreed it was a non-story that didn't deserve further coverage.

"Our excellent reputation helped pull us through on this one," said the company's CEO to his management team. "We knew there was no connection between the drug and consumers' sex drive, but we could have easily been slaughtered in the media or the courts on this. Our credibility and reputation helped give us the benefit of the doubt. Let's do everything we can to preserve those valuable commodities in our business."

Three lessons to learn

The example of the pharmaceutical company helps reinforce these three points:

1) **Any allegations can snowball into an avalanche of media attention.** Any allegations, even false ones, can draw substantial media interest. Litigation provides the news media with a timely angle needed to demand significant media coverage. Consider your vulnerabilities in this area. Develop some worst-case scenarios for your business and consider how you would manage them.

2) **Help educate the news media with facts and background.** When the media considers a possible story, such as the allegations against the pharmaceutical company's tennis-elbow drug, they often are just seeking facts and background to help them decide whether it's a story worth pursuing. The pharmaceutical company was able to show the media – through specific facts and written materials – that no connection could exist between the drug and the reduction of consumers' interest in sex. The key is to be prepared in advance of a crisis with information materials that can be immediately put to use. Remember, most crises can be avoided through advance preparation and fast action.

3) **The news media are affected by a company's reputation just like other publics.** Contrary to popular belief, most news media are not 100% objective journalists all the time. Reporters and editors rely on their best judgment everyday to assess the newsworthiness of a story; whether to take a hard-nosed, negative stand in reporting something; and, when to do a profile showcasing a company or its products in

a positive light. These decisions are based on their professional instincts and best judgment. Those are shaped by what they hear, read and sense about a possible situation or topic. Most businesses underestimate the importance of their reputations, credibility and trust as it relates to the news media and future positive or negative coverage about their organization. As the pharmaceutical company CEO said to his management team, do what you can to preserve these valuable commodities as you grow your business.

◆

Example: Losing with the media

The dental practice is well regarded in the healthcare community and has grown to enjoy a broad patient base in the community. Despite the group's outstanding record, it occasionally is accused by a patient of making a mistake and – in rare occasions – of malpractice.

The group of dentists has received little interest from the news media since it was established 15 years ago. The health-beat reporter from the local newspaper has asked to meet with the group's top dentists to report on the newest developments in the area of family dentistry; however, no one was willing to invest the time to do so. Other media have asked the dentists to identify someone to appear on health panels – sponsored by the local media – at schools and community centers. But no dentists from the practice were ever available to help.

The practice is led by a 40-year veteran who is only three months away from his 65th birthday and retirement from the business. He is a friendly fellow that shuns publicity and the limelight, and is looking forward to his retirement on the boat and golf course. Unfortunately, a patient has sued the dentist for misdiagnosing what developed into a case of mouth cancer. The patient has been told the cancer has spread and is now committed to destroying the reputation of the dentist – in addition to receiving a large cash settlement.

After receiving calls and written information from the patient, several local reporters call the dentist for his comment and reaction to the litigation. He instructs his receptionist to inform the reporters he has no interest in talking with them and, if they persist, to slam the phone in their ears. This occurs, only making the reporters more interested in the story. They wait for the dentist in the parking lot to ask them some questions on the way to his automobile. He curses at them saying, "I have nothing to say to you. She's a crazy woman trying to get money from me. I'm only three months away from retirement. Leave me alone or I'll sue you!"

As you might expect, the news media ran several negative stories about the dentist and the practice group. Patient demand dropped in half, and several dentists left the group, since their reputations were being tarnished as well.

"If he had just handled the situation better with the media," said one of the dentists as he left the office for the last time, putting his office belongings in the backseat of his car.

Three lessons to learn

The dental group learned these lessons too late to help save its practice:

1) **A positive reputation takes a long time to earn and a short time to lose.** The dentist who had a successful 40-year career recognized that his outstanding reputation could be tarnished by the malpractice lawsuit by one of his patients – only months before he was planning to retire. However, he failed to realize that the way he managed the situation would have a greater impact on his reputation than on the lawsuit itself. This is why having *The Crisis Counselor* mindset – no matter what type of business you are in – will help guide you from inadvertently stepping on a landmine while working your way through your crisis.

2) **Advance preparation helps ensure your first few steps are the right ones.** The dentist and his group would have surely handled the problem more effectively if they had thought about their vulnerabilities in advance, and considered the best ways to manage media inquiries related to malpractice allegations. Doing so outside of the pressure of a current crisis situation almost always leads to

more rational thinking. They could have discussed the pros and cons of cooperating with reporters who inquire about such a case, and may have determined a much different way of managing the situation.

3) **You'll lose every time when you treat the media like the enemy.** Some businesses make the mistake of rudely dismissing the media, which causes a reporter to become motivated to dig more into the situation and to place a more negative slant to the story than originally intended. The dentist and his medical group could possibly have persuaded the reporter that – in the business of working on people's teeth – it's not unusual for patients to sue their dentist. They could have said that it rarely occurs in their case, but it is somewhat standard practice in their industry. If it was done nicely with full cooperation, it is possible the reporter may have agreed and recognized that the story wasn't newsworthy after all.

◆

What's the best way to handle the news media during a crisis?

The most effective way to work with the news media during a crisis is to:

- **Treat them the way you would want to be treated.** Put yourself in the reporter's position. Recognize the reporter's job and respect his responsibilities in covering your company's crisis.

- **Return their calls promptly and courteously.** Reporters understandably hate when companies are pleasant and upbeat when they try to convince them to do a "positive" feature on the company, but then are uncooperative and evasive when the media are interested in a potentially negative angle about the business. This comes with the territory. It's important to cooperate with them in both circumstances.

- **Reveal any information the media could easily get elsewhere.** Recognize that if they are likely to learn about the information through some other source, you will be better off communicating it yourself. This allows you to properly position it, communicate your core messages and reinforce that you are being forthright and honest. This approach will help prevent the reporter from feeling that she needs to work extra hard to get the information elsewhere.

- **Make it easy for them to understand your company, products and industry.** Provide them with easy-to-understand fact sheets, backgrounders and other information that will make it easy for them to convey it to their readers, listeners or viewers. This will help reduce the chance of an error or misinterpretation to slip into your story.

- **Show patience and understanding when they keep asking questions or don't seem to grasp what you're saying.** It's much better to patiently answer all questions, and review difficult points or concepts several times, than to suffer the consequences of a misinformed story. One-page, bulleted fact sheets could help a great deal as well.

- **Don't act like you're intimidated or afraid of them.** This will be a sign that you have something to hide (that they might like to uncover). Answer the questions in a relaxed and comfortable manner.

- **Treat them like a respected peer – not like an enemy or an adored icon.** Consider reporters a respected peer or colleague. The media is not the enemy, nor should they be put on a pedestal.

- **Know which mistakes to correct.** If you are displeased with a story reported on your business, recognize the difference between *factual* errors (that should be corrected) and disagreements with the tone, style and content of the story (which are the media's prerogative). If a material factual error was made, contact the reporter to mention it to him and – when appropriate – nicely ask if a correction could be published (or aired). If you aren't satisfied with the response from the reporter, decide whether to contact his editor, write a letter to the editor correcting the error or drop it altogether.

In what ways can we communicate with the news media during a crisis?

Companies communicate their information and perspectives through the news media in one or more of the following ways:

- **News releases.** This is a company-produced news story announcing information or perspectives about the organization. It usually is one or two pages long and becomes the official position of the company. It typically is distributed to a number of news media via a media-distribution service – such as PR Newswire or BusinessWire – or is faxed or mailed to specific news media. A news release works best when the company desires to communicate the same information to more than one media simultaneously and – in most cases – is used only when you hope the release will encourage media coverage.

- **Individual media contact.** One-on-one phone calls and meetings should be considered when offering special access or information to a single media outlet. This method, often referred to as "offering an exclusive," can help obtain more in-depth coverage from an important media outlet because it feels no other media have the information. Also, individual media contact works best during a crisis when it's in the company's best interest to provide greater background and information to specific reporters or when a factual error reported in a story needs to be corrected.

- **News conference or media briefing.** The company should consider conducting a news conference or media briefing during a crisis when a high level of interest has been sparked by the crisis. The decision whether to conduct a news conference or media briefing during a crisis is a difficult and extremely important one. On one hand, if the media interest is high and news crews and reporters are likely to cause significant turmoil and disruption to your company, you may be better off conducting a news conference. The other reason to do so is to – once again – attempt to reduce the amount of time your company is placed on the defensive. On the other hand, in a crisis, you don't want to needlessly conduct a news conference that could magnify the problem and encourage a greater amount of negative media coverage.

- **Media interviews.** You should have one or more company spokespersons prepared to cooperate with requests for media interviews. These spokespersons could range from the Chief Executive Officer to a public relations representative. Although occasions may exist where the company may be better off declining the interview request, it is always best to reinforce your key messages and confirm any information possible. If you decide *not* to appear on camera or on the radio, or to respond "on the record," do so by being cordial and explaining why you feel it's inappropriate at this time.

- **Electronic mail.** A growing number of reporters and editors prefer receiving e-mail correspondence, and can be communicated with in that manner. This is most appropriate when your messages are relatively brief and straightforward.

- **Editorial board visits.** These are meetings that can be requested with writers and editors of the editorial pages of major newspapers or, in some cases, from major-market television stations. You should consider proactively contacting one or more of them when you feel your crisis – and/or your *management* of it – is likely be the subject of a future editorial. In most cases, the editorials may be more accurate and possibly include some of your key messages if you initiate an editorial board meeting.

- **Satellite media tours.** Satellite time can be reserved to schedule interviews with television news reporters or producers from important markets who want your company spokesperson. The spokesperson stays in one location and various television stations schedule to interview the person during times set in advance. This can be considered during a crisis if you feel the television stations from other markets have been misreporting your situation due to their inability to travel to your location.

- **Video news releases.** A video news release is a television news story or background video footage produced by the company for distribution to a number of television stations. Although these are rarely used at major networks or even large-market stations in most cases, they could be considered to help further reinforce your key messages through television stations. Such a video release should be considered in a crisis if your company has video footage that is important to the management of your crisis, and have chosen not to provide access to television crews to photograph the information themselves.

- **Op-ed articles.** These are original opinion-editorial articles provided to a small number of newspapers or magazines. They provide opportunities for someone from your company to offer the company's perspective and analysis on the crisis. This should be considered only with crises that have major community impact and prolonged media coverage.

- **Letters to the editors.** Letters to editors should be reserved only for commenting on stories previously reported in specific publications. If you plan to use the opportunity to criticize a past story, stick to correcting the factual errors written in the article and try to avoid any personal or emotional criticism that could hurt your future relationship with the reporter or publication.

- **Position papers.** These are usually comprehensive analyses of a company's position on a specific issue. They can be distributed to key reporters, editorial-page writers and editors with a cover letter. Position papers should help reinforce your key messages and be limited in length – with no more than three pages.

- **Q&A document.** It is more effective to *anticipate* media questions and answer them before you are put on the defensive. A document with answers to likely questions could be distributed with news releases or other media information. The Q&A provides opportunities to reinforce your key messages and would be an effective leave-behind piece when meeting with reporters and editors.

- **Media background information.** It is important to do whatever possible to ensure the news media understand the facts about your company, products, people and industry. This is particularly important during a crisis, when limited time exists for the media to do their homework. Companies should consider producing – well in advance of a crisis – one-page fact sheets, backgrounders, biographies of key executives and other information. They can be distributed to reporters who are covering your company's crisis and may go a long way to ensuring accurate reporting.

Who should be our company spokesperson in a crisis?

It depends on the situation. Your choices of spokespersons could be among the following types of people:

- Chief Executive Officer
- Chief Operating Officer
- An Executive or Senior Vice President
- An operations manager
- A plant or product manager
- An engineer, chemist or physician
- A public relations officer
- Your legal counsel

But how do you know which one to use at any given time?

It all depends on the nature and severity of the crisis, and what you want to convey by using the specific spokesperson. Here are some suggestions to consider:

- **Using the CEO.** Consider using the CEO as the primary spokesperson if the crisis is extremely serious, and it's important to demonstrate the company's leadership, concern, empathy and compassion. If the nature and severity of the crisis fall short of that, then use someone else at the outset of a crisis. The CEO is your "ace in the hole," and you won't have someone else to use if you've already played the CEO card.

- **Using someone from public relations.** Of course, not every business has an on-staff public relations professional or a relationship with a public relations firm. However, if you are fortunate to have one, consider using a public relations spokesperson in some situations. An appropriate time would be if you want to communicate only a statement, position or message from the company, and avoid answering more than a few basic questions. If you have the use of a public relations person, she should be used to help *screen* the media calls – even if she won't be an official spokesperson. The screening process involves being the first contact point in the business, to answer media calls, determine the general types of questions the reporter would like answered and to arrange for the spokesperson to talk with the reporter.

- **Using someone with product knowledge.** This could be a Vice President of Operations, VP-Manufacturing, VP-Engineering, VP-Marketing or a number of other positions in your business. Consider using this type of person when complex information needs to be described in a credible and knowledgeable manner – to prove that your business is informed and competent.

- **Using your attorney.** Use your legal counsel as a spokesperson only when highly complicated legal provisions and regulations need to be communicated and would be too difficult for others to express accurately. Otherwise, you're almost always better off with someone else as a spokesperson since an attorney – identified as such – can convey a sense of avoiding legal troubles at any cost.

Example: **Who should be the spokesperson?**

The paints and coatings company – one of the leaders in the aerospace business – has been located at its current manufacturing site for the past 35 years. It purchased the land and an existing facility, and recently expanded the plant to add another 150,000 square feet.

No one who works at the paints and coatings company today was with the business when it acquired the site 35 years ago. But, one thing is clear, a sufficient environmental inspection and analysis weren't conducted and the company today is facing the consequences of buying land contaminated with chemicals buried on its property. Today, the buried chemicals – despite being in drums – are seeping through the land and leaking into groundwater and other industrial and nearby residential properties.

The community is beginning to learn of the situation and public dissent is starting to erupt like a poorly buried barrel of contaminated paint. The news media is asking questions, and the paints and coatings company is struggling with how to handle the inquiries.

The company's CEO, Executive VP, VP-Manufacturing, VP-Environmental, VP-Public Relations and General Counsel have discussed who should respond to media questions and eventually be interviewed. They agreed each of them are knowledgeable about the situation, have rehearsed the core messages and answers to expected questions, and are equally capable of representing the company in a favorable manner.

It was decided the first to first respond to the questions should be done by the VP-Public Relations. This will ensure timely responses are made to inquiries but not to draw needless attention to the situation by involving the CEO. They also didn't want to use the company's "ace in the hole" too early, in case she was needed if the pressure intensifies.

If the media pressed to interview someone in great detail, the group decided the VP-Environmental could best provide the technical background and demonstrate credibility through his life-long concern of maintaining high environmental standards.

Then, it was decided, if the scrutiny continued and public concern escalated, the CEO would be brought in to reinforce the company's commitment to environmental safety regardless of the cost to ensure those standards are met.

Three lessons to learn

The paints and coatings company followed a thought process from which we can all learn:

1) **Think through who is best *qualified* to be a spokesperson.** When deciding on the best spokesperson, consider who is best qualified for the task. The paints and coatings company had to decide who was most knowledgeable about the situation. It decided the VP-Environmental would know the most about the area, but the public relations person is most experienced at working with the news media. And, the President is most qualified to speak on behalf of the organization. In their own ways, each is highly qualified, but who is the most *appropriate*?

2) **Consider who is most *appropriate* to be the spokesperson.** Who is the most appropriate person at each step along the way? Who would be the most credible? Who would make us look like we know what we're doing? In the case of the paints and coatings company, it was decided the most appropriate spokesperson in the early, routine stage would be the VP-Public Relations. The VP-Environmental would be used if media wanted greater information and someone to interview on-camera. And the President would be most appropriate if the problem escalated to crisis proportions, with the President offering her personal commitment to fixing the situation.

3) **Decide at which point the spokespersons will change.** The paints and coatings company drew clear distinctions between each of the spokespersons and their roles. If you have a situation where different spokespersons will be used, work to define when you will use one over the other. If possible, this should be done *before* the crisis occurs to avoid any needless confusion once the crisis erupts. In this case, the paints and coatings company had sufficient time to discuss it and work it through – but, the luxury of time won't be available during most crises.

◆

What other things should we consider when deciding who our spokesperson should be?

You will want to consider several other factors in determining the potential effectiveness of your spokesperson – whether it be the CEO or someone else in the business. These include:

- **Ability to quickly learn and express information effectively.** Consider the person's ability to remember and effectively communicate your *core messages*, and how well she can express company-preferred answers to routine *and* difficult questions.

- **Credibility and believability of the person.** Select a person that is seen as credible and knowledgeable. An uninformed, ineffective spokesperson can quickly convey the message that the company is sorely unprepared to manage the crisis.

- **Ability to listen carefully.** The spokesperson should be able to listen well. The listening skills are needed when you decide to make changes to your messages or the way you'd like to answer specific questions. Also, a good listener can recognize sensitivities when addressing specific publics who have their specific concerns, questions and suggestions. This person can perceptively address those concerns without much provocation, which can help defuse criticism and frustrations before they make the crisis even more difficult to manage.

- **Ability to express compassion, warmth and patience.** An effective spokesperson needs to have the ability to show compassion, warmth and patience. You want people to believe your spokesperson and, to do that, they need to *connect* with the person. This connection is in the form of respect, believability and trust of the spokesperson. If your spokesperson is cold and impersonal, the chances are slim that he will win a great deal of support for your business.

- **Willingness to take direction and coaching.** Some people take direction and coaching well, while others resist any suggestions or instructions from anyone. Recognize this important trait – and the person's ability to think on his feet – in selecting your spokespersons. They need to accept input, suggestions and even criticisms without missing a beat or holding grudges. You won't have time to play games during the crisis.

- **Accessibility and availability when needed.** You don't want to select and train an outstanding spokesperson and then determine she is unavailable when needed. Your spokesperson should be accessible – by telephone or in person – and willing to be contacted at home, during the middle of the night or on weekends or vacation/holiday.

- **Ability to keep cool under extreme pressure.** An effective spokesperson must be able to maintain composure under the stress of representing the entire business. The pressure may likely include being interviewed by the news media, speaking in front of hostile community groups and symbolizing the company's position on a controversial issue.

- **High stamina to work long hours.** Based on the specific crisis at hand, the spokesperson might need to work 15-20 hours a day – leaving only a few hours for rest – before returning back to the job.

It takes a tremendous amount of stamina and strength to remain fresh and effective, and is an often overlooked trait for a company spokesperson.

What sort of training should we consider for our spokespersons?

Training for your spokespersons should be to:

- **Review and rehearse your *core messages.*** Make sure they understand the points you need to reinforce. Work with them to learn how to communicate the core messages when asked questions that may or may not be natural opportunities to reinforce the points.
- **Develop and rehearse answers to routine and difficult questions.** First determine the preferred answers to questions you expect to arise and the ones you hope don't. The spokespersons need to be prepared for both. Then, work with the spokespersons to practice answering the questions accurately and confidently.
- **Practice making transitions from undesired questions to communication of the core messages.** Work with the spokespersons on ways to communicate the core messages – no matter what is asked. One way to do this is by using a transition statement to link a question that is asked to something you would prefer to answer. Politicians use this technique particularly well. An example of a transition statement is: "That's an interesting question. What we find most people are interested in is ..." In some cases, the spokesperson will be asked again to answer the original question after deflecting it the first time. However, in most cases, this doesn't occur.
- **Teach your spokespersons ways to avoid being placed on the defensive.** It is important to train your spokespersons they need to retain as much control as possible during an interview or speaking appearance. This means not always directly answering the question that is asked, and ensuring that the core messages are communicated – no matter what is asked. In addition, they should know how to handle a hostile encounter with a reporter, community resident or employee.

- **Work on ways to answer questions that shouldn't be answered at this time.** The spokespersons should know how to respond to questions that can't be answered or requests for information that can't be confirmed. They should know to avoid saying, "No comment." And they should know how to convey a sense of openness, honesty and accessibility even when being unable to directly answer the question.
- **Work on body language.** Teach other important tips and techniques on eye contact, posture, breathing, relaxation and other ways that can be either empowering or destructive in an interview or speaking appearance.
- **Practice ways to react to reporters' "tricks of the trade."** These include a variety of techniques reporters may use to get someone to share information voluntarily or to trick them into revealing something against their better judgment. (See the next two questions for more details.)

Why do reporters "stoop" to using tricks to get their information?

Not all do. Many reporters receive plenty of cooperation in covering more *positive* stories that involve less investigative work and are inherently less controversial. Therefore, those contacted by the reporters for information are usually more cooperative. It is when reporters receive far less cooperation that they may instinctively use a variety of subtle but tricky ways to obtain information from an unsuspecting person.

Reporters find that not everyone is always willing to divulge the information they consider to be newsworthy and important. They are in an increasingly competitive industry that pressures them to uncover newsworthy information that will "scoop" or beat out their competition. Reporters, and their media outlets, are judged by their ability to "break" stories and issues not previously covered by the competition. As in any other industry, if they are beaten by the competition on a frequent basis, they find themselves updating their resumes and searching for another job.

What are some techniques reporters may use to trick someone?

These are just a few of the methods a reporter may use when talking with you or one of your spokespersons – along with some suggested ways to counter them:

- **The "false-premise."** This is when a reporter will intentionally preface a question with a statement to test whether or not you will correct the statement. The actual question might be fairly unrelated to the premise but the reporter will insert it to determine your reaction. If a reaction doesn't come, the reporter feels he has the start of an important piece of information.

  Example: "Since you have very few minorities and women in your senior management, what type of board members is your company seeking?"

  Counter: If the premise is incorrect, make mention of it immediately before answering the question that is asked. Don't agree to a false premise.

- **The "hypothetical situation."** This is one of the most common ways the media attempts to get you talking about something you might prefer to avoid. They may ask a question related to something that may or may not ever occur, hoping you will comment on it and say something newsworthy.

  Example: "If your stock price drops to an all-time low, would you consider selling your worst-performing subsidiary to generate additional cash?"

  Counter: Mention to the reporter that you won't discuss a hypothetical situation, and fight the temptation to do so.

- **The "I've heard a rumor."** Some reporters may seek a reaction to something they may have contrived, simply to see if it leads anywhere with the executive. The reporter may feel the person isn't likely to confirm the rumor itself, but could inadvertently talk her way into an equally juicy story angle.

  Example: "The rumor is you plan to drop the product line altogether if it continues to receive such negative reviews. Is this true?"

  Counter: Disagree with the rumor, if it isn't true, and be careful what you say after you have disclaimed the rumor. Always have a positive statement you could make about your business in response to any question. In this example, you could say: "Not at all. In fact, we are extremely pleased with the sales of the product in the southern part of the country. We are excited about its future prospects as we expand into additional regions."

- **The "comment on the competition."** This is most often posed as a way to achieve some conflict and controversy between companies in the same industry. The questions might be asked innocently about the competition's new advertising campaign, chief executive officer or decision to move into a new market.

  Example: "What do you think about the way they are handling their takeover attempt? They sure could learn some lessons from your company."

  Counter: Make it a standard practice not to discuss your competition's business. As clear cut as its situation might appear, you don't have the advantage or insight of being part of its company or knowing exactly what went into the decision it made. You don't want your competitors dissecting your business, so it's best to avoid doing it to them.

- **The "tough guy/gal."** Some reporters, on rare occasions, will attempt to bully you into giving them the information they are seeking. This often is in the form of a threat to run a story or obtain the information elsewhere even if you aren't willing to cooperate. They may seem particularly annoyed at you or mention they are under an extremely tight deadline.

  Example: "What are you afraid of anyhow? This is another example of how your company looks like a buffoon against your competition. I'm giving you a chance to correct that. Do you want that opportunity or not? I need to know right now."

  Counter: Calmly explain to the reporter that he can do whatever he'd like, but you won't go against your best judgment just because that is what he would like. Mention why you prefer not to discuss the situation further. Don't take any gruff but do it in a cordial and professional manner.

Is it okay to say "no comment" to the news media?

It's only okay if you want to appear guilty, untrustworthy and evasive. You can always communicate *something* if you're prepared for it. Several ways exist to avoid saying anything harmful, or even directly answering the question asked, without saying "no comment."

Example: Saying "no comment" without saying it

Here's a way of not saying much to a media inquiry, but without giving the impression you have something to hide:

> **"As you know, we are currently investigating the situation and plan to determine specifically what went wrong and why. Until the investigation is completed, it is premature to discuss the situation further. You can be assured we will communicate any appropriate information after the facts have been confirmed and when it is relevant to the situation."**

Three lessons to learn

Three lessons emerge from this example:

1) **There's always a better alternative to saying "no comment" in response to a reporter's question.** This example shows a way to avoid saying anything definitive about the situation, without the impression of guilt or evasiveness. If you can't discuss a specific area, mention why you are unable to do so.

2) **Leave the reporter with the impression of being open, honest and accessible.** By avoiding the words "no comment," and explaining what you can and cannot discuss in reply to a specific question, a spokesperson comes across much more credible and believable. Consider what you will say in reply to a question you'd rather not answer.

3) **Know when to stop talking.** The other advantage of developing a response, in advance, to a question you'd rather not answer, is to make it concise enough that the reporter can't read something in to what was said. Try to find the fine line between being concise and saying something that doesn't sound like you are being evasive – and leave it at that.

How do we know if we are being successful in our communications with the news media during a crisis?

You will likely know by the answers to the following questions:

- Has the media coverage continued after the first few days of the crisis?
- Are the number of negative stories increasing or decreasing?
- Are reporters no longer calling to ask for comments or information, and are using others as sources for their stories?
- How would you characterize your relationships with the news media with whom you've been dealing? Cordial and professional? Antagonistic and untrustworthy?
- Are any of your core messages being used in the stories?

Can we really *trust* the media to report accurately on our crisis?

It depends on the media outlet, the reporter, editor, timing and circumstances. Although most media attempt to be objective and fair, often a story can be told with two or more different slants to it. Your company may not like the way the story was reported, but that shouldn't be misinterpreted as betraying a trust. Nevertheless, reporters and editors are like any other profession – *some* can be more trusted than *others*. Therefore, treat them all professionally and be prepared to respond to questions confidently and effectively. Are they *all* to be trusted? No, but neither are all crisis-management experts!

Should we ever go "off the record" with media?

"Off the record" is like "no comment." You see more of it in bad television shows than you do in real life.

However, disagreement exists among some public relations professionals about whether it is smart to go "off the record" with news media. I *have* gone "off the record" with news media during crisis situations, but very infrequently and only in a way that wouldn't have been catastrophic if the request was not honored. Since, as my previous answer stated, some reporters and editors can be more trusted than others, my recommendation is to avoid going "off the record."

Is talking "on background" the same as going "off the record" with a reporter?

It depends on the reporters' interpretation of the two. My interpretation is that it means close to the same thing. Talking "on background" with a reporter typically means you don't expect or desire to be quoted while providing background information and perspective. "Off the record" usually refers to the same expectation, but typically involves communicating an opinion as opposed to factual information. The difference is that you expect the reporter will use the background information – yet without attribution to you – while you wouldn't want the reporter to use the "off the record" comment, even without attribution of any kind.

Then is it okay to talk to a reporter "on background"?

Yes, if the background information being provided wouldn't be harmful to your situation if attributed to you.

What should we do if the news media messes up the facts or takes a negative approach in reporting our crisis?

If the story includes a significant factual error that deserves correction, you should first discuss it with the reporter who made the mistake. Discuss the options available to have the mistake corrected, if it warrants one, and if the correction wouldn't draw more attention to something you'd prefer wasn't reported on in the first place. In many newspapers, for instance, "corrections" are made in a separate heading elsewhere in the publication. However, the reporter should know about the mistake before writing another story on the subject.

If a newspaper won't publish or air a correction, your next options are to talk to an appropriate editor or write a *letter to the editor.* If you "go over the reporter's head" to his/her boss, be mindful of the long-term effect that might cause to your relationship. Make sure the correction will be worth the possible long-term impact.

In the case of a story being published or aired that you felt had an unnecessarily negative slant to it, putting your company in a bad light, you should consider **1)** doing nothing about it; or **2)** talking with the reporter in a professional, non-confrontational manner. A third, less desirable, option would be writing a letter to the editor – but, stick with the facts and don't let strong emotions get into the letter.

What can be done *before* a crisis to help increase the opportunity to receive fair treatment by the news media *during* and *after* a crisis?

Key reporters and editors should be considered another important group whose opinions and trust in your business are important to its future success. Here are some areas to consider in managing relationships with key reporters and editors *before* a crisis occurs:

- **Get to know reporters assigned to cover your business or industry.** Don't wait for a crisis to meet reporters or editors who cover your business and/or industry. Schedule an informal meeting to establish rapport and to provide some perspective on your business and industry.

- **Work to have a cordial, business relationship with key reporters and editors – responding to their requests in a professional and timely manner.** Answer their phone calls, in both good and bad times, and respond to their questions in a patient and professional manner.

- **Provide opportunities for the CEO to be interviewed by key reporters, when requested and appropriate.** Don't hide the CEO or overprotect her in meeting with reporters and editors. Select the highest-priority media – starting with any beat reporters assigned to your business and/or the industry – and arrange for informal meetings for each to get to know each other.

- **Seek opportunities for co-sponsoring events or becoming a partner on community projects with local news media outlets.** In many markets, the local media sponsor projects in schools, businesses or the community. Take advantage of improving your credibility and bond with specific media outlets by seeking ways to join them in their involvement (i.e., sponsorship dollars, executive participation, volunteering facilities).

- **If you disagree with a story about your business, and feel the reporter should be corrected, be sure you point out the *factual* errors only and go to the reporter first (rather than his or her editor). Do this in a professional manner without antagonism.** Reporters and editors will remember if they felt mistreated by you. This could affect the way you and your business are treated when you are most vulnerable during a crisis. Treat them well – you'll need all the support you can get when a crisis occurs.

Can you give a *real-life* example of a company effectively managing its relationships with key media, and how it benefited them?

McCormick & Company, Inc., the world's largest spice company, faced an unexpected crisis in July 1994 when its chief executive officer died of a heart attack. Bailey A. Thomas, 63, was a 33-year McCormick & Co. executive admired greatly by employees, customers and others.

Thomas' untimely death was covered extensively by the local Baltimore, Maryland, media, and it was important to the company that coverage was fair, objective and respectful.

"We were very touched by the quantity and quality of the coverage," said Allen M. Barrett, Jr., Vice President-Corporate Communications, McCormick & Co., Inc. "Positive editorials ran in three different newspapers, and a front-page story was published in the *Baltimore Sun*. The coverage was very meaningful to our organization."

Barrett credits the media response to the company's efforts to achieve positive relationships with key reporters and editors. He said, "We try to instill the attitude that members of the news media form a customer constituency who are important to our company. We recognize they are trying to do their job. We believe in *building* bridges with reporters, not *burning* them. They are important links to our various audiences, and we help ensure they receive the straight scoop from us."

What other tips can you give about working with the news media during a crisis?

Some *additional* tips include:

- **Be sensitive to their deadlines.** Return their phone calls promptly and don't tie them up on the telephone if you sense they are rushing to meet a deadline.

- **Don't assume they know more than they do – try to educate them about your problem, company, products and industry.** Unless the reporters are extremely familiar with your business and its industry, take the time to provide sufficient background information.

- **Limit your core messages to five or less and keep reinforcing them.** Make it as easy as possible for the media to understand your key points. Keep reinforcing them and, if appropriate, provide the media with a news release and/or fact sheets that also reinforce the messages.

- **Be forceful and firm with reporters and editors, but avoid antagonism and confrontations if at all possible.** You don't have to be a doormat to the media. If you think they've overstepped their bounds or are being particularly unfair, you can honestly let them know how you feel. However, this is a sensitive area. Do so on an even keel and without unnecessary emotion.

- **Don't ever mention a possible connection between your company's news coverage and your future advertising support of the media outlet.** In most media, no relationship exists between the editorial and advertising sides. One of the worst mistakes you can make is telling a reporter or editor that your "company is a major advertiser and, therefore ...." This will only infuriate the reporter and editor, and will paint you as a naive amateur.

- **Don't ask a reporter or editor if you can review a story in advance.** This is another cardinal sin that understandably upsets the media. They have no obligation to review a story with you in advance, and most would be seriously reprimanded or perhaps terminated if they did. Work with the media the best you can, and cross your fingers before you read about it like everyone else.

- **Never threaten a reporter or editor.** As mentioned before, treat the media the way you would want to be treated. Threatening a reporter or editor will get you nowhere – except for perhaps trouble with the law – so avoid doing this at all costs.

- **Don't try to fake it.** If you don't know the answer to a question, admit it and say you will contact them as soon as you can get the answer. Then, follow through with it.

- **Fulfill all commitments and promises.** Credibility and trust are important factors in dealing with the news media. Once these are lost, you will surely pay the price and have difficulty in winning it back.
- **Avoid risky remarks.** Stay away from comments that can be misinterpreted by a reporter or editor – such as off-color jokes, sarcastic comments or flippant remarks about bribes or kickbacks.
- **Maintain an appropriate distance.** Don't attempt to get buddy-buddy personal with a reporter or editor – unless such a relationship is established prior to or naturally after several years of working together.

Communicating with *other* publics

In some businesses, you could communicate effectively with employees, customers and the news media during and after a crisis, but still suffer significant damage if other important publics are ignored. Every organization needs to determine the publics who feel they have some stake in the success of your business – or that *your* success has a major stake in the success of *their* business. Some organizations call this group of publics "stakeholders" and recognize the need to communicate with all their stakeholders in times of crisis.

How you communicate with your other publics, and when to do so, are important questions when winning their support is critical to your crisis survival.

It's often the other, less noticeable publics that can erode an organization's support and trust in a community. It's like your home. Isn't it much easier to notice when your house needs a new coat of paint than when termites are destroying the entire two-story frame? You need to broaden your perspective and recognize that it's often the secondary publics that can cause some significant dissension and disharmony within your business.

This section describes some other publics – beyond the employees, customers and news media – you should consider addressing when your business needs their support the most.

With what other publics – beyond employees, customers and news media – should we consider communicating during a crisis?

Other publics with whom to consider communicating, depending on the company and nature of the crisis, include the following:

- Shareholders
- Regulators
- Financial and market analysts
- Community leaders
- Business leaders
- Government officials
- Board members
- Labor officials

Example: Secondary publics need not be forgotten

The advertising agency is one of the most successful in its industry. However, a negative story in a major business publication has reported on its current loss of business. It seems the agency has lost four of its major accounts during the past two months, and total agency billings have been reduced by 45 percent. The story reports the agency is in major financial trouble, and several other clients and senior executives are considering bolting as well.

The agency's previously outstanding reputation has been tarnished, its leadership wants to immediately conduct an aggressive communications campaign to dispel any doubts and misconceptions about the future health of the advertising agency.

The management team knows it has to make a positive impact with its primary publics – the agency's employees, current and prospective clients, and select reporters from local and industry news media that cover news about the agency.

"But, let's make sure we don't forget some of the others who benefit from the success of our agency," said one senior executive. "They can be important allies to us."

The team discussed who would fall under that category, and agreed their communications program also would focus on their *secondary* publics as well. These were identified as: advertising reps and general managers/ publishers at the various media outlets from which the agency purchases media; printing company reps and senior management; photographers; producers and senior executives at production companies; talent (i.e., actors, actresses, models); and, other business leaders in the marketplace.

"But, what do we want to ask them to do?" said another senior executive. "Why do we have to ask them to do something? Isn't it enough to simply tell them about our situation?" said one of the Vide Presidents. "Heck, they may already have heard about it and probably have made up their own minds. Do we really need to do anything else?"

Three lessons to learn

The advertising agency example helps reinforce the following points:

1) **Don't forget the "secondary" publics, which can be important allies and can help influence your most important publics.** It's easy to forget about second-priority publics when you are so focused on reaching your primary publics. In the case of the advertising agency, the principals there knew that their most-important publics were the agency's employees, current and prospective clients, and select reporters from local and industry news media that cover news about the agency. However, they recognized other publics could affect how their primary publics view their situation. They set forth a plan to contact advertising reps and general managers/publishers at the various media outlets from which the agency purchases media; printing company reps and senior management; photographers; producers and senior executives at production companies; talent (i.e., actors, actresses, models); and other business leaders in the marketplace. Don't forget your "secondary" publics in a crisis.

2) **Give them a "call to action."** When your publics are contacted by voice or in writing, they will want to know what you'd like them to do. Don't make the mistake of simply informing them about a situation without asking them to do something. In the case of the advertising agency, it might be as simple as asking for their continued support. Another technique is thanking them for something you'd like them to do. For instance, "Thank you for your referrals and kind words about our agency." Give them something to do.

3) **Get to them quickly before they come to their own conclusions.** It is important to contact your secondary publics as quickly as you would your primary publics. Otherwise, they will likely hear about the crisis second- or third-hand and may be offended you didn't communicate directly with them.

◆

Do we need to communicate with all of these publics during a crisis?

Much depends on how each are affected by the crisis. Each should be segmented and analyzed individually using the same criteria as we used to guide our communication with employees, customers and media. They include:

- If you were any of them, would you expect the company to communicate with you about the crisis? Would you be upset if the company didn't?
- Is it likely they will learn about the crisis through some other way? If so, wouldn't it be better to have it positioned initially by you in *your* way?
- Might any of them be effective *allies* for your company?
- Can any help communicate your *key messages*?

How should we consider communicating with them during a crisis?

They can be communicated with in some of the same ways as customers and even employees. Review the list of ways suggested earlier in this chapter, and determine if some are applicable for these second-priority publics. Also, as part of your crisis-*planning* process, you might consider asking representatives from some or all of these publics on ways they prefer to receive information about the company. This can be done through informal discussions, telephone surveys or focus groups.

Nevertheless, you can be quite confident that these publics can be reached via telephone, fax, courier, regular and overnight mail and – in an increasing number – the Internet.

Closing thoughts

Crisis communications is often the only aspect of crisis management considered by many businesses. Most never consider ways to plan for the crisis, or whether ways existed to help prevent the problem from occurring in the first place. However, most are familiar with the need for "disaster control," or what can be done to help reduce the potential damage after the crisis has occurred.

Cookie-cutter approaches won't work here. Every crisis is different from others because every business is unlike any other. And, to make matters even more challenging, the decisions on how and what to communicate (to whom) must be made quickly, decisively and confidently. The window is a small one to prove the crisis is being managed competently. Failure to meet expectations of your key publics – employees, customers, news media and others – can make a previously strong corporation back-pedal and eventually fall flat on its back.

Judgment, instincts and planning are three areas described here that can help you and your organization when you ask the question at the outset of a crisis: "Now, what do we do?"

Lastly, you might be saying after reading this chapter: "I agree these things should be done, but I won't have the time or the expertise to make them happen when a crisis occurs." If you're in that situation, you might retain the services of a respected public relations firm or hire one or more professionals on staff. But, don't wait for a crisis to occur before doing so. Tell them what you have in mind and work with them on a specific budget – to help prepare in advance for a crisis and to further establish goodwill with each of the major publics. Assess your situation today and make something happen.

Tips to consider

- **Segment your key publics as much as possible and determine which messages should be communicated to each audience.**
- **Don't inadvertently ignore some key publics.**
- **Set objectives and strategies for each major public.**
- **Identify no more than five key messages to communicate to the key publics.**
- **Determine specific tactics to use for communicating with your various publics.**
- **Develop in advance all or part of the written materials that will be needed in the event of a crisis.**
- **Recognize your window to communicate confidently and effectively is usually less than 24 hours – depending upon the severity of the crisis.**
- **Convey a sense of accessibility, sincerity and concern during the crisis.**
- **Apologize if a mistake was made that caused inconvenience or problems for others.**
- **Recognize that employees are your organization's most-important asset – communicate with them as your first priority.**

- **Use the Internet to help reach your key publics.**

- **Train your spokespersons in both *content* and *technique.***

- **Think through the questions that will likely arise and ensure you've thought through the answers.**

- **Ensure all those speaking on behalf of your organization during a crisis are answering questions in a consistent and accurate manner.**

- **Never say "no comment" when asked a question from the news media.**

- **Don't go "off the record" with a reporter.**

- **Recognize the difference between *legal* risk and *reputation* risk.**

- **Listen to your key publics and make the appropriate adjustments.**

- **Communicate with your "secondary" publics as well as your primary ones.**

- **Retain the services of a public relations firm or hire one or more on-staff professionals to help.**

- **Don't stop communicating.**

CHAPTER 7

Monitoring, evaluating and making adjustments

How will we know whether or not we are successfully managing our crisis?

Take a few minutes to answer these questions to get you warmed up for learning how to monitor and evaluate a crisis:

1) Can a crisis be monitored and evaluated before it is actually over?

2) Is it possible to truly evaluate the success in managing a crisis?

3) Is the only way to evaluate success in a crisis by asking your employees?

4) Should the CEO be the only one in the organization to set attainable goals to meet during a crisis?

5) Is the best way to evaluate a newspaper article on your company by measuring the story's size and the publication's circulation?

6) Are telephone surveys useful ways to measure public opinion about your organization?

7) Does an effective evaluation of a crisis typically cost several thousands of dollars?

8) Is customer satisfaction the only true test of how well a crisis was managed?

9) Is it possible to begin the evaluation process even before the crisis occurs?

10) Can traits such as reputation, credibility and trust be evaluated?

Answers:

1) **Y;** 2) **Y;** 3) **N;** 4) **N;** 5) **N;** 6) **Y;** 7) **N;** 8) **N;** 9) **Y;** 10) **Y**

Evaluation:

0 - 4 correct answers:	You're far from an expert in this area. You'll need to carefully read this chapter.
5 - 7 correct answers:	You'll need some help in this area. Keep reading.
8 - 10 correct answers:	You have a good foundation, but I bet you'll learn a few things as you read on.

So, now your business has experienced a crisis. It probably wasn't much fun. And, you probably can't wait to move on to something else or to pretend it never happened at all.

However, in reality, most crises don't go away easily. They can leave a dirty, untidy mess from which it isn't easy to recover. Employee morale might be low. Sales could be soft. Trust and credibility in your business might be shaken.

But, how do you know what type of adjustments to make in your strategy? What signs or symptoms will indicate the crisis and its impact have ended? How can you measure your performance in managing the crisis? In which ways can you best learn from the experience so you will be better prepared and capable of managing the next crisis that strikes your business.

This chapter offers some thoughts, suggestions and examples to help lead you through the important process of monitoring and evaluating the crisis, and making adjustments if necessary.

How will we know when our problem should still be considered a *crisis*?

You will know it by answering some of the following questions:

- Are we still asked a lot of questions about the problem?
- Is employee morale continuing to be affected?
- Are the news media still interested in the situation?
- Are rumors still circulating about the crisis?
- Have company sales and share price rebounded to pre-crisis levels?
- Are you finding that the crisis no longer grabs as much attention and focus from your managers as it once did?
- Do your instincts and judgment indicate that the crisis is no longer a major issue in your organization?

The Crisis Counselor mindset

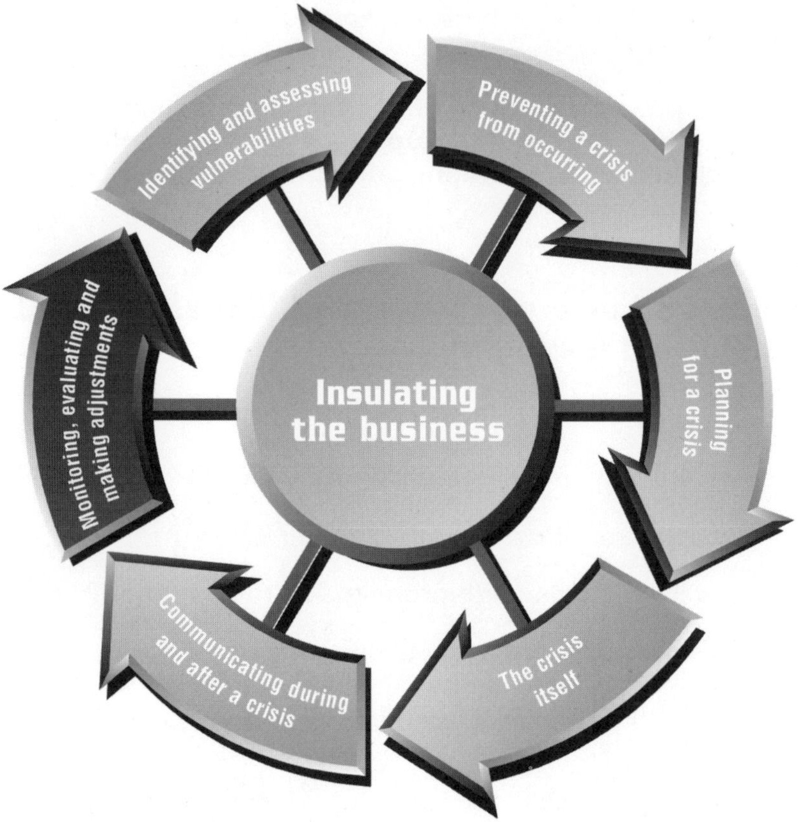

What do you mean by *monitoring* and *evaluating* a crisis?

The process of *monitoring* and *evaluating* a crisis means to:

- Determine how the crisis has affected your key publics' behaviors and opinions, and the extent to which your sales and share price have been impacted.
- Measure and track ways the crisis has affected your business.

- Use the information and perspectives gained in the monitoring process to make necessary adjustments in strategy and tactics.
- Help identify when the crisis stage has ended and when it is in your best interest to move onto other issues.

What are some ways to monitor and evaluate a crisis?

Some effective ways to monitor and evaluate the impact of a crisis on your business include the following:

- **Measure and track sales, profits and share prices during and after a crisis.** What effect is the crisis having on these areas? Did they once suffer but have clearly rebounded back to previous levels?
- **Document the nature of the calls from news reporters and others asking questions or seeking information.** What questions are being asked? What type of information are they seeking? Which of your core messages are being understood and accepted, and which are not? What type of media and other people are calling? Do you sense their frustration, confusion or hostility is increasing in intensity?
- **Use a news-media monitoring service to provide copies of media coverage on your crisis.** Are you seeing most everything that is reported about your crisis? Would a media monitoring service (e.g., Luce, Burrelle's, Bacon's, Video Monitoring Service) help ensure you are provided with copies of all pertinent media coverage on your business? Has the media coverage of the crisis stopped or is it continuing to be covered or discussed in the media?
- **Establish separate telephone *hotlines* for employees and customers to call with questions and comments about the crisis and your management of it.** Are you providing sufficient opportunities to obtain feedback from your most important publics, so you can determine whether and when the crisis is no longer an issue with them? Can you clearly draw distinctions between the types of questions being asked by your publics? What suggestions or comments are being offered?

- **Conduct focus group sessions (with 12 or less people in each group) to obtain opinions from employees and other key publics.** Would it be helpful to hear first-hand comments and questions about the crisis and your business from a segmented group of individuals? The focus group format allows you to probe into the opinions and attitudes of your employees and other publics. It also provides an opportunity to learn their suggestions and test some ideas for possible future plans.

- **Prepare a written survey questionnaire to distribute to employees.** You might ask your employees to answer some questions on a survey and return the questionnaire in a suggestion box or an envelope earmarked to a specific person or department. What issues do they think are most important to address in their division or department? How would they rate employee morale, teamwork, management support, quality of decisions made and the like?

- **Conduct a survey to determine the opinions and attitudes of your external publics.** How do your customers, prospects, community residents, or other opinion leaders feel about your business at this time? What type of effect did the crisis have on their awareness, opinions and attitudes about your business? What are some of their suggestions for the future? Hire a public-opinion research firm to develop a survey questionnaire and conduct the interviews by telephone.

- **Use an Internet monitoring service to help identify what is being said about your situation on the Internet (i.e., usergroups, chat forums and home pages).** What is being communicated over the Internet regarding your business and its recent crisis? Is it apparent your core messages are being accepted and communicated by others? What questions, complaints or opinions are being mentioned? Consider hiring a company that specializes in the monitoring and reporting of communications on the Internet – such as Minnesota-based eWorks, Inc.

Example: The tipsy employee and the bulldozer

The excavating company was having a difficult time disciplining its first-shift bulldozer operator. He had an alcohol-dependency problem that often emerged on a Monday morning, after a weekend of drinking, or after a liquid lunch at a bar near the worksite. He was disrespectful to his onsite supervisor and, at times, would close his eyes for a quick cat nap while the bulldozer's engine was on. An accident was only a knee-jerk away, his supervisor would say.

The supervisor's fears were realized one day when the operator was excavating a road near an upscale subdivision. The road was about 20-feet higher than the homes below, with both separated by a small fence and a median of well-kept grass. On this day, the fully inebriated operator – fresh from knocking down another liquid lunch – felt the effects of the sun, the heat and the Jack Daniels. He nodded off while his bulldozer kept moving forward. The bumps and knots on the hill didn't wake the operator as it plowed ahead another 25 feet, until the bulldozer tumbled off the side of the hill and crashed down into the front yard of an unsuspecting neighborhood resident.

The operator was thrown from the bulldozer and somehow suffered only some minor cuts and bruises from the fall. The sound of the three-ton bulldozer crashing onto the ground below shook the neighborhood, and the impact ripped open the sod in the front yard like a hammer going through toilet tissue. Luckily, the family that owned the home was away on vacation, and its three young children who often played kickball in the front yard were far away riding a merry-go-round in a neighborhood park.

Nonetheless, the neighborhood was furious, particularly after it heard from police that the bulldozer operator was drunk. The family returned from vacation early after hearing about the incident, and later joined with the neighborhood association to show their outrage. The association filed a lawsuit against the excavating company on grounds that it shouldn't have allowed the operator to work after it recognized that he had a drinking problem. It demanded the county road commission find another company to complete the road work. It wrote letters to their local political officials, and held a town-hall meeting that was covered heavily by the news media.

The excavating company suffered the wrath of the community, and its reputation was seriously damaged. It responded with a crisis-management approach that included personal visits to the neighborhood by the company's CEO and other senior executives, and information on how it has improved its hiring and disciplinary policies. It fired the bulldozer operator. It ran an ad in the local newspapers apologizing to the community, highlighting the company's previously flawless safety record, and asking it for another chance. A special phone line was established by the excavating company to answer questions and inquiries from local residents. Its CEO promptly returned all phone calls from the news media and answered all questions.

The company won over many of its critics by agreeing to follow through with an idea emerging from the special phone line – to purchase an empty lot in the neighborhood and turn it into a park area complete with picnic facilities and a new baseball field.

A few weeks after the incident, the community began to show strong support for the company.

"You know, that's a pretty darn good company," many of the residents were saying. "We need companies like that working in our area. It had one bad employee and it probably won't let that happen again. Let's give the company another chance."

The company was monitoring the crisis. Phone calls into the special phoneline dropped from about 10 calls a day with complaints and questions in the first two weeks to one or two calls of support after the fifth week. Phone calls from the news media and local politicians stopped after the first week.

"When can we forget about this incident and move onto other things?" asked the company's senior executives to themselves. "How long do we need to keep operating the phone line? Should we run another ad? What should we do now?"

The CEO said, "All the signs seem to indicate that we can move on. I don't think we need to run the ad again. The calls from the phone line indicate that it's no longer an issue for people But, before we make any final decisions, let's call back the first 20 people who called the phone line with complaints. Have someone develop 10 questions we can ask each person about how they think we did in handling the problem and what they think we need to do now. Then, make sure to send them a thank-you note from either the senior executive who called them or signed by me personally."

The firm's Director of Marketing developed the questionnaire, and the phone calls were split between two Senior Vice Presidents. The thank-you letters were mailed the same day the calls were made.

The phone calls indicated all 20 people were satisfied that their complaints were addressed appropriately. No one felt it was necessary to continue the special phone line or running the ads. Most said it would gladly support the use of the company for a future excavating job in the community. Four felt the CEO should run for Mayor.

Three lessons to learn

The example of the excavating company reinforced the following lessons as they relate to monitoring a crisis:

1) **Build in ways to obtain feedback.** The excavating company knew the value of obtaining feedback when it established the special phone line, had the CEO and other senior executives meeting personally with community residents, and made phone calls to obtain feedback. Build in these type of feedback vehicles in your planning, so they can be quickly integrated when the crisis occurs.

2) **Consider a number of vehicles in evaluating the crisis.** Don't make the mistake of relying on only one way to monitor and evaluate your performance. It is the cumulative effect of a number of vehicles that will demonstrate your commitment to communication and obtaining feedback. And, a checks-and-balances system will be established naturally by implementing two or more different ways to monitor and evaluate the crisis.

3) **When in doubt, ask people how they feel.** The excavating company had a number of different ways to monitor and evaluate its crisis, but the CEO wanted still another way to obtain direct and accurate feedback (through the 20 phone calls). Most people like to be asked their opinions and for their advice. When in doubt, ask for their thoughts.

◆

When should we begin to monitor and evaluate our crisis?

You should begin to monitor and evaluate the crisis as soon as possible. The process should have been integrated as part of your crisis-management *planning* (i.e., documenting major decisions made in planning meetings). It will help provide a *discipline* in your organization to document, track and measure important aspects of the crisis and your management of it.

What sort of reports can we generate to senior management regarding the monitoring and evaluation process?

You could consider one or more of the following ways to report on the impact of the crisis:

- Reports and graphs tracking sales, profits and share prices (versus comparable pre-crisis periods).
- Lists of media inquiries including the reporters' names, titles and phone numbers, along with the media outlets' names and the nature of the calls.
- File booklets of newspaper and magazine stories related to the crisis, along with transcripts from television and radio coverage.
- Analyses of the media coverage in determining the effectiveness of communicating key messages and the accuracy of the reports.
- Quantitative and qualitative reports of phone calls received on the telephone *hotlines* for employees and customers.
- Analyses of focus group sessions.
- Summaries of the written employee surveys.
- Reports on the results of the telephone surveys of your external publics.

- Updates on and samples of information about your crisis communicated on the Internet.
- Periodic crisis-management updates on your overall goal, crisis objectives, strategies, tactics and evaluation tools. (Remember, you may need to make some adjustments to each along the way. These updates encourage you to remain flexible and objective with your approaches.)

How frequently should we develop these monitoring and evaluation reports?

It depends on the nature of the crisis. You should conduct some form of reporting on a *daily* basis in fast-changing and dynamic crises. The best decisions are made based on accurate information, and this type of reporting and analysis can help ensure you're best equipped to make sound choices. Reports on a weekly, monthly or quarterly basis may be more appropriate during and after a slower-moving, less-damaging crisis has occurred.

Isn't it unrealistic to expect we'll have sufficient time and resources to conduct this level of monitoring and evaluating during a crisis?

No, it's not unrealistic if one or more of these ways are integrated at the outset into your crisis-management process. Someone should be pre-assigned the responsibility to conduct the monitoring and evaluation process. It should be someone who will not be on the front lines during the crisis, and will likely be able to make sufficient time to conduct this. You may wish to have an outside counseling firm assist in this area.

How should we assess the information to determine our next steps in managing the crisis?

You need to use the information to objectively answer the following questions:

- Are we communicating effectively with each of our internal and external publics?
- Which of our most-important publics are *most* and *least* supportive of our company at this time? How much equity do we have in our *banks of goodwill* with each?
- How effectively are we communicating our key messages? What is the current understanding of those among our internal and external publics?
- Has the media coverage been primarily positive, negative or neutral? What can we do to improve the media coverage?
- What questions arise more frequently than others, and in which ways can we be more effective in *proactively* addressing these points?
- What is the primary criticism we receive about the crisis and our management of it, and should we consider making any adjustments?
- Should we become more or less aggressive in any of our approaches?
- Does the crisis appear to be going away or is it picking up momentum?
- What are we doing right? What can we learn from those things?
- Are we appropriately funding – in terms of budget and time – the crisis-management initiative?
- Are any other crises in our organization likely to arise in the short term? If so, what can we do to prevent them from occurring or causing significant damage?
- Should we make any other adjustments?

In which ways might we consider adjusting our *management* of the crisis?

The management of the crisis can be adjusted in several ways, including:

- Increasing or decreasing the level of communication to employees, customers, prospects, suppliers, community leaders, the news media or any other publics.
- Refining your *key messages* and the way they are communicated.
- Using your spokespersons in a different way. (Is it time to begin using the CEO in all or certain circumstances? Should others be considered?)
- Developing new *strategies* and *tactics* to fit the changing situation.
- Improving the monitoring, evaluating and reporting of the crisis.

Example: The fruit & vegetable market and the murders

The local fruit and vegetable market was one of the small town's most popular attractions and successful businesses. Nearly every one of the town's residents would visit the fruit market at least once a week to buy bananas, pears, green beans, peas or anything else that would help round out a meal or curb an appetite.

The market experienced little crime or safety problems. Sure, the odd 12-year old would steal an apple under his shirt now and then, but nothing too serious. But, everything changed the day murder struck the unsuspecting fruit and vegetable market.

One of the market clerks, who was a 50-year-old woman working behind the cash register and food scale, had an ongoing battle with her husband of 25 years. She claimed he often hit her after a tough day of work at his job in the paper mill, and she often threatened to divorce him and to tell everyone in town how he treated her. After a particularly difficult night of yelling, hitting and throwing things, the woman came into work with small cuts, deep bruises and puffiness around the eyes from too much crying and too little sleep.

Suddenly, her husband threw open the front door to the market and yelled for his wife. He found her weighing plums for a gray-haired, older gentleman in the front of the market. She glanced up just in time to see him pulling out a small handgun he used to shoot rabbits in the woods behind their house. He shot her three times, and – amid screams of terror from customers and employees – he also shot the customer she was waiting on. Bodies fell and blood stained the floor like the tomatoes that sometimes rolled off the shelves. Chaos ensued.

The market owner's son, a 20-year-old, shot-put star on the local college's track team, dove at the man with the gun and knocked it out of his hand. A shaken employee called the police and the man was arrested – eventually indicted on the murders of his wife and the customer.

"Nothing like this has ever happened in our town," echoed most of the town's residents.

"It will take a long time to recover from this," most everyone agreed.

The fruit and vegetable market, announced its owner, would immediately close down for an unspecified period of time. The core messages communicated by the owner included: **1)** That everyone there was sorry such a situation occurred; **2)** Their thoughts and prayers were with the victims' families; **3)** Its ongoing concern lies with their employees and customers; and **4)** The store will be closed for an indefinite period of time, and perhaps may never re-open.

Employees and customers were provided free trauma counseling at a nearby school. The owner responded to all requests from the local newspaper and radio station, and thanked the community for its strong support. All of the fruit and vegetables were packed into a truck and were driven to the big city, two hours away, to donate the food to a shelter for the city's homeless. The owner's wife and family continued to answer phone calls from loyal customers and worried employees. They documented every phone call. The owner's son developed a chart at the end of every day, summarizing and analyzing the following questions: Who called? What did they say? What were their concerns? Did they express an opinion? The owner and the family reviewed the charts and discussed possible next steps.

The family would ask themselves the same questions each night. What should we do? Have we been doing the right thing? Do we need to adjust our thinking in any way? What are our next steps?

Their strategy never wavered through the first week or two. No one calling the store felt the owner or the business was to blame in any way. Everyone strongly encouraged the owner not to give up on the business, and to eventually re-open it. Letters to the editor of the local newspaper and phone calls to the radio station reinforced the same thoughts. Employees began calling in greater numbers saying they were ready to return to work sometime soon.

"Should we consider re-opening afterall?" the owner asked his family. "We don't want people to think we are being insensitive or dispassionate to the victims and their families. We don't want customers to be afraid to shop here, and employees scared to work in the market. Perhaps we should wait a little longer before we make the decision but, in the meantime, change slightly the messages we are communicating."

The new messages were: **1)** This has been difficult for our employees, customers and the town; **2)** We have received an unbelievable amount of support and love from the community; **3)** Most everyone is encouraging us to re-open the market; **4)** We haven't yet decided whether to do so, but will make a decision sometime soon on it, as we consider further input from our employees and customers; and **5)** We must not forget the victims of this terrible crime, and we must continue to pray for them and their families.

The owner and his family communicated those messages for another week. More phone calls came into the market, and positive responses were called in to respond to comments expressed on the local radio station. The decision was made to re-open the fruit and vegetable market within the next week – after new shipments could re-stock the shelves.

"I'm glad we remained flexible and were willing to change our position along the way," said the owner to his wife. "It was a good move to document the phone calls received and to follow what was being said in the newspaper and on the radio station. Let's run a newspaper ad and radio commercial to thank everyone for their support, and let's make this the best grand opening this town has ever seen."

Three lessons to learn

The example of the fruit and vegetable market helped reinforce a few excellent points about monitoring and evaluating a crisis, and making the proper adjustments along the way. Those include the following three points:

1) **Remain objective and be willing to adjust.** It's important to keep an open, objective mind during a crisis. No room exists for stubbornness when input and feedback are guiding you in a clear direction. Business owners and executives too often are unwilling to remain flexible when managing a crisis. Your *Crisis Counselor* mindset should be to seek input, to consider important guiding signs and to make adjustments when necessary. Don't let ego and stubbornness get in the way of effectively managing the crisis. The owner of the fruit and vegetable market was originally inclined to never re-open the store, but recognized the importance of communicating and listening to people along the way.

2) **Ask yourself questions and base your answers on information and instincts.** The market's family asked itself questions every night, after considering the input and calls received during the day. What should we do? Have we been doing the right thing? Do we need to adjust our thinking in any way? What are our next steps? They answered those questions based on the input received (via the telephone, newspaper, radio station, one-on-one discussions) and their instincts and experience. Consider as much information as possible but use your experience to help you remain decisive and confident with any decision you make.

3) **It's okay to change strategy but be decisive and clear about your position.** Changing strategy is not the same as being wishy-washy or indecisive. A good basketball coach may have a strategy before the game that he is convinced will help his team dominate the other. However, he may completely change the strategy if his team is down by 20 points in the first half. The same is true in a crisis. An initial strategy may not work as effectively as thought. When that occurs, you have to be willing to change approaches to follow and messages to communicate. The important point is that when a new strategy is set, move forward in a confident and aggressive manner – until the point occurs when you feel it should be changed once again.

◆

Is it possible to make the situation *worse* by making adjustments?

Sure it is. This can occur in one or both of the following ways:

- By making *too many* adjustments – confusing your key publics or giving the impression the crisis is being mismanaged by your company.
- By prematurely giving up on a strategy or tactic – shifting to something less effective than your initial plans.

So, when do you know when it's best to make adjustments?

You have to base the decision on the following:

- The information and analyses about the impact of the crisis.
- The answers to the questions you've previously asked yourself.
- The professional judgment, instincts and experience of your crisis-management team members.

When is it okay to *stop* monitoring and evaluating the crisis?

You no longer need to evaluate the crisis when your data, research and other information have indicated the *aftermath* from the crisis is over. The crisis itself could have long ended, but the aftermath may likely include continuing rumors and speculation, weakened customer trust and loyalty, employee morale problems and lack of credibility with the news media and other publics. If the aftermath continues, the *management* of the crisis has not ended. Be careful you don't prematurely end the monitoring, evaluation and management of the crisis and its aftermath.

How do you know when the crisis has ended?

Your data, research and other information will indicate when the crisis and its aftermath have ended. But, you'll likely know by answering the following questions:

- Are our employees and customers – along with other key publics – allowing us to get on with *business as usual*? Or, do they continue to ask questions and mention issues related to the crisis?
- Have our sales, profits and other indicators rebounded effectively?
- Has the media coverage on the crisis long ended?
- Is it extremely unlikely the crisis will recur if you move onto other things?

What should be our next steps, if we deem that our crisis is officially over?

The next steps should include those areas covered in the next chapter. However, here are a few tips to hold you over until then:

- Critique what you've learned from the crisis experience and make any necessary adjustments for the next time (i.e., strategies, tactics, personnel, counselors, suppliers).
- Determine other ways to improve your crisis-preparedness (i.e., materials needed, training of spokespersons and other staff, added resources and expertise).
- Begin the crisis-management process over again (i.e., identify your vulnerabilities, work to prevent the problems from becoming crises, and plan what you'd do in the event of a crisis).
- Build up the equity stored in your *banks of goodwill* with each of your key publics (i.e., initiate an ongoing public relations program for your company).

Closing thoughts

Someone has suffered a heart attack and is wheeled into the emergency room for immediate surgery. A heart surgeon washes his hands, snaps on his gloves and considers his strategies before picking up the scalpel. The strategy may work just as expected, or a whole new strategy may be needed. The decision on strategy is based, of course, on how the patient reacts to the surgery. The surgeon carefully monitors the patient's vital signs and – if he isn't responding as expected – may completely change the strategy. An angioplasty surgery may turn into a triple by-pass operation if it is necessary to save the patient.

The effective management of a crisis in a business is no different. The leader managing the crisis has to have a strategy going into the situation, and must monitor the organization's vital signs as the crisis evolves. Information to help the business make the best decisions has to be gathered and analyzed quickly. Decisions must be made with the speed, confidence and decisiveness of a heart surgeon. And, the business leader must recognize the importance of doing so.

This chapter offered several suggestions on ways to monitor and evaluate the crisis, and on how and when to consider making adjustments along the way. Don't allow a false sense of security to creep in before a crisis, just because your organization has a crisis plan. You will most likely need to adjust your strategies once the crisis train has taken off and you are holding on for the ride. It is those making smart and quick adjustments that are likely to be most successful in managing the crisis. Those who are rigid and unwilling to remain flexible are those who will find themselves with a much larger crisis to manage than the one they began attempting to control.

Tips to consider

- **Monitor and evaluate the perceived impact of the crisis and your management of it.**
- **Begin the monitoring and evaluation process as soon as the crisis occurs.**
- **Integrate the monitoring and evaluation process into your advance crisis-management planning to help ensure it is conducted once the heat is on, and to ensure someone is responsible for it.**
- **Conduct an evaluation methodology with as many major tactics as possible.**
- **Remain flexible – with a willing attitude to make adjustments – in the areas of strategies, tactics and evaluation.**
- **Use information, data and analyses to answer questions related to the effectiveness in communicating with your priority publics, ensuring an understanding of your key messages, and making necessary adjustments.**
- **Strive to be as objective as possible when evaluating data, analyzing information and trusting your best judgment.**
- **Include the Internet as an important way to help monitor the impact your crisis is having on various publics.**

- **Monitor and analyze media coverage based on content, positive or negative tone, key messages communicated, media reach and overall impact.**

- **Critique what you've learned from the crisis experience and make adjustments for the next time.**

- **Determine other ways to improve your crisis-preparedness.**

- **Begin the crisis-management process over again – particularly as it relates to identifying other potential vulnerabilities in the business.**

- **Work to build back up the goodwill equity from each of your key publics.**

CHAPTER 8

Insulating your business

In addition to the areas covered in the previous chapters, are there other steps companies can take to prepare themselves for a future crisis?

Yes. Take a few minutes to consider whether these statements are true or false:

1) Although a business can't completely eliminate the possibility of suffering a crisis, it *can* insulate itself from suffering needless damage from it.

2) After your crisis has ended, it's best to forget about crises, and move on to other things.

3) Crisis planning should be conducted only when a serious problem has clearly emerged in your business.

4) Your crisis-management team should meet only when a potential or existing problem has emerged.

5) *Positive* points about a company are almost always neglected in a crisis.

6) Although it's nice to do, establishing rapport and cordial relationships with key reporters during non-crisis periods won't likely help much during a crisis itself.

7) Training sessions during non-crisis periods can help a company stay crisis-ready, even if every crisis is slightly different from any other.

8) Effective, ongoing communications programs need to include strong mechanisms for achieving input and feedback.

9) Various research tools can help take the guess work out of crisis planning and ongoing communications.

10) Ongoing public relations programs are great for achieving visibility, but don't play much of a role in crisis management.

Answers:

1) **T**; 2) **F**; 3) **F**; 4) **F**; 5) **T**; 6) **F**; 7) **T**; 8) **T**; 9) **T**; 10) **F**

Evaluation:

0 - 6 correct answers:	Is it a tad drafty in your organization? Please read through this chapter carefully, and see if you can improve on your company's insulation.
7 - 8 correct answers:	Pretty good. But, you'll learn more by reading through this chapter.
9 - 10 correct answers:	Your organization is, or soon will be, insulated well against a potential crisis.

A house needs to be insulated to ensure it can withstand extreme and unpredictable weather. Failure to have the proper insulation will make for an uncomfortable and possibly dangerous winter and summer. And fuel and electricity costs alone will far exceed the cost to properly insulate the house. Nearly every homeowner knows this, and very few are foolish enough to build a home with no insulation.

Unfortunately, many business owners aren't so smart. Some don't realize that businesses, like houses, need plenty of insulation to help the survive the extreme and unpredictable.

This chapter describes how a business should properly insulate itself to help it succeed in both crisis and non-crisis times. This concept of insulating a business is the single most important factor in whether a business can survive a crisis.

What type of insulation does a business need?

A business needs sufficient amounts of goodwill stored up to act as insulation when it needs strong support from those who are important to the success of the business – employees, customers, investors, suppliers, politicians, community leaders, the news media and others. Goodwill is when the business has the reputation of being credible, trustworthy, honest, caring, forthright, accessible, cost-effective, efficient and successful. These traits don't mean a business is infallible, but it does mean it will receive every benefit of the doubt in the early stages of a crisis.

Remember the bully in elementary school. The pug-nosed redhead with freckles and a crew cut. If the teacher heard of someone on the playground throwing rocks, or pulling hair or picking a fight, it was the bully who often was to blame – even if he wasn't anywhere near the scene. If someone ratted on the bully, it didn't take much to convince the students, teacher and principal that the bully was guilty and deserved to be severely punished. The bully had a lousy reputation because he did several things to deserve it and failed to do anything positive to compensate for the negatives.

When a business isn't properly insulated, it almost always receives immediate criticism and little support in the times of crisis. A business without the proper insulation finds its publics jumping to a "guilty" verdict well before it can do much about it. The key to effectively managing a crisis is to be in full control and confident, and that can occur only with the support and teamwork of those important to the success of your business.

In addition to building and maintaining a strong base of goodwill, an organization needs to establish a Crisis Counselor culture in the company. Its executives need to identify vulnerabilities, prevent them from turning into crises, plan for the inevitable crisis, communicate effectively when a crisis occurs and evaluate and make adjustments along the way to successfully manage the crisis.

***The Crisis Counselor* mindset**

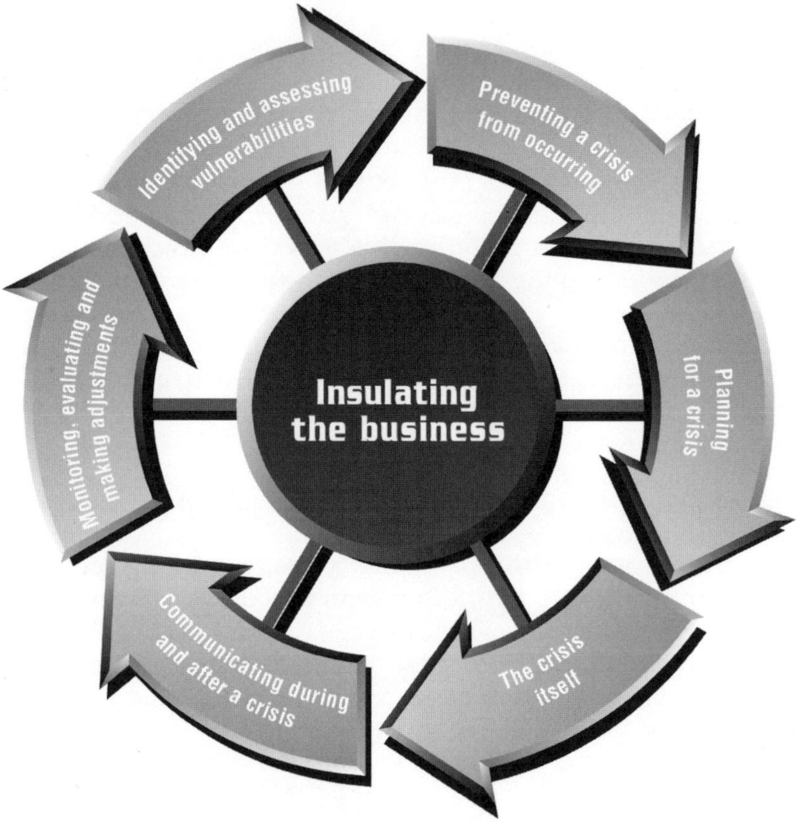

Why is this so important?

The single most important factor in how your company will survive a crisis is predicated on the amount of insulation it has stored and built up as it enters a crisis. Insulation is acquired through days, weeks, months and years of establishing trust, loyalty and credibility with each of your key publics. This is your *bank* of goodwill that, someday, will be tapped and tested. Your business will be considerably more likely to survive, and perhaps even thrive during a crisis, if the bank account remains solid and robust during a crisis. If your business has a bank account of goodwill that runs dry, meaning you no longer have the support and trust needed, a crisis will almost certainly take control of your company and very quickly destroy it. *Goodwill* is receiving the "benefit of the doubt" and the "second chances" your business will need when it makes a mistake or is suffering a crisis.

The combination of a strong base of goodwill with a solid Crisis Counselor culture and performance provides a business the best opportunities to successfully manage a crisis. Without one or both of these, a business has little chance to survive a crisis with its reputation and credibility intact.

What are the best ways to help insulate a business from the damaging effects of a crisis?

The two most-important ways are to establish and maintain:

- A crisis-management culture in your organization.
- A high level of goodwill with each of your company's key publics (i.e., employees, customers, suppliers, news media, civic and community leaders).

What are some ways to establish and maintain a crisis-management culture in our company?

Some of the best ways to establish and maintain a crisis-management culture in your organization are to:

- Conduct *The Crisis Counselor* system within your business.
- Implement a formal vulnerabilities analysis at least once every year.
- Conduct annual research to assess your company's reputation and the amount of goodwill you've earned with each of your priority publics.
- Work to prevent warning signs from igniting into crises.

- Even during *non*-crisis times, conduct quarterly meetings with your crisis-management team.
- Ensure crisis-management activities are budgeted appropriately.
- Make sure your spokespersons are properly trained and ready to represent the company with key messages, and answers to both routine and difficult questions.
- Update your crisis-management plan and crisis-response manuals, and ensure those responsible for implementing it are properly trained.

How can a business establish and maintain high levels of goodwill with its key publics?

You can do so by the following:

- Conduct your company in a socially responsible manner.
- Treat your key publics the way *you* would want to be treated if you were in their place.
- Conduct an ongoing public relations program to bolster the relationships, trust and credibility you possess with each of your key publics.
- Provide ways to make it easy for your key publics to ask questions, offer suggestions and provide input to your company.
- Heed warning signs, and address them directly and decisively.
- Work to measure and evaluate your major communications activities, and make adjustments as necessary to improve their impact on your key publics.

Example: The engine block company running on all cylinders

The manufacturer of engine blocks was one of the area's top companies. Its CEO and management team often had spirited debates and healthy discussions on issues affecting the company's productivity and growth. They would disagree on whether to expand their largest plant, the site to build a new one and ways to sell more engine blocks to their loyal customers.

But, they always agreed with one aspect of their business. "You don't fool around with relationships," they would say.

The company worked hard to earn the trust and loyalty of their employees, customers, suppliers and the news media. They never really thought too much about crisis situations or public relations, but knew that strong relationships usually meant a healthy business.

They would often leave time in their management meetings to run through each of their key publics: "How do our employees feel about us? What is employee morale like at this time? What questions are we getting from our customers? What can we do to make our customers feel better about our company? Are there any problems with our suppliers? What are we hearing from the media covering our industry? What is our reputation like these days?"

They realized after a while they needed some help to ensure everything possible was done to nurture good relationships with its key publics. The company hired a local public relations firm that helped develop a strategic plan with specific objectives, strategies and tactics. A variety of activities were implemented each month by the public relations firm, reporting to the Executive VP/Chief Operating Officer. The activities included the following:

- **Employees.** Its 280 plant employees and 60 office staff members had a tremendous amount of respect and loyalty for the company. The public relations activities included regular "coffee" visits in the lunchroom with the CEO; a company newsletter mailed to employee homes; a scholarship program for employees' children; a number of employee awards; memos and news releases posted on bulletin boards; semi-annual employee surveys to determine how they feel about the company and its work environment; an advisory group of employees who offer suggestions and new ideas; ongoing training to help employees develop new skills and open up new opportunities within the company; and an employee stock ownership program to help everyone feel they have a financial stake in the company.

- **Customers.** The company's customers are the purchasing representatives and platform engineers from the automotive manufacturers. They like the company's engine blocks and have grown to respect its sales staff and management team. The activities implemented to target customer contacts include special visits and open houses at their facilities; regular letters and e-mail updates; an annual customer survey; a quarterly newsletter for customers; exhibits and displays at trade shows; an annual report; co-sponsorships of customer golf outings and other events; continuous customer training to determine new ways to exceed their expectations; and financial and personnel support for charity activities actively supported by their primary customers.

- **Suppliers.** The engine block manufacturer considered 25 suppliers to be its most important. Those suppliers had to be dependable and supportive to enable the company to manufacture the engine blocks to customer specifications. And, the major suppliers were frequently talking with the purchasing agents and platform engineers, and had a high level of influence over the company's primary customers. The activities targeting suppliers included: an annual supplier "thank you" party; update letters reinforcing key messages; an annual supplier survey (written questionnaire); a special supplier golf outing held by the company; and a year-end holiday gift to thank them again.

- **News media.** The news media covering the company included reporters from two engine trade publications, three automotive magazines, the daily newspaper's business section and a weekly community newspaper. The activities targeting the media included a company media kit; an updated questions and answers document for the media; biographies and photos of the company's management team; one-on-one breakfast meetings between the CEO and each reporter; media visits to the plant; and, sponsorship of select media luncheons on key issues important to the industry and/or community. In addition, the company worked hard to ensure all calls from the news media were returned quickly, and that the company responded professionally in goods times and in bad.

The engine block manufacturer also recognized that relationships with other publics were important, and implemented activities throughout the year to target:

- prospective customers;
- directors of the company board;
- shareholders;
- local political and community leaders;
- local residents living around the company's plant facilities;
- industry leaders, including board members from the industry's trade association;
- prospective employees and management candidates; and
- current and prospective investors in the company.

"I credit the excellent relationships we've established, and our work to nurture those relationships throughout the years, with our company's outstanding growth and success," said the President & CEO.

"We've worked hard to earn their loyalty and trust, and you'd be surprised how often having that has helped us out of a jam. We never underestimate the value of those positive relationships, and our work to enhance those relationships on an ongoing basis is the best money we spend all year," he added.

Three lessons to learn

The example of the engine block manufacturer, and the efforts to insulate its business, reinforces the following key points:

1) **Don't forget all your most important publics.** Break out and set in priority order the publics who are most important to your business. To whom do you count on that will most affect whether your business succeeds or fails? What can you do throughout the year to earn their credibility, trust and loyalty? The engine block manufacturer recognized that *several* publics were important to the success of its business, and the relationships had to be nurtured with consistent communications throughout the year.

2) **Provide several ways for input and feedback.** Resist the temptation to communicate solely by telling people want you want them to know. This may express a message, but it won't enhance a relationship. You also must provide ways for people to offer their input, ideas, suggestions and feedback. The engine block manufacturer used several ways to accomplish this, including: telephone surveys, mailed survey questionnaires, advisory panels and one-on-one meetings.

3) **Make this a priority.** The effort to establish goodwill and insulate a business is among the most important ways to build and grow your business, and should be treated as such. Establish a budget. Set a timeline. Hire a public relations firm to help, if necessary. Make it a priority.

◆

How can conducting an ongoing public relations program help insulate a business in a crisis?

By planning and implementing an *effective, ongoing* public relations program, your company will:

- Segment and target your priority publics (e.g., employees, customers, prospects, news media, community leaders, suppliers) to ensure they receive a consistent stream of useful information about your business.
- Ensure vehicles are in place to encourage and obtain *feedback* from your key publics.
- Provide opportunities to communicate your positive messages throughout the year.
- Help showcase the competency and quality of your people – through your spokespersons – which can provide a warm, human persona to an otherwise cold, faceless organization.
- Integrate a culture of measuring and evaluating the various communications activities conducted throughout the year, and provide *quantitative* and *qualitative* input for making new decisions and adjusting previous actions for the future.

Example: The radio station and its community goodwill

The radio station enjoyed consistently higher ratings than any other in its market. Its General Manager would say he graduated from the "school of hard knocks" and had built up plenty of calluses from making mistakes in other markets. He would frequently remind his staff that "we have plenty of people to please." He'd say, "We need to do good things and tell people about them in ways that are credible and appropriate for our business."

The station had a Public Relations Manager on staff who was supported by a staff member with the title of Community Relations Coordinator. They were responsible for raising the visibility of the radio station throughout the market area, and helping ensure current and prospective listeners and advertisers understood what made the station different and better than its competitors.

The Public Relations Manager and Community Relations Coordinator included a variety of strategies and tactics in their plans that would be the blueprint for the year. They worked closely with the General Manager to ensure their plans were consistent with those of the station's senior leadership. The plans included ways to increase coverage in the local daily and weekly newspapers; showcasing the station's talent at charity events, mall promotions and school appearances; and, working with current and prospective advertisers to increase their loyalty to the station.

The activities implemented included the following:

- Semi-annual focus group sessions and telephone surveys of listeners, non-listeners, current advertisers and companies advertising on other stations to assess opinions and attitudes about the station.
- Updated core messages to communicate by on-air and sales staffs.
- A comprehensive media information kit with updated fact sheets and backgrounders on the history of the station and its differentiating features and community involvement; charts on audience numbers and demographics; reprints of positive media coverage about the station; and updated biographies and photos of on-air talent and station management.

- A program for its largest advertisers that includes visits by on-air talent to their corporate events; free training seminars for its top executives on communicating effectively on the radio and in front of large groups; and use of the station's studios for taping corporate audio and video programs.
- A quarterly *audio* newsletter to current and prospective advertisers, newspaper and trade reporters, and key business and community leaders – in an audio cassette format that includes highlights from the past quarter; interviews with senior management; positive testimonials from advertisers and listeners; reports on quarterly audience numbers; and recent and future community events sponsored by the station.
- A multi-faceted program in the area's elementary, middle and high schools, which include coloring books and workbooks; visits to the schools by the on-air talent and management staff; tours and visits to the station; internships; and voice and presentation clinics by the on-air talent.
- Active involvement in local community charity organizations – including hands-on assistance from staff; emcee duties by on-air talent; and promotion of charity events on the station during heavy listening periods.
- Updating and improving the station's Internet website to generate a greater number of visits, increased excitement for station activities and feedback from its listeners.

"Our public relations and community relations activities have played a major role in the success of our station," the General Manager told a local business reporter. "I've learned throughout the years that you have to earn your listeners' trust. They won't just hand it to you."

The Public Relations Manager responded in the same interview: "We've worked hard to ensure we don't simply rely on the station itself as our primary communications vehicle. We are like any other business. We need the third-party credibility of having other people saying nice things about us – community leaders, advertisers, newspaper columnists and others – and we are always looking for new and creative ways to earn as much goodwill as possible with our most important publics."

Three lessons to learn

Lessons learned by the radio station included the following:

1) **Include the direct involvement of the CEO and senior management.** The General Manager learned from previous experiences that the positive visibility, credibility and reputation of the radio station are among its most important commodities. And that's true with any business in any industry. However, they won't likely occur without making them a top priority in the company. The direct involvement of the CEO and senior management is necessary to help set and communicate the core messages; agree to the strategies, objectives, tactics, budget and timeline; and insist that the organization makes this a major priority.

2) **Don't get lulled into a one-dimensional approach.** The radio station could have easily decided to communicate only through its own broadcasts to shape public opinion about itself. However, it realized the importance of reaching out to its publics in a variety of non-traditional ways that carry third-party credibility – such as seeking positive media coverage, obtaining ideas from focus groups and surveys, assisting charity organizations and large advertisers, and including positive testimonials from advertisers and listeners on the audio-cassette tapes. Don't make the mistake in your business of relying on only one or two ways to enhance the relationships with your key publics.

3) **Keep the variety fresh and make adjustments as necessary.** The radio station's Public Relations Manager said, "... we are always looking for new and creative ways to earn as much goodwill as possible with our most important publics." The station used a variety of ways to enhance the relationships – from communicating on audio cassette, in person at corporate or charity events or through its website on the Internet. It is important to maintain a fresh variety of activities and to make adjustments along the way when it becomes necessary to improve or replace them. Ask a sample of your publics along the way how they feel about what you are doing, and seek their recommendations for the future. This can be done through one-on-one interviews, focus groups, telephone surveys and advisory groups.

◆

How should a business determine what type of public relations action to take?

Public relations offers a variety of ways to improve the relationships with your most important publics. How can you achieve a better relationship with your publics? Sometimes this can be accomplished by sharing information, describing your position on an issue, showing that you care about them, obtaining some third-party notoriety or visibility that might impress them or supporting a mutually favorite charity.

The decision on what tactics to implement should be dictated by measurable objectives and a smart strategy for targeting specific publics.

What are public relations *objectives*?

Those are concise descriptions of what you hope to achieve. Examples of public relations objectives include those beginning like the following:

- Increase the visibility of ...
- Enhance the understanding of ...
- Achieve a change of behavior in ...
- Increase the public support for ...
- Obtain the approval of ...

Then what are *measurable* objectives?

Objectives aren't useful if they are so general that it is unclear whether or not they have been achieved. For instance, consider this objective: "Increase the visibility of our business through the end of this year." That objective is so general it would be unclear when it has been met. Has it been met if one newspaper story is published about the business? How is visibility defined so it is clear whether or not it has been achieved?

Measurable objectives are those which can clearly be evaluated and quantified, so little doubt exists when they are achieved.

What are some examples of *measurable* objectives?

A few examples include the following:

- Improve the awareness of our business 25 percent in our community by January of next year.
- Increase by 35 the number of members in our coalition between now and August 31.
- Reduce the number of complaints received on our customer phone line by 40 percent this month.
- Persuade two customers to offer testimonials in our customer newsletter before the end of the year.

What is meant by a *strategy* for targeting specific publics?

A strategy is simply the overall *approach* your business takes in an effort to make an impact on specific publics and meet the objectives you've identified. Public relations strategies describe the *direction* your business will take, not necessarily what activities will be implemented during the course of action (which are referred to as *tactics*).

What are examples of some public relations strategies?

Examples of public relations strategies are the following:

- Seek the close involvement and participation of the neighborhood block clubs within a five-mile radius of our factory in determining the best solutions to our environmental problem.
- Use our best employees to provide testimonials on why they like working at our company.
- Target editorial-page editors at college and university newspapers to obtain their support for our organization's cause.
- Focus all communications efforts on our suppliers to encourage them to spread the word about our new product line within the industry.

What are some examples of public relations *tactics* our company could consider throughout the year?

A list of examples could quickly turn into "1,001 PR Tactics" – a somewhat meaningless hodgepodge of activities without corresponding *objectives*, *strategies* or targeted *publics* or *audiences*. Nonetheless, they could include any number of activities such as:

- One-on-one informal meetings
- Media briefings
- News releases
- Focus group sessions
- Employee newsletters
- Internet websites and databases
- Open houses
- Update letters to customers and others
- Video presentations
- Position papers

- Op-ed articles
- E-mail notes
- Telephone surveys
- Sponsorships
- Brochures and pamphlets
- Annual reports
- News conferences
- Exhibits and displays
- Newspaper advertorials
- Radio and television talk-show interviews
- Toll-free telephone hotlines
- Appearances at local schools and community events
- Media information kits
- Grassroots coalitions and letter writing
- Contributions of resources or money to help community or social causes
- Fact sheets
- Internet-updated kiosks placed in high-traffic pedestrian areas (i.e., malls, fairs, large office complexes)
- Minority-outreach activities
- CEO interviews distributed on audio cassette tapes
- Media training of your spokespersons and senior executives
- Editorial board meetings
- Road-show presentations to industry/market analysts

What other recommendations can you make to help us insulate our company from the damaging effects of a crisis?

Here are some final words of advice to help ensure your company is properly insulated from the damaging effects of a crisis:

- Work to always have a solid, ongoing understanding of your key publics and their perceptions of your company.
- Don't allow your business to get lulled into a false sense of security when things are going well.
- Make the protection and maintenance of your company's reputation among the highest priorities in the business.
- Recognize the long-lasting effects of how well you communicate and manage during a crisis – your publics will undoubtedly have long memories, and it will be difficult to reestablish lost credibility, loyalty and goodwill.
- Explain to your key publics – particularly your employees – how you arrived at a major decision, not simply what the decision is.
- If a mistake is made, the company should admit the error and describe the steps being taken to correct it and ensure it won't occur again.
- Conduct a comprehensive critique of the management of a crisis, and make necessary adjustments for the next time.
- Meet during non-crisis times with key reporters covering your business to brief them on your business and establish trust and rapport which will be helpful when a crisis occurs.

Closing thoughts

Most organizations don't link the need to conduct ongoing public relations activities with the intention of managing a crisis well. They see public relations as simply publicity or "free" media coverage. Public relations is too often seen as only something you do with discretionary funds in a business to get the company's name in the newspaper or to promote a new product without advertising. However, the greatest benefit of an effective public relations program is helping to insulate the business with the goodwill it will need when a serious problem arises and a crisis strikes.

We reviewed in this chapter the need to ensure your organization has sufficient insulation to withstand the turbulent and stormy times that every business faces at some point. Insulation is established by a business simply doing good things and telling people about them in a credible, appropriate manner. An ongoing public relations program in your business will help ensure this is done with the continuity and effectiveness needed to achieve meaningful results. Otherwise, you are betting the insulation will occur by accident – yet the odds are strongly against the possibility of that occurring without a focused effort.

The other way to insulate a company to protect it from suffering needless damage in a crisis, as discussed in this chapter and throughout most of *The Crisis Counselor,* is simply to be prepared for it in advance. Too many businesses make the mistake of shrugging off the need to prepare for a crisis in advance. Preparation is often ignored despite how much can be done well before a crisis ever strikes. And, the difference between being prepared and ill-prepared for a crisis is a major factor in whether the crisis is well managed by a business.

Put into motion today ways to thicken your company's insulation of goodwill and to become as prepared and ready for a crisis as possible. Don't make the mistake of waiting until it's too late, and then regretting your failure to take these easy steps before a crisis strikes.

Tips to consider

- **Recognize that the single most important factor in surviving a corporate crisis is the amount of goodwill you have earned with each of your key publics as you enter the crisis.**

- **Establish a *Crisis Counselor* culture in your organization.**

- **Schedule a formal vulnerabilities analysis in your business at least once a year.**

- **Conduct annual research to assess your publics' perceptions of the company.**

- **Budget sufficient funds and time to ensure the crisis-management process is effectively conducted in your company.**

- **Conduct quarterly meetings with your crisis-management team, even during non-crisis times.**

- **Update your crisis-management plans and crisis-response manuals throughout the year.**

- **Ensure your CEO and other company spokespersons are properly trained to communicate specific key messages and answer routine and difficult questions effectively and confidently.**

- **Conduct ongoing public relations activities to bolster relationships, trust and credibility with each of your key publics.**

- **Provide several ways for your key publics to ask questions, offer suggestions and provide input to the company.**

- **Heed warning signs and move quickly.**

- **Measure and evaluate major communications activities, and make adjustments as necessary to improve their impact on your key publics.**

- **Make the protection and maintenance of your company's reputation among the highest priorities in the business.**

- **Learn from your mistakes.**

CHAPTER 9

Putting it all together

This final chapter offers some summary points from *The Crisis Counselor* to piece together the various advice you've read throughout the book. These should help you consider those that will improve your organization today and ensure it can survive a crisis in the future:

What are the most important points covered in *The Crisis Counselor*?

The importance and value of the points covered in *The Crisis Counselor* are based on the impact they may make on you and your organization. Those probably include the following:

- A *crisis* is anything that has the potential to negatively affect the reputation or credibility of a business.

- Every business will face a crisis at some point. It's those that are best prepared that will survive – and perhaps even thrive – during a crisis.

- Business crises aren't just of the high-profile variety covered on the front page of newspapers. They include employee layoffs/ downsizings, corporate lawsuits, negative media coverage, damaging rumors, product defects or quality problems, poor employee morale and others.

- *Crisis management* is a function that works to minimize the potential damage of a crisis in a business.
- *The Crisis Counselor* philosophy extends far beyond just "disaster control." It includes identifying vulnerabilities, preventing crises from occurring, recognizing and isolating the crisis, communicating effectively during a crisis, monitoring and evaluating a crisis, making necessary adjustments, insulating the company with goodwill and starting the process over again.
- Effective businesses should establish a crisis-management *culture* of crisis planning, preparation, communications and evaluation on an ongoing basis.
- *Warning signs* precede nearly every crisis. Senior management should notice them and attempt to solve the problems before they erupt into crises.
- Establish a crisis-management team within your organization, and have it meet regularly – even in *non*-crisis times.
- Conduct crisis training within your organization at least once a year.
- Segment your *internal* and *external* publics – those most important to the success of your business – and ensure they are addressed with effective communications before, during and after a crisis.
- Develop specific core messages that are important to communicate about your business – or about the crisis itself – and ensure those representing your organization to the news media, customers, employees and others are proficient at communicating the core messages.
- Convey a strong sense that you'll be accessible and communicative during a crisis – and that you're not defensive or running scared from the situation.
- Communicate all the bad news at one time, if possible, rather than encouraging a continuation of negative media coverage and other damaging results.
- Monitor and evaluate all major activities conducted before, during and after a crisis.

- The single, most important factor in surviving a corporate crisis is having previously earned a substantial amount of goodwill from each of your key publics. They will be more willing to continue their support and give you the benefit of the doubt during a crisis, if you have previously earned a high degree of trust and credibility with them.
- Conduct ongoing public relations programs targeted to each of your key publics so you can establish and maintain high levels of goodwill equity.
- Nothing in your business takes longer to rebuild than a damaged reputation, credibility and trust.

How can I get others to appreciate the importance of crisis management in my organization?

You can start by doing the following:

- Mention crisis management and question your company's crisis preparedness at your next board, senior-management, staff, office or department meeting.
- Show how other companies – in and outside your industry – have suffered from damaging crises. In particular, point out some mistakes you feel could have been avoided with advance planning.
- Volunteer to organize the crisis-management planning initiative or to lead others to do so. In many organizations, crisis-management planning isn't done primarily due to the lack of anyone taking the initiative to start the process.
- Identify some vulnerabilities – and possible crisis warning signs – you see within the organization. Mention how you would help solve the potential problems or would lead others to do so.
- Encourage them to read *The Crisis Counselor.*

How can I contact you to ask a question or make a suggestion for future editions of *The Crisis Counselor*?

You can contact me by mail at the address below or through the Internet at **jcap@caponigro.com** or visit our company's website at **www.caponigro.com**.

Jeffrey R. Caponigro
President & CEO
Caponigro Public Relations Inc.
4000 Town Center
Southfield, MI 48075-1208

I hope to hear from you. Best of luck to you and your business.

◆ ◆ ◆ ◆ ◆

Glossary

Business crisis. An event or activity with the potential to negatively affect the reputation or credibility of a business.

Core messages. A small number of specific points to be communicated about a company's products, services, people or position on key issues.

Crisis Counselor. A business owner, executive, franchisee, sales person, marketing or public relations professional, accountant, CEO, CFO or others who – through their crisis-management principles and actions – prevent and manage problems that arise in their everyday business lives.

***The Crisis Counselor* mindset.** A thought process that involves a series of steps to help prevent, manage and thrive on business crises.

Crisis management. The function that works to minimize the potential damage of a crisis in a business, and helps gain control of the situation.

Crisis management plan. A strategic plan describing the steps the business will take to effectively manage a crisis situation and to establish specific staff responsibilities for each area.

Crisis management team. A small group of people assembled in a business responsible for helping to plan for and manage a crisis.

Crisis-response manual. A printed manual – tailored for each individual who has responsibilities in the crisis-management plan – to provide specific step-by-step guidance on actions to take during a crisis situation.

Crisis simulation. An important practice drill that establishes a crisis scenario and assesses the crisis-preparedness of an organization through role playing and critique.

Editorial-board visit. A meeting with reporters, writers and editors – from major newspapers or, in some cases, from major-market television stations – who are responsible for setting the editorial position of the media outlet and/or reporting the news.

Focus group session. A meeting facilitated by a single person who seeks to obtain the opinions and attitudes of a segmented group of people.

Goodwill. The credibility a business earns by doing good work and making it known in an appropriate manner.

Interactive voice response. Artificial intelligence programming that allows computers to interact with people, take information, process the data and send out appropriate responses as either a voice file or hard copy document.

Media training. The focused effort to train a company's spokespersons on effectively communicating with and through the news media.

News release. A company-produced news story announcing information or perspectives about the organization.

Op-ed article. An opinion article written for the editorial page of one or more newspapers or magazines by an individual that offers an opinion on a specific issue.

Position papers. A comprehensive analysis of a company's position on a specific issue.

Publics. Individuals or groups of people or organizations with similar characteristics that are important to the success of your business.

Public relations objectives. Concise descriptions of what you intend to achieve with your public relations initiatives.

Public relations strategy. The overall *approach* your business takes in its public relations effort to make an impact on specific publics and meet the objectives you've identified.

Satellite media tour. The activity to schedule interviews with television news reporters or producers from important markets interviewing your company spokesperson. The spokesperson stays in one location and various television stations interview the person – via satellite – during times scheduled in advance.

Spokesperson. The person who represents your organization and answers questions from the news media and others. Depending on the nature of the crisis, this could be one or more of the following: the company's owner, the Chief Executive Officer, a plant manager, a department director, a public relations representative, an attorney, marketing representative or company executive.

Stakeholders. The publics who feel they have some stake in the success of your business – or that *your* success has a major stake in the success of *their* business.

Turning point. The point in a crisis when the crisis is either neutralized, abolished or escalates in intensity.

Video news release. A television news story or background video footage produced or paid for by the company for distribution to a number of television stations.

Vulnerability. An area in a business susceptible to becoming a serious issue, challenge or problem for the organization.

Vulnerabilities analysis. The process to identify the most significant vulnerabilities existing in a business and setting them in priority order to ensure they are being addressed properly by management.

Warning signs. The signals that usually precede a crisis.

Index

A

accidents, 5
annual report, 58, 267

B

Bacon's, 15, 233
Baltimore Sun, 218
Barrett, Jr., Allen M., 218
benchmark, 54
Burke, James E., 24
Burrelle's, 15, 233
BusinessWire, 13, 200

C

Caponigro Public Relations Inc.
  address, 276
  Internet address, 276
Caponigro, Jeffrey R.
  address, 276
  Internet address, 276
Chief Crisis Officer. *See* Crisis Counselor
Chrysler Corporation, 24
communications
  admitting mistake, 159
  editorial board, 201
  level during a crisis, 154
  interactive voice response, 131
  messages, 157, 163
  methods, 175, 186, 200
  reports, 238
  satellite media tour, 201
  tips, 157, 163, 172, 180, 186, 190, 198
  video news release, 201
  with customers, 181, 190
  with employees, 165, 180
  with media, 191, 198, 200
  with other publics, 220
corporate
  business plan, 84
  downsizing, 3
  financial downturn, 4
  name change, 12
  reputation. *See* reputation
  spokesperson. *See* spokesperson
  takeover, 7
crisis
  accessibility, 154
  adjustments, 241, 245
  characteristics, 137,231
  costs, 13
  definition, 3
  end of, 246
  impact of, 10
  initial action steps, 147
  monitoring, 232, 233, 245
  more difficult to manage, 142
  most vulnerable businesses, 44
  objective, 146
  opportunities in a, 24
  planning for, 101,107
  positive benefits, 24
  prediction of, 44
  prevention, 83, 88, 94
  rationale for failing to plan for, 102
  stages, 142
  strategy, 146
  timeframe, 139
  warning signs. *See* warning sign
  well-managed, 30
Crisis Counselor, The
  definition, 19
  role, 19
  selection of, 18, 21
Crisis Counselor mindset, *The*
  definition, 16
crisis management
  accessibility, 192, 198
  budget, 96
  buy-in from others, 131, 171, 275
  definition, 15
  insulation, 253, 255, 260

materials, 20
mistakes, 27
role of employees, 165, 171
spokesperson. *See* spokesperson
crisis management plan
components, 115
definition, 114
ensuring usage, 117
crisis management team
definition, 109
CEO, 111
meeting frequency, 114
size of, 110
crisis-response manuals, 118
components, 118
distribution, 119
updating, 120
crisis-simulation training
components, 124
definition, 120
example of, 122
customer
loss of a major, 6
customers
communicating with. *See* communications

D

DataTimes, 15
death
employee, 241
senior executive, 6, 90
DesignCAD, 95
disaster
Act of God, 7

E

employee
communication, 83
input from, 54
loyalty, 11
morale, 4, 83
eWorks, Inc., 15, 234
examples
"no comment", 213
accident, 235
advertising agency, 222
assault, 22
association, 48
bank, 8
construction, 235
crisis management team, 22, 112
crisis-simulation training, 122
customer service, 35, 48, 59, 154, 182
customer support, 188
death of employee, 241
death of senior executive, 90, 218
discrimination, 8
downsizing, 143
embezzlement, 86
employee support, 167
employee support, lack of, 169
employee violence, 105
environmental business, 75
environmental hazard, 204
goodwill, 194, 218, 235, 257, 261
healthcare, 167, 196
Internet provider, 35
law firm, 169
lawsuit, 194
manufacturing, 69, 90, 112, 126, 161, 178, 204, 257
McCormick & Company, Inc., 218
media outlet, 140, 261
media training, 126
media coverage, negative, 196
newspaper, 140
non-profit organization, 86
pharmaceutical, 194
prejudice, 140
quality, 161, 178
retail, 122, 154, 182, 188, 241
Secretary of State's office, 105
sports team, 59
transportation, 143
university, 22
vulnerabilities analysis, 69, 75
ViaGrafix Corp., 95

F

feedback. *See* publics
Find/SVP, 15
Forbes, 45
Fortune, 101
Fourth Wave Group, 132
Fram, 47

G

General Motors, 24
goodwill, 25, 30, 83, 86, 103, 142, 240, 253, 275
government
  investigation, 6

H

harassment, 4
hotline, 187, 233, 238, 267

I

Iaccoca, Lee, 24
Internet
  communications tool, 177, 187
  corporate website, 177, 187, 224, 239, 266
  monitoring service, 15, 234

intranet, 173, 177
Investor's Business Daily, 45

J

Johnson & Johnson, 24

L

legal advice, 163
Lexis-Nexis, 15
Luce, 15, 233

M

MAID's Profound®, 15
McCabe, Doug, 95
McCormick & Company, Inc., 218
media
  factual error, 216
  information materials, 202, 208
  inquiries, 27
  methods, 200
  monitoring, 15
  no comment, 28, 212, 213
  off the record, 215
  on background, 215
  techniques used by, 210
  tips, 198, 210, 216, 218
media training
  components, 125
  definition, 125
Microsoft Corporation, 95

N

National Association of Retired Persons, 7
National Highway Traffic Safety Administration, 178
NBC, 24
NHTSA, 178

O

objectives
  definition, 264
  measurable, 265

P

Pearce, Harry, 24
PR Newswire, 13, 200
publics
  definition, 32
  goodwill. *See* goodwill
  input from, 55
  segmented, 33
  targeted, 32
  ways to obtain input from, 58

Q

quality problems, 5

R

reputation, 6, 10, 18, 26, 32, 84, 125, 158, 255, 275
rumors, 5

S

satellite. *See* communications
Securities and Exchange Commission, 45

spokesperson, 31, 109, 125, 128, 147, 164, 174, 201, 203, 208, 256, 270
stakeholders. *See* publics
strategy
  examples, 266
  definition, 265
survey
  focus group, 55, 165, 224, 234
  questionnaire, 55
  sample size, 56
  telephone, 55

T

tactic
  examples, 266
Thomas, Bailey A., 218
Tylenol, 24

U

U.S. Postal Service, 46
United Automobile Workers of America, 7

V

ViaGrafix Corp., 95
Video Monitoring Services, 15, 233
vulnerabilities
  ways to determine, 53, 55
vulnerabilities analysis
  budget, 57
  definition, 55
  frequency, 77
  how to conduct a, 55
  informal, 74
  priority categories, 65
  questions for customers, 62
  questions for employees, 61
  questions for media, 63
  questions for suppliers/vendors, 64
  timeframe, 57
  ways to obtain input, 58

W

Wall Street Journal, The, 45
warning sign, 35, 44, 47, 51, 62, 82, 89, 95, 135, 138, 255, 274